W9-AOH-832

INTERNATIONAL DICTIONARY
OF FINANCE

The
Economist
Books

INTERNATIONAL DICTIONARY OF FINANCE

Graham Bannock and William Manser

JOHN WILEY & SONS, INC.

New York • Chichester • Weinheim • Brisbane • Singapore • Toronto

This book is printed on acid-free paper. ∞

THE ECONOMIST IN ASSOCIATION WITH
PROFILE BOOKS LTD

Published by John Wiley & Sons, Inc.

First published in 1989

This edition was previously published in the U.K. by Profile Books
by arrangement with Penguin Books, 1999

Copyright © Graham Bannock and William Manser 1989, 1995, 2000

The greatest care has been taken in compiling this book. However, no
responsibility can be accepted by the publishers for the accuracy of the
information presented. Where opinion is expressed it is that of the
contributors and does not necessarily coincide with the editorial views of
The Economist Newspaper.

This publication is designed to provide accurate and authoritative
information in regard to the subject matter covered. It is sold with the
understanding that the publisher is not engaged in rendering professional
services. If legal, accounting, medical, psychological or any other expert
assistance is required, the services of a competent professional person
should be sought.

ISBN 0-471-36328-6

Printed in the United States of America

10 9 8 7 6 5 4 3 2 1

FOREWORD TO THE FIRST EDITION

This book is intended as a source of reference for all those concerned with finance. It is entitled 'International Dictionary of Finance', rather than 'Dictionary of International Finance', because it is concerned not solely with transnational finance, but also with domestic financial matters in the major countries, particularly in the United Kingdom and the United States. No one involved in business finance, savings and investment or public finance can now neglect the international dimension.

Money markets, commodity markets, securities markets, banking and *insurance*, the five principal subjects of the book, have always involved international connections. Some or parts of these markets have always been fully international, but we are now well on the way to the globalization of virtually all financial markets, as barriers to entry fall with the abandonment of exchange controls and the deregulation of these markets in the United States, Europe and Japan. These developments are now being given additional impetus by the adoption of the Single Act of the European Community, which is intended to bring about by 1992 the full integration of the capital markets of the EC member states. Just as the regulation of markets following the Second World War led to innovation in finance – notably the development of the Euromarkets – so too has deregulation stimulated further innovation. Each phase of change has generated new terminology, which has been further enriched by the cross-fertilization of languages, business cultures and electronic technology.

The specialized terminology of finance is vast and expands daily, and we have had to be highly selective, even within the five core areas mentioned above. We have attempted to include all the more common terms which market operators and those in financial institutions are likely to encounter in English-speaking countries.

We have also included key terminology in accounting, business finance, investment appraisal, public finance, savings and investment, statistics and technology. We have not assumed much prior knowledge of the subject, and the dictionary is specifically directed at businessmen, students and the investing public as well as at financial professionals who may need to verify terms outside their own specialized field.

Happily for English speakers, their language is dominant in international finance, but we have been careful to note where US and British terminology differs. Where a term is not generally common to both countries we have indicated this by (US) or (Br.) after the entry. We have also included a large number of the key foreign-language terms, including institutional terms, with an indication of their national reference thus: (Aus.) Australia; (Bel.) Belgium; (Den.) Denmark; (Fr.) France; (Ire.) Ireland; (It.) Italy; (Jap.) Japan; (Neth.) Netherlands.

All terms, even where commonly abbreviated (for example, SEAQ), are defined under the full term to which the abbreviation is cross-referenced thus: ►Stock Exchange Automated Quotation System. Cross-referencing is elaborate, both in the interest of avoiding repetition and to enable the reader to pursue objects in greater depth and in their wider context. All cross-references are indicated by a single arrow for 'see' and a double arrow for 'see also'. Where a cross-reference is given in parentheses, it refers only to the phrase or sentence immediately preceding it and not to the whole entry.

While we, as authors, though professionally experienced in research on financial matters, cannot be expected to be expert across the whole of such a broad field, we have sought advice and help from many people and published sources, too numerous to mention. We do, however, wish to thank our editor, Andrew Franklin, for his enthusiasm and support through a lengthy task.

GB, WM
London, September 1988

INTERNATIONAL DICTIONARY
OF FINANCE

A

'A day' (UK) 29 April 1988, when the ➤Financial Services Act came into force.

à la criée (Fr.) ➤open outcry; one of the three methods of quotation on the French ➤stock exchange, the others being ➤*par casier* and ➤*par opposition*. Normally used in the ➤*marché à terme.*

'A' shares ➤share.

abbreviated accounts (UK) Under ➤directives of the EU incorporated in UK company law (➤incorporation), small and medium companies are permitted to disclose less information for public inspection than larger firms. The shorter accounts they file are known as abbreviated accounts. Small and medium companies are defined in terms of ➤turnover, ➤assets and employment (small: 50 or fewer employees, and medium: 250 or fewer employees).

ABI ➤Association of British Insurers.

above the line ➤below the line.

Abschlag (Ger.) ➤Discount.

absolute liability ➤strict liability.

accelerated accrual Use of a denominator less than 60 in the ➤accrual rate applied in the calculation of an employee's pension (➤pensions). If the denominator is, e.g., 40, then an employee having served for 40 years would receive 100% of their final salary as pension.

accelerated depreciation ➤capital allowances.

acceptance The act of accepting, i.e. agreeing to honour, a ➤bill of exchange. By extension, the document itself.

acceptance credit A use of ➤acceptances whereby a set ➤credit period is accorded the buyer by means of a documentary letter of credit, or ➤documentary credit. A bank or ➤accepting house is itself the drawee of the bill, subject to ➤clausing and to the documentary credit. The bank or accepting house normally ➤discounts the bill and remains responsible for payment of the bill at ➤maturity, making arrangements with the buyer for the latter's payment in turn. Should the buyer fail to pay, the bank's liability to pay remains, contrary to the practice for a simple acceptance.

1

accepting house An institution specializing in accepting or guaranteeing ➤bills of exchange. All accepting houses have taken on other functions as the use of bills of exchange has declined, returning to their original, wider function of merchant banking (➤merchant banks).

accommodation bill (Jap.) A ➤bill of exchange accepted by a bank (a ➤bank bill or ➤banker's acceptance) based on a number of ➤trade bills.

account 1. A record of financial transactions as in a bank account (➤see current account; ➤➤banking) or ➤balance sheet. **2.** An arrangement between a seller and a buyer under which a period of ➤credit is allowed before payment, e.g. the period in which ➤London Stock Exchange transactions take place and after the end of which ➤settlement must be made. Up to the end of the account, transactions are made without payment, and account dates are thus of vital importance to speculators. Until recently there were 24 account periods in a year. Other countries have different systems for settlement. ➤➤account day.

account day (UK) The day on which all transactions made during the previous ➤account at the ➤stock exchange must be settled (hence *settlement day*). On the ➤London Stock Exchange, as in the US, the markets use rolling accounts (➤settlement) which are settled after a fixed number of days after the transaction: at present five days, or 'T+ 5' (eventually T+ 3).

accounting equation, basic ➤balance sheet.

accounting principles Policies used in drawing up the ➤annual accounts or other financial statements and covering such matters as the valuation of ➤assets, accruals (➤accrual accounting) and the treatment of Research and Development expenditure. ➤accounting standards; generally accepted accounting principles.

accounting standards The ➤Accounting Standards Board (ASB) sets accounting standards for the UK. It issues *Financial Reporting Standards* (FRS) and in 1990 replaced the Accounting Standards Committee (ASC) which issued Statements of Standard Accounting Practice (SSAP). ➤➤Financial Accounting Standards Board; International Accounting Standards Committee.

accounts payable Amounts owed to trade creditors and included as current ➤liabilities in the ➤balance sheet.

accounts receivable Invoiced or billed amounts owing to a business which are outstanding from ➤debtors and included under current ➤assets in the ➤balance sheet.

accrual rate The rate, i.e. the number of years of service, at which an employee's rights to a pension (➤pensions) accumulate throughout their period of employment. Normally this number is expressed as a fraction of 60 and then applied to the employee's final salary to arrive at the pension. Thus a person who has served 40 years will receive 40/60ths of their final salary as their pension.

accruals accounting Where expenses have been incurred, or income is due, but not paid or even invoiced at the time accounts are drawn up but are nevertheless included in the accounts. For example, accountancy fees or the cost of electricity consumed in an accounting period can be included in the accounts as liabilities even though these costs have not been paid and invoices have not yet been received.

accumulation units ➤unit trust.

acid ratio The ratio of current ➤assets minus ➤stock to current ➤liabilities. Used as a crude test of ➤solvency.

ACII Associate of the ➤Chartered Insurance Institute.

acquis communautaire (Fr.) 'Community attainment'. A term in common use in ➤European Union (EU) circles to refer to all that has been achieved by the Union (formerly the European Community) to date – invariably as part of a statement that past successes should not be allowed to go to waste.

acquisition accounting ➤consolidated accounts.

ACT ➤corporation tax.

Act-only policy Motor ➤insurance that offers the strictly minimum cover required by law.

actif (Fr.) ➤Asset.

action group A group of ➤Names on certain heavily loss-making Lloyd's ➤syndicates taking joint action, including litigation, against alleged fraud or negligence on the part of the market operators.

actionnaire (Fr.) ➤Shareholder.

actions (Fr.) Shares in the ➤equity capital of a business. ➤ordinary share.

active underwriter The Lloyd's ➤working member authorized by the ➤managing agent to underwrite on behalf of the members of a ➤syndicate. An active underwriter is usually assisted by up to 10 working members.

actual A ➤commodity immediately or very quickly available for delivery, sold on a ➤commodity market. Also termed *physical* and *cash*. ➤➤forward; futures; option.

actual price The price of a ➤commodity available for immediate sale and delivery. Also known as *cash*, *physical* or *spot* price. ➤➤forward; futures; option.

actuary A senior ➤insurance company official, expert in statistics and particularly in those of ➤mortality and loss incidence, responsible for estimating future ➤claims and disbursement requirements and for calculating necessary fund and ►premium levels. Actuaries may not call themselves such unless they have passed the examinations of the Institute of Actuaries. Actuaries are also employed in ►savings banks and may in any case move from insurance companies and savings banks to positions elsewhere, particularly in the financial services industry.

ad valorem 'By value'. An *ad valorem* tax is a tax (►taxation) on the price of a good or service. The *ad valorem* principle is used, e.g., in import ►tariffs and ►value added tax.

adaptive expectations hypothesis (US) A theory of ►rate of interest prediction based on the assumption that the future course of a target variable can be discerned from previous patterns.

ADB ►Asian Development Bank.

ADEF (Fr.) ►*Agence d'Evaluation Financière*.

adjustable rate mortgage (ARM) (US) A ►mortgage loan in which the ►rate of interest is adjusted in line with market interest rates at predetermined intervals. ►Floating rates are, of course, common practice in the UK and elsewhere.

adjustable rate preferred (ARP) stock (US) A form of ►preference share for which ►dividends are linked to the ►rates of interest on ►Treasury bills. ARPs carry a 'collar' that sets the minimum and maximum dividend rates that will be paid. ARPs may be convertible into common ►stocks at a fixed price at a specified date or dates.

adjustment credit (US) ►Loans of a few days' duration only from the US ►Federal Reserve to banks and other ►deposit-taking institutions for the purpose of meeting a shortage of ►reserves.

ADR ►American depository receipt.

advance corporation tax (ACT) ►corporation tax.

adventure A legal term referring to a project or venture, as distinct from an item of property or other consideration, that is the subject of an ►insurance policy.

AEX The ►Amsterdam Exchanges.

AFBD Association of Futures Brokers and Dealers. ►Financial Services Act.

Affärsvärlden General Index The Stockholm Stock Exchange ►share index.

affiliate ►subsidiary.

after-hours trading ►24-hour trading.

aftermarket Dealing in ►securities immediately after a ►new issue.

AG (Ger.) ►*Aktiengesellschaft.*

age admitted A phrase in a ►life insurance policy indicating that the assured has provided evidence of their age, no further proof being needed when a claim is made.

Agence d'Evaluation Financière (ADEF) (Fr.) The French ►rating agency.

agency (US) Of a ►security, one issued by an agency of the US government. Most are in the form of ►bills and are issued mostly by Eximbank (►Export–Import Bank), the ►Government National Mortgage Association, the ►Federal home loan banks and farm credit banks.

agency bill A ►bill of exchange drawn on a local branch (e.g. in London) of a bank based abroad.

agency loan A loan of the ►European Investment Bank, available only to public bodies, which may be subdivided into smaller components for various purposes.

Agenda 2000 ►European Union (EU).

agent A person authorized by another person (a ►principal) to carry out transactions with third parties on their behalf, e.g. a ►broker.

agent de change (Fr.) ►Stockbroker; an official member of the French ►stock exchange, or *bourse.*

agente de cambio y bolsa (Sp.) ►Stockbroker. ►►Madrid Stock Exchange.

agente di cambio (It.) ►Stockbroker.

aggregation risk The potential multiplying of risk where securities trading takes place in more than one market where problems could arise.

agio A turn or ►spread, usually in the sense of a banker's return on the difference between the ►rate of interest they pay on ►deposits and that on the ►loans they extend.

AGM ►annual general meeting.

agreed value policy An ►insurance policy in which the sum of money to be paid in the event of loss or damage is specifically stated.

AIBD ►International Securities Market Association.

AIM ►Alternative Investment Market; ►Amsterdam Interprofessional Market.

AITC ►Association of Investment Trust Companies.

Aktie (Ger.) ►Share.

Aktiengesellschaft (AG) (Ger.) Public limited company. ►incorporation.

Aktionär (Ger.) ►Shareholder.

ALFI The Luxembourg Investment Funds Association.

aliquot A small sample taken from a gold bar for the purpose of *assay* (i.e. determination of the fine gold content).

all or nothing A theory of money measurement in which all money forms are regarded as equal. Also known as the *simple sum theory*.

All Ordinaries ►Australian Stock Exchange.

All Ordinaries Index The main Australian ►share index.

all risks insurance ►Insurance covering a generality of ►risk, i.e. loss or destruction, rather than one confined to specific ►perils, such as theft or flood.

Allfinanz (Ger.) ►Insurance and ►banking operation within the same institution. ►►bancassurance.

allocated capacity That part of the ►overall premium limit of a member of ►Lloyd's that is allocated to ►syndicates.

allotment letter A letter addressed to a subscriber to an issue of ►shares informing him of the number of shares that has been allotted, accompanied by a cheque for the balance of subscription monies if the issue has been ►oversubscribed or a request for payment of the amount due as appropriate.

ALM ►Association of Lloyd's Members.

alpha coefficient A statistical measure of the price volatility of a ►share against the volatility of all shares or selected risk-free shares. It identifies the price fluctuations inherent in the ►security as distinct from those in the market as a whole (*systematic risk*), which are measured by the *beta coefficient*. These terms are used in ►portfolio theory.

alpha securities, stocks (UK) A discontinued classification of some 130 ►equity shares most actively traded on the ►London Stock Exchange by at least 10 ►market makers of which at least six had to quote on SEAQ (►Stock Exchange Automated Quotation System) firm ►bid and ►offer prices in a minimum quantity of 1,000 shares. Details of transactions in alpha stocks had to be notified and were displayed on SEAQ within five minutes of the trade. The term was part of a three-category classification of shares. *Beta stocks*, of which there were some 550, required only six market makers of which at least four provided firm prices on SEAQ. *Gamma stocks* (1,500 in number) required two market makers quoting at least indicative prices on SEAQ that had to be firmed up on inquiry. *Delta stocks* (130 in number) were the least actively traded stocks, for which market makers quoted prices only on inquiry so that prices were not shown on SEAQ. Trading volumes were shown on SEAQ only for alpha stocks. This classification system was replaced on 14 January 1991 by a new system called ►normal market size.

alphabet brokers (US) A popular term applied to the dominating ►insurance brokers in the USA, commonly known by their initials, e.g. Marsh McLennan (M.M.), Alexander & Alexander (A.&A.), Johnson & Higgins (J.&H.).

Alternative Investment Market (AIM) (UK) A market for small and young companies introduced in 1995 by the ►London Stock Exchange in replacement of the ►unlisted securities market. The AIM enables companies to raise ►capital, secure a listing and offer shares for trading, without the rigorous listing requirement required by the main exchange. Companies gain entry chiefly by the disclosure of information. Such information includes evidence of establishment as a public company, with freely transferable shares, under the laws of its country of incorporation; the publication of annual and interim accounts; and the observance by the directors of a model code. In addition, AIM companies must appoint a nominated adviser (►normal) and a nominated broker; the first of these advises and informs the directors of their responsibilities under AIM rules; the second promotes trading in the shares of the firm.

American depository receipt (ADR) (US) A ►certificate registered in the holder's name or as a ►bearer security giving title to a number of ►shares in a non-US-based company deposited in a bank outside the USA. These certificates are traded on US ►stock exchanges.

American Stock Exchange (AMEX) (US) The smaller of New York's two ►stock exchanges, listing mainly smaller and younger companies than those listed on the ►New York Stock Exchange (NYSE). Also referred to as the Little Board and the Curb Exchange.

American style option An ►option which can be exercised at any time during its life until expiry date.

AMEX ►American Stock Exchange.

AMEX Major Market Index (MMI) A ►share index measuring the average prices of 20 major industrial ►stocks quoted on the ►New York Stock Exchange. ►Futures based on the ►AMEX MMI are traded on the ►Chicago Board Options Exchange.

amortize, amortization ►sinking fund.

amount at risk The real ►liability of the insurer in a life policy, given that reserves against the sum payable increase steadily through the duration of the policy. At any one time, therefore, the amount at risk is the balance of the sum payable not covered by ►reserves and thus potentially falls on the *net worth* (►net assets) of the company.

Amsterdam Exchanges (AEX) An ►equity and ►derivatives market formed in Amsterdam through the merger in January 1997 of the ►Amsterdam Stock Exchange and the ►European Options Exchange.

Amsterdam Interprofessional Market (AIM) A method of transacting large business at negotiated ►commission, initiated on the ►Amsterdam Stock Exchange in 1986, between banks and commission houses, and institutional investors. The method dispenses with the service of ►brokers, or *hoekmen*.

Amsterdam Stock Exchange The 35 or so members of the Amsterdam Stock Exchange, the world's oldest exchange, are known as *hoekmen* or *hoeldieden*. These members act as ►market makers specializing in ►single-capacity dealing in particular ►stocks on the ►trading floor through a screen-based ►quotation system set up in 1990. ►Block trading is carried out off the floor in the ►Amsterdam Interprofessional Market (AIM). The second-tier market (►unlisted securities market) known as the *parallel market* was closed to new entrants in 1993. The Exchange was in January 1997 merged with the Amsterdam-based ►European Options Exchange to form the ►Amsterdam Exchanges (AEX).

Amsterdam Treaty An agreement signed in 1997 between member governments of the ►European Union (EU) intended materially to carry forward the work of the ►Maastricht Treaty. In the event some progress towards a common immigration policy, and a more unified approach to foreign policy and security matters, was made. Some co-ordination of efforts to reduce unemployment across the EU was also agreed. It was also agreed that after entry into Economic and Monetary Union (►Maastricht Treaty) member states would observe a 'stability pact' under which national budget deficits would not exceed the ►convergence limit of 3% of GDP, with a fine in case of default in the absence of mitigating circumstances such as severe recession.

anbei kabunushi (Jap.) An inter-company shareholding rarely traded on the ►stock exchange.

Andean Pact A grouping of Bolivia, Colombia, Ecuador, Peru and Venezuela, founded under the Cartagena Agreement in 1969, with the purpose of assisting economic integration between its members.

Anlage (Ger.) ►Investment.

Anleger (Ger.) Investor.

Anleihe (Ger.) Borrowing, ►bond.

annual accounts All limited liability companies (►incorporation) must file accounts or financial statements for public inspection each year. For larger companies, and especially quoted companies which need to distribute accounts to shareholders, the annual accounts (or report and accounts) are elaborate documents including reports of the directors and auditors and notes as well as ►balance sheets, ►profit and loss account (P&L) and ►sources and uses of funds statements. Smaller companies file ►abbreviated accounts.

annual depreciation allowance ►capital allowances.

annual general meeting (AGM) All public limited companies (►incorporation) in the UK are required by law to invite all ►shareholders to a general meeting with directors each year. (US = *annual meeting, annual stockholders' meeting*.) Among other things the meeting elects directors, appoints ►auditors and fixes their remuneration.

annual percentage rate (APR) The true statement of the annual cost of financial charges levied on ►consumer credit, as required by the ►Consumer Credit Act in the UK and the ►Truth in Lending Act in the USA. The lender's administrative costs, profit margin and interest charges on the loan are normally incorporated in an added charge payable throughout the term of the contract and expressed as a percentage of the value of the transaction. Until legislation was adopted, the percentage was often shown as a rate per month, a figure clearly smaller than the rate per year. The legislation made annual quotation compulsory.

annuitant Person in receipt of an ►annuity.

annuity 1. A regular annual payment of money. 2. A future stream of guaranteed annual income purchased by an immediate lump-sum payment. The lump sum is calculated by ►discounted cash flow and varies according to the ►rate of interest. Annuities can be *certain* or ►terminable life, ►immediate, ►deferred or ►perpetual. Some annuities offer protection against the erosion of the real value of income at higher cost, e.g. by a guaranteed increase of 5% or some other percentage each year, or the income may be tied to the profits of a life fund. ►►life assurance.

ANRPC ►Association of Natural Rubber Producing Countries.

anti-trust legislation ►trust.

APACS ►clearing house.

Apec ►Asia Pacific Economic Cooperation Forum.

APCIMS (UK) Association of Private Client Investment Managers and Stockbrokers.

appreciate To rise in value, as of a ►security on the ►stock exchange or a ►currency against other currencies in the ►foreign exchange market.

appropriations ►below the line.

APR ►annual percentage rate.

arbitrage Use by arbitrageurs (►ARBs) of the difference between the value of, or return on, ➤assets in order to obtain a profit, namely: **1**. The purchase of a currency or ➤money-market asset ➤forward at three months and the sale of the same asset forward at six months, with the intention of securing a profit on the immediate cost, as against the contracted subsequent price, of the asset. **2**. The sale and purchase of matching assets in different currencies in order to obtain a profit on an anomaly in exchange rates. **3**. The switching of funds between money-market assets in order to obtain a profit on the differences in the yield or the ➤discounted value of the assets. **4**. A ➤swap of ➤securities. **5**. The purchase and sale forward of ➤commodities or the purchase and sale of these in different ➤commodity markets.

ARBs Arbitrageurs (➤arbitrage) who buy ➤shares in companies subject to ➤take-over bids.

arithmetic average ➤average.

arithmetic mean ➤average.

ARM ➤adjustable rate mortgage.

arm's length As between financially unrelated parties.

ARP ➤adjustable rate preferred stock.

Article 65 ➤Securities and Exchange Act.

articles of association ➤memorandum of association.

articles of incorporation ➤memorandum of association.

as-you-like option An ➤option in one form that, at the choice of the holder, can, within a specified time limit, be changed into another form. Also known as a *chooser* or *call-or-put* option.

ASB Accounting Standards Board. ➤accounting standards.

ASC ➤Australian Securities Commission.

Asia Pacific Economic Co-operation Forum A grouping of the governments of 18 countries bordering the Pacific, comprising those in the Far East, Australasia and the Americas, for the purpose of the liberalization of trade and investment.

Asian Development Bank A bank to provide financial aid to the ➤developing countries of Asia established in 1966 by 32 governments mainly in the Asian area but including those of the United States, the UK and Switzerland.

Asian option ➤average rate options.

Asian style option An ➤option which is automatically settled, if expiring ➤in the money, as the difference between the ➤strike price and the average value of the underlying asset in an agreed price period.

asked price ➤offer price.

asset Something that has value or earning power. On the ➤balance sheet of a company the following categories of assets are distinguished: *current assets* – cash, bank deposits and bills receivable; ➤trade investments; *fixed assets* – land, buildings, plant and machinery, vehicles and furniture; *intangible assets* – ➤goodwill, patents, etc. Financial assets are titles to cash such as a ➤bank deposit or income and/or ➤capital gains such as ➤ordinary shares.

asset allocation ➤investment approaches.

asset-backed security An ➤issue whose ➤security or ➤collateral is the return on a financial ➤instrument, e.g. a ➤mortgage, ➤credit card receivables or a ➤currency hedge.

asset stripping Usually the acquisition of a company at a price less than its break-up value and the sale of some or all of the ➤assets to realize a ➤profit.

assignment The transfer of rights and obligations in property to a third party, as in the assignment of a lease or an insurance policy.

associate company (UK) A company over which another company has some influence, normally through a minority shareholding of less than 50% but more than 20%. ➤➤consolidated accounts.

Association of British Insurers (ABI) A trade association formed in 1985 by a merger of the British Insurance Association (BIA) with a number of other representative bodies in the insurance industry, including the Life Insurance Association and the Life Offices Association. With some 440 members, the ABI represents virtually the whole of the British insurance industry. Its objects are: to represent members' interests to government and to political and trade bodies in general; to provide a range of services to members, including technical guidance, statistics, investment information and standards, e.g. in international trade, training and accounting; to promote knowledge of the industry in the general public.

Association of Futures Brokers and Dealers ➤Financial Services Act.

Association of International Bond Dealers ➤International Securities Market Association.

Association of Investment Trust Managers (AITC) (UK) An association of UK ➤investment trusts established in 1932 to further the interests of member companies. AITC offers representation to the ➤London Stock Exchange, the ➤Accounting Standards Board, the Inland Revenue and other government departments, and the European Commission. The AITC provides advice, information and technical guidance. Membership comprises over 300 ➤investment trusts, and accounts for 94% of the value of all funds under management.

Association of Lloyd's Members (ALM) A voluntary and non-official association of ►external members of ►Lloyd's, formed to inform and advise members on Lloyd's issues, and to represent the views of members to the market's authorities. The ALM has some 9,000 members and has been acknowledged by the market authorities as making a useful contribution to the formulation of policy. It is not to be confused with the various 'action bodies' formed to pursue loss-making members' grievances against syndicates and agents.

Association of Natural Rubber Producing Countries (ANRPC) An intergovernmental organization, comprising India, Indonesia, Malaysia, Papua New Guinea, Singapore, Sri Lanka and Thailand, formed in 1970 to bring about co-ordination in production and marketing, to promote technical co-operation among member countries and to achieve fair and stable prices. The member countries account for approximately 90% of world supply. In 1982 a Standing Committee on INRO Matters (►International Natural Rubber Organization) was formed to co-ordinate members' position on subjects discussed at that body. The association consists of an assembly and an executive.

Association of Payment Clearing Services (APACS) ►clearing house.

Association of Tin Producing Countries (ATPC) A market grouping of tin-mining countries (Australia, Bolivia, Indonesia, Malaysia, Nigeria, Thailand and Zaire) accounting for 60% of world production, formed after the collapse in 1985 of the International Tin Council and the release on to the world market of buffer stocks of 100,000 tonnes. The aims of the ATPC are to reverse the resultant fall in price (from $12 per kg in 1981 to $5 per kg in 1993) by means of export quotas. However, economic decline in industrialized countries and increased exports from non-ATPC sources (Brazil, Burma, China, Peru, Portugal, the former Soviet Union, the USA and Vietnam), often at lower prices, largely nullified the quota scheme.

Association of Unit Trusts and Investment Funds (AUTIF) (UK) Founded in 1959 as the Association of Unit Trust Managers, AUTIF is a trade association representing 98% of the industry and comprising 138 organizations, including banks, building societies, insurance companies, stockbrokers and investment management houses. The objects of the association are to represent the interests of the industry vis-à-vis government, the media, other trade bodies, consumers, institutional investors and others; to promote knowledge of, and confidence in, the industry; to provide technical and statistical information to the industry; to set standards where appropriate; and to publish relevant literature.

ASX ►Australian Stock Exchange.

at best An instruction to a ►broker to buy or sell a ►security at the best price they can get at the time of the ►order.

at call ➤call money.

at-the-money The ➤exercise price of a ➤derivative that is closest to the market price of the underlying instrument.

Athens Stock Exchange Like ➤stock exchanges in many countries, the Athens exchange (the only one in Greece and founded in 1876) has been modernized and adopted electronic trading.

ATPC ➤Association of Tin Producing Countries.

ATX Index (Austria) The main Vienna Stock Exchange ➤share index.

au jour le jour (Fr.) ➤Overnight money.

auction system ➤order driven.

audit The verification of accounts by an external qualified accountant. Larger limited companies (➤incorporation) are required under the Companies Acts to have their accounts audited by a member of a recognized accountancy body. The auditor's report is intended to give an opinion on whether or not the accounts give a 'true and fair view' on the affairs of the business and also that the accounts comply with the requirements of the Companies Acts.

audit trail An important advantage of the ➤market maker or ➤quote-driven system of ➤securities dealing is that computer files can be maintained of price quotations and transactions so that irregularities may be investigated along the audit trail, which is the name given to the successive entries in this system, which when necessary are followed through by an investigator or auditor. Checks may be made, e.g., to ensure that when dealers buy or sell from their own account from or to a client they have done so at a price that is fair in relation to the prices being made by other market makers at the time.

auditor An accountant or firm of accountants appointed by the directors on behalf of the ➤shareholders of a company (➤annual general meeting; incorporation) to verify that the accounts of the company present a 'true and fair view' of its financial affairs. Audits are a legal requirement for all companies in the UK but only for those registered with the ➤Securities and Exchange Commission in the USA.

Aufgeld (Ger.) ➤Premium.

Aufsichtsrat (Ger.) Supervisory board of a company.

Auftrag (Ger.) ➤Order.

Ausgabe (Ger.) ➤Issue.

Ausland (Ger.) Abroad.

Auslandskassenverein (Ger.) The ►Kassenverein for foreign ►securities.

Auslandsobligation (Swiss) A ►foreign bond (8 to 15 years' ►maturity) or ►note (3 to 8 years) issued in Switzerland.

Austraclear The Australian clearing house for ►commercial paper.

Australian Associated Stock Exchange ►Australian Stock Exchange.

Australian Ratings The ►rating agency set up in Australia.

Australian Securities Commission (ASC) The supervisory body for securities transactions in Australia.

Australian Stock Exchange (ASX) There were six stock exchange ►trading floors in Australia: in Adelaide, Brisbane, Hobart, Melbourne, Perth and Sydney. The formation of the national stock exchange in April 1987 amalgamated the six state exchanges, loosely federated in the Australian Associated Stock Exchange (AASE), into one body. Floor trading ceased in 1990 when the new Stock Exchange Automated Screen Trading System (SEATS) came into operation (►automated screen trading). The exchange is regulated by the Australian Securities Commission. The barometer for the Australian Stock Exchange is the All Ordinaries Share Price Index, a weighted ►share index of 250 companies. There is a second board market in shares in ►unlisted companies.

authorized capital (UK) The amount of share ►capital fixed in the ►memorandum of association and the articles of association of a company as required by the Companies Acts (►incorporation). US = *authorized capital stock.*

authorized capital stock (US) ►authorized capital.

authorized foreign exchange bank (Jap.) A bank licensed by the Ministry of Finance to lend and borrow in foreign ►currencies at ►short term. Such licences are granted to most commercial banks, as well as to ►long-term credit banks, ►trust banks and ►*sogo* banks.

AUTIF ►Association of Unit Trusts and Investment Funds.

Automated Bankers Clearing System (BACS) ►clearing house.

automated screen trading (AST) An electronic dealing system in which orders to buy or sell are entered, matched and executed by keystrokes on a computer system and at prices shown on video terminals. Such a system dispenses with ►trading floors, telephone dealing and paperwork and therefore with ►back offices and can operate worldwide on a 24-hour basis (►24-hour trading). At present automated screen trading in the major markets exists only in a limited way, e.g. under the ►National Association of Securities Dealers Automated Quotation System and in the ►Stock Exchange Automatic Execution Facility, but it is expected eventually to be available on all ►stock exchanges. The ►Chicago

Mercantile Exchange introduced AST for out-of-hours trading in 1989 (►post-market trading). The first AST was in the New Zealand ►futures market in 1985 (►automated trade system), and the second was in the ►Swiss Options and Financial Futures Exchange, which commenced operations in 1988. ►►Toronto Stock Exchange.

automated trade system (ATS) (NZ) An electronic system for trading on the ►New Zealand Futures and Options Exchange. The market in New Zealand is very small and geographically dispersed, which makes such a system important.

automatic teller machine (ATM) A computerized machine used for banking transactions, e.g. paying or withdrawing money, statement inquiries and transfers; operated by magnetic plastic cards and ►personal identification numbers (PINs).

aval A guarantee of payment of a ►bill of exchange under the commercial law of many European countries outside the UK, normally given by a third party, often a bank, for all or part of the nominal value of the bill. The existence of an *aval* is signified by the phrase '*pour aval*' or '*bon pour aval*' inscribed on the bill, followed by the signature of the party giving the *aval*. ►►acceptance.

avant-bourse (Swiss) ►Swiss stock exchanges.

average 1. A single number calculated to summarize a group of numbers. An *arithmetic mean* is the sum of the values of the items in the group divided by the number of items. The *median* is the middle value in a group of items ranged in order of size. The *mode* is the most frequently occurring value in such a group. A *geometric mean* is the root of the *n*th product of a series of numbers multiplied together, where *n* is the number of values in the series. **2.** A term used, particularly in marine insurance, for the apportionment of a partial loss. *General average* describes a case where a part of a ship or its cargo is abandoned in order to save the ship and cargo as a whole; the owner of the abandoned portion is entitled to proportionate compensation from the other owners concerned. For this purpose the services of an *average adjuster*, somebody who is not necessarily an advocate but is well versed in the law of average, are used. Where a part of the ship or its cargo is lost not in order to preserve the remainder, then a situation of *particular average* is deemed to exist, and no claim on other owners is allowable.

average adjuster ►average.

average rate option An ►option that is ►settled on the basis of the difference between the ►striking price and the average market value of the underlying security. Also known as an *Asian option*.

avoir fiscal (Fr.) A tax credit, equal to 50% of dividends paid, allowed non-French holders of French ►securities. ►►tax credit.

azione (It.) ►Share.

B

back ►backwardation.

back office The department in a firm of ►stockbrokers that deals with ►settlement procedures, such as the forwarding of ►share certificates to clients and the maintenance of ►accounts. Sometimes referred to as 'the cage' in the USA, where a section dealing with cheques and certificates is protected by a metal grille.

back-to-back loan Borrowings in one currency that are matched by borrowings in another currency to overcome ►exchange control in aid of investment.

back-up credit A credit guarantee provided by a bank or ►syndicate of banks underpinning a ►Euronote facility or ►note issuance facility. The credit is operated where some or all of the notes fail to find a purchaser.

backward price (UK) ►crossed.

backwardation (UK) **1.** On the ►stock exchange, a sum of money paid by a ►bear to a ►bull for the right to delay delivery of ►securities sold forward at a fixed price. **2.** The situation in a ►commodity market where ►spot prices are higher than prices quoted for future delivery. **3.** ►crossed.

BACS ►clearing house.

badges of trade (UK) Criteria set out in 1954 by the Royal Commission on the Taxation of Profits and Income to define the distinction, in the ►securities and ►commodity markets, between trading and investment. Investment incurred the generally lower capital gains tax (►capital gain) upon realization of a gain; while trading is regarded as current business, the profits on which are subject to income tax or ►corporation tax. The definition is needed to establish a dividing line between frequent investment transactions and trade. Commodity market dealings are normally assessed as trade. Security market dealings can fall into either category.

Baht The national ►currency of Thailand.

baisse (Fr.) A fall, normally in the ►stock market.

balance In financial accounting, the balance is the amount required to be inserted in one of two columns of *debits* and *credits* to make the totals equal (►double-entry bookkeeping). A bank balance is the amount standing to the credit or debit (►overdraft) of a customer. ►►balance of payments.

balance commerciale (Fr.) Visible, or merchandise, balance. ►balance of payments.

balance of payments The total movement of goods, services and financial transactions between one country and the rest of the world; the term commonly used for the record of such movements. In money terms, therefore, the balance of payments is the total of all receipts from abroad, and of all payments to recipients abroad. All receipts and payments of whatever nature are included, whether they be payments and receipts for non-commercial purposes, such as legacies and for pensions; for goods sold or services rendered; for investment purposes; on behalf of government; or of private persons and agencies.

The balance of payments record or account is conventionally divided into the ►current account, or payments and receipts for immediate transactions, such as the sale of goods and rendering of services; and the *capital account*, or the money movements not immediately devoted to trade, such as investment. The current account is subdivided into the merchandise, or visible account (often also termed the trade account), comprising the movement of goods; and the invisible account, comprising the movement of services, transfers and investment incomes. Services comprise transport, travel, banking, insurance, broking and other activities; transfers comprise money movements for the transmission of legacies, pensions and other non-commercial items; investment income consists of the interest, profits and dividends deriving from capital placed abroad.

The capital account is normally divided into long-term and short-term capital, the former relating to capital employed for investment purposes, the latter to bank advances, trade credit and the like. Long-term capital is again subdivided into *direct investment* capital, or capital employed for the establishment of commercial premises and industrial plant; and *portfolio investment* capital, or capital employed for the purchase of bonds and shares.

A balance of payments account will normally resolve the various subordinate accounts into balances or net receipts and payments, summing these to an overall balance, subject to a balancing item (UK), net errors and omissions, or statistical discrepancy (US), against which the net overflow from or net inflow into the country's ►reserves is noted. The balance of payments account is also referred to as the *external account* of a nation.

balance sheet A statement of the wealth of a business or organization at a particular date, usually the end of the ►financial year, as distinct from a ►profit and loss account, which records changes over a period. The balance sheet is in two parts: ►assets on the left-hand side or at the top, and ►liabilities on the right-hand side or at the bottom. The assets of the company – ►debtors, cash investments and property – are equal to the claims or liabilities of the persons or organizations owning them: the ►creditors, lenders and ►shareholders. This is the principle of ►double-entry bookkeeping.

According to the basic accounting equation, assets equal liabilities plus equity;

therefore, assets minus liabilities equal ➤equity. Equity, shareholders' interest or *net worth* (which are all the same thing) may not reflect true market value, since assets are normally written into the balance sheet at historical cost (➤costs, historical) without any adjustment for *appreciation* (➤appreciate; inflation accounting). ➤➤Fourth Directive.

balancing item ➤balance of payments.

balloon payment The final payment on a ➤loan that is substantially larger than earlier payments. Designed to defer the burden of debt repayment.

ballot ➤oversubscribed.

Baltic Exchange Full title: Baltic, Mercantile and Shipping Exchange. A London market now primarily dealing in ship charters. It originated as the Baltic Coffee House, an 18th-century meeting place for merchants interested in trade in produce from the Baltic countries, then amalgamated with the London Shipping Exchange in 1899, and thereafter dealt primarily in shipbroking, although the London Grain Futures Market also trades on the exchange. Most shipbroking business is, however, now conducted by telephone, off the floor of the exchange. ➤➤Futures and Options Exchange; Grain and Feed Trade Association.

bancassurance The merging of banking and assurance business within a banking business or a building society. Assurance services provided include life assurance and ➤pensions. The emergence of bancassurance was due to the entry of banks into house loan business and the recognition both by such banks and by building societies that with their many outlets they were well placed to sell the life assurance policies used as collateral for mortgages. Ger. = *Allfinanz*.

band 1. The range of ➤maturities in which the Bank of England conducts transactions daily with the ➤money market, principally the ➤discount houses, in ➤Treasury bills, ➤eligible bank bills and ➤local authority bills, in order to influence ➤short-term interest rates. There are four bands: Band 1, 1 to 14 days; Band 2, 15 to 33 days; Band 3, 34 to 63 days; Band 4, 64 to 91 days. **2.** The range within which a ➤managed currency was permitted to move under the ➤Bretton Woods system. **3.** The range within which member countries' currencies are permitted to move under the ➤European Monetary System (EMS).

Bangkok Stock Exchange ➤Securities Exchange of Thailand.

bank ➤banking.

bank advance ➤bank loan.

bank bill A ➤bill of exchange accepted by a bank.

bank charges Fees and other charges made by banks (➤banking) for their services and debited (➤double-entry bookkeeping) from customers' accounts, now commonly after the customer has received an itemized statement of charges.

bank credit proxy (US) A term used by the ➤Federal Reserve to refer to the total deposits of member banks, accepted as a proxy for total credit extended.

bank deposit The amount of money standing to the ➤credit of a customer of a bank. Bank deposits are simply IOUs written in the books of a bank and do not necessarily represent holdings of cash by the bank (➤banking). A deposit may be on ➤current account or ➤deposit account. These two types of account are known as *demand deposits* and *time deposits* in the USA. ➤➤deposit; sight deposit.

bank draft A ➤cheque issued by a bank, in effect a certified cheque in which the recipient may have confidence. Banks will issue drafts for customers for a fee where a ➤creditor will not accept an ordinary ➤debtor's cheque.

Bank for International Settlements (BIS) An institution, effectively a ➤central bank for central banks, with head office in Basle, set up on the basis of a proposal by the Young Committee in 1930. The original purpose was to enable the various national central banks to co-ordinate through their own central bank the receipts and payments arising mainly from German war reparations. It was hoped that it would develop beyond this, but many of the functions which it might have performed were in fact taken over by the ➤International Monetary Fund (IMF) after the Second World War. However, the BIS has in recent years played a more active part in attempting to mitigate the effects of international financial ➤speculation and acts as a trustee for international government loans. In addition the Bank has carried out financial transactions for the ➤Organization for European Economic Co-operation, ➤Organization for Economic Co-operation and Development, ➤European Payments Union, ➤European Monetary Agreement, ➤European Coal and Steel Community and the IMF. From 1973, the bank acted as agent for the European Monetary Co-operation Fund (➤European Monetary System). In 1995, the ➤European Monetary Institute took over the bank's responsibilities in this area. Although major functions of a central bank for central banks are performed by the IMF, the meetings of the central board have been an important means of central bank co-operation, especially in the field of offsetting short-term monetary movements of a speculative kind. In 1996, the BIS had 32 members but in that year invited a further 9 financial institutions to subscribe to the bank's equity, in Brazil, China, Hong Kong, India, Korea, Mexico, Russia, Saudi Arabia and Singapore. ➤Capital Adequacy.

bank loan A ➤loan by a bank, normally for a fixed period and for a specific purpose. The term *bank loan* is also loosely used to include ➤overdrafts, bank ➤mortgage loans and ➤personal loans, as well as ➤term loans, though it is more common to use the generic term *bank advances*. Bank loans are normally secured (➤collateral security) and repaid in regular instalments, with interest charged at rates that vary with the bank's ➤base rate.

---

bank mandate ➤mandate.

Bank of England The ➤central bank of the UK. Founded in 1694 by a group of private bankers, chiefly to raise money for the Crown, it was chartered first to operate as a commercial *joint-stock bank* (➤commercial banks). In succeeding centuries its royal charter favoured the circulation of its notes, and it became a leading banker to other banks. The Bank Charter Act of 1844 recognized it as the central note-issuing authority and the ➤lender of last resort. By 1870 it was recognized as responsible for the general level of interest rates, which it regulated through the ➤bank rate, and thus for the general state of ➤credit in the country. By the early 20th century the Bank of England was recognized as the central organ for the execution of national financial and monetary policy, under the overall direction of the government. In 1946 the bank was nationalized, thus completing its identification with the state. The ➤Banking Act 1979 provided formal definitions under which the bank exercised its supervision of commercial banking practices. In mid 1997 the UK government announced that the bank's responsibility for supervision of the banking system would pass to the Financial Services Authority (➤Financial Services Act). At the same time the bank was made solely responsible for determining UK interest rates, a function until then exercised by the ➤Treasury. The bank thus became independently responsible for UK monetary policy (➤Monetary Policy Committee).

Bank of France The ➤central bank of France, established in 1800 and the oldest in the world after the Bank of Sweden and the ➤Bank of England. In January 1994 the French authorities appointed a nine-member council of the bank, which with other measures is intended to give it a high degree of autonomy in the formulation of monetary policy in conformity with the ➤Maastricht Treaty.

Bank of Japan (BOJ) Japan's ➤central bank, which acts as ➤lender of last resort, manages ➤monetary policy and issues ➤currency. It does not regulate the banking system, which is the role of the Banking Bureau.

bank rate The interest rate at which the ➤Bank of England lent to the commercial banking system as ➤lender of last resort. First recognized in 1702, it remained in existence for 270 years, until 1972 when it was replaced by the ➤minimum lending rate (MLR). The bank's lending under bank rate took the form either of direct loans against collateral or of the discounting of ➤eligible bills. For this reason it was frequently referred to as the *discount rate*.

banker's acceptance (US, Can.) A ➤bill of exchange or *time draft* drawn on and accepted by a Canadian or US bank, usually as part of a ➤line of credit under a ➤letter of credit or ➤acceptance credit. Synonymous with the UK term ➤acceptance.

banking The business of taking ➤deposits and making ➤loans. As ➤financial intermediaries, banks may also offer a whole range of other financial services, such as ►insurance, ►credit cards and ►foreign exchange, but their distinguishing characteristic is their role in the ►money supply through the creation of deposits. When a bank makes a loan it incurs a book debt to a customer in return for a promise to repay it. The ability of a bank to create money in this way is limited in many countries by government controls on lending (►credit control) as well as by its obligation to pay out ►current account deposits in cash on demand. Since the bank's customers meet most of their needs for money by writing ►cheques on their deposits, the cash holdings the banks need are only a small fraction of their total deposits (►liquidity ratio). The settlement of debts arising between banks through cheques drawn on one bank and deposited in another is made through a ►clearing house. Banks are supervised and regulated in most countries by the ►central bank, which acts as ►lender of last resort.

The traditional distinctions between banks and other financial intermediaries are breaking down; e.g. in the UK ►building societies now offer cheque accounts. In some countries banks are not allowed to hold ►equity stakes in their client companies or to act as ►investment banks (►Glass–Steagall Act), and some US states have *unit banking* laws that require each bank to be a single enterprise without branches. Germany, the Netherlands and Switzerland have *universal banking* systems that allow banks to act as investment banks and to provide a very wide range of other financial services. ►►Banking Act 1979; commercial banks; telephone banking; wholesale banking.

Banking Act 1979 (UK) Legislation defining a bank (►banking) and a ►licensed deposit-taker for the purposes of supervision and ►regulation by the ►Bank of England. The Act defined a bank as a deposit-taking institution with either a wide range of banking services or a highly specialized banking service according to a number of specific criteria, and with net ►assets in excess of certain limits. The Act was made necessary by the ►European Union's First Banking Co-ordination ►directive. ►Banking Directives.

Banking Directives Several ►directives of the European Union intended to remove impediments to the provision of banking services across borders in Europe. The Second Banking Directive (1989) allows banks to offer services anywhere in the ►European Union (EU) provided they are authorized in their home state (the principal of mutual recognition). The Second Directive has provisions for minimum capital for credit institutions and gives the EU the right to suspend licences for banks headquartered in countries outside the EU where those countries do not give equal treatment to EU banks. Other banking directives include Own Funds, Solvency Ratio, Large Exposures, Money Laundering, Deposit Insurance, Capital Adequacy. The *Investment Services Directive* (1993) has similar objectives to the Second Directive for firms providing investment products such as ►unit trusts and allows, for example, cross-border access to ►stock exchanges.

banknote A note issued by a bank promising to pay the bearer the ►par value of the note on demand. At one time banknotes were exchangeable for gold, but now the promise to pay simply means that they are legal tender.

bankruptcy A declaration by a court of law that an individual or company is insolvent, that is, cannot meet ►debts on the due dates. A bankruptcy petition may be filed either by the debtor or by their creditors requesting a receiving order. An inquiry into the debtor's affairs is then conducted by, in the UK, the official receiver; the business has then passed into receivership. If the receiver thinks fit, they may call a meeting of the debtor's creditors and, if the creditors wish it, declare the debtor bankrupt. The debtor's assets are then realized and distributed among the creditors either by the receiver or by a trustee appointed by the creditors. In the case of a company it goes into ►liquidation.

US procedures are similar to those of the UK, but under Chapter 11 of the Bankruptcy Reform Act 1978 a firm may apply to the court for protection from its creditors while it carries out a reorganization of its affairs so as to be able to pay off its debts. In a similar way companies in the UK may now be placed under administration rather than go into liquidation. The Insolvency Act 1985 and 1986 codified existing law and made the handling of the affairs of insolvent debtors the responsibility of a registered insolvency practitioner. The Acts introduced a wide range of sanctions against directors who act negligently, as did the Company Directors Disqualification Act 1986.

Bankruptcy Reform Act 1978 ►bankruptcy.

banque d'affaires (Fr.) ►Merchant bank.

Banque de France ►Bank of France.

BAPEPAM ►Jakarta Stock Exchange.

Bar (Ger.) ►Cash.

Barber case ►equalization of pensions.

Bardepot (Ger.) A regulation requiring West German borrowers on foreign markets to deposit part of the proceeds in a non-interest-bearing account at the ►Bundesbank; introduced to deter foreign inflows into West Germany, and thus to contain the West German balance of payments surplus. Withdrawn in the 1970s.

bargain (UK) A purchase or sale on the ►London Stock Exchange.

Bargeld (Ger.) ►cash.

barratry A ►peril in marine insurance policy consisting in a deliberately wrongful act by the master or crew of a vessel involving a loss to the owner or charterer of the vessel.

barter ►countertrading.

base period The reference date for which an ➤index number of a time series is calculated.

base rate (UK) The rate of ➤interest that forms the basis for the charges for ➤bank loans and ➤overdrafts and the deposit rates of the ➤commercial banks. Actual rates are set at up to about five percentage points above base rate according to the creditworthiness of the borrower. In the USA the *prime rate* is the rate at which a bank will lend to its most creditworthy customer. Though to some extent now superseded by ➤cost of funds rates, the prime rate is still an important indicator of ➤money-market trends. ➤➤bank rate.

base-weighted indices ➤Index numbers in which the weights used are those of the reference or base year against which changes are to be measured. ➤weighted average.

basic balance The balance struck of the ➤current and ➤long-term capital accounts combined of the ➤balance of payments.

basic rate of tax ➤income tax.

basis (US) The difference between the ➤futures price and the ➤spot price.

basis point 1/100th of 1%. A measure normally used in the statement of interest rates; e.g. a change from 5.75% to 5.81% is a change of six basis points. First used in the USA, now common elsewhere.

basis price 1. In the ➤commodity markets, the price agreed between the seller and buyer at which an ➤option can be exercised; generally the market price of the commodity at the time the option is sold; also known as the ➤striking price. 2. The basis on which a ➤dealer in the ➤over-the-counter market attempts to match buyers and sellers of a ➤security. Thus, their estimate of the market price.

basket trade (UK) A trade in securities involving all the shares comprising the FT 100 share index. ➤Financial Times Shares Indices.

Basle Agreement ➤capital adequacy.

Basle Concordat An understanding reached between the monetary authorities of the major countries in 1975 under which each authority is responsible for the supervision of foreign branches established by its domestic banks.

baud, baud rate The number of ➤bits (units of information) per second that can be sent down a transmission line, such as a telephone line. Used in rating the capacity of equipment such as a ➤modem.

bear A speculator who sells ➤securities because they expect a fall in prices; the antonym of ➤bull. A bear who sells securities that they do not possess is described as having *sold short* (➤position). If they do possess the securities that they sell, they are described as a *covered* or *protected* bear. A *bear raid* is an attempt by a number of investors acting in collusion to drive down the price of a share by selling stock. This has been done to defeat a ►take-over by depressing the shares of the predator. A *bear market* is one in which prices are falling. ►►bear squeeze.

bear call spread The holding of a call ►option against the sale of another call option of the same maturity but with a lower ►exercise price; the intention is to profit by a fall in the value of the underlying ►asset.

bear market ►bear.

bear position ►position.

bear put spread The simultaneous purchase and sale of put options with the same expiry date but with an ►exercise price for the purchased put ►option higher than for the sold put option. The operator expects a fall in the value of the underlying ►asset.

bear raid ►bear.

bear squeeze The purchase of ►securities, ►currency or commodities in the markets by the authorities, thus raising prices and squeezing the ►liquidity of speculators who have been selling short (►position) in the expectation of falling prices.

bearer security A ►share or ►bond that is not registered in the name of the holder, who can sell it or claim ►dividends on simple presentation to a bank or ►broker. Common on certain continental European ►stock exchanges, bear securities have the attraction that the tax authorities cannot identify the owners. For this reason dividends and interest on bearer securities are usually subject to a ►withholding tax. In most countries owners of securities are registered. ►Registrar.

bed and breakfast (UK) The sale of a ►security on one day and its repurchase the following day in a previously agreed transaction for the purpose of establishing a ►capital gain or loss. A transaction of this kind does not establish a loss or gain for tax purposes in the USA but until recently did so in the UK.

Beige Book (US) A familiar term for the report on local economic and financial conditions prepared by the district banks of the ►Federal Reserve System and supplied to members of the ►Federal Open Market Committee before each meeting. It is one of three information documents so supplied. ►►Blue Book; Green Book.

Bel-20 (Bel.) The ►Brussels Stock Exchange ►share index.

below the line Items in the ►profit and loss account which are underneath the line at which the total trading profit for the period is struck. In reported results for a ►quoted company, extraordinary items that arise from transactions which are outside the ordinary trading activities of the company (e.g. the sale of an office building) may be taken below the line for the purposes of calculating ➤earnings per share, whereas exceptional items that do derive from the ordinary activities may be taken above the line for that purpose. Appropriations such as ➤dividends, transfers to ➤reserves or ➤taxation are below the line.

bénéfice (Fr.) ➤Profit.

beneficial interest Ultimate ownership of property. For example, UK directors of companies are required to declare beneficial interests in their companies even where these shares are held by ➤nominees or in ➤trust.

Berne Union The International Union of Credit and Investment Insurers, an international organization for both government and private export credit (➤Export Credit Guarantee Department) and other trade insurance bodies.

BEST ➤Stock Exchange Automatic Execution Facility.

best price ➤order.

beta coefficient ➤alpha coefficient.

beta stocks ➤alpha securities, stocks.

BFE Baltic Futures Exchange. ➤Futures and Options Exchange.

bid price The price at which a ➤market maker will buy ➤shares or a ➤dealer in a ➤commodity market will buy commodities. ➤Unit trust managers also quote a bid price at which they will repurchase units sold to the public. ➤offer price.

bid rate The ➤rate of interest offered for a ➤deposit. ➤London interbank offered rate (LIBOR).

Big Bang (UK) The term used to encapsulate the changes culminating on 27 October 1986 with the abandonment of the ➤commission agreement between members of the ➤London Stock Exchange and of strict segregation of ➤jobbers and ➤brokers. In July 1983 the government agreed to exempt the stock exchange from the provisions of the Restrictive Practices Act in return for lifting a number of restrictions. In 1982 the Stock Exchange Council had raised the limit placed on any one outside shareholder from 10% to 29.9% and in 1985 decided that this limit would also be abandoned. Many banks and other financial institutions have acquired interests in, or control of, stock exchange companies since March 1986. Other changes associated with the Big Bang have been in the closure of the trading floor of the stock exchange in favour of electronic off-the-floor telephone dealing and a major expansion in dealings in international ➤securities.

Big Board ➤New York Stock Exchange.

Big Four 1. The four dominating Japanese securities houses: Nomura, Daiwa,

Nikko and Yamaichi. **2.** Also used of the four biggest UK commercial banks: Barclays, Lloyds, Midland and National Westminster.

BIIBA ►British Insurance and Investment Brokers Association.

bilan (Fr.) **1.** ►Balance. **2.** ►Balance sheet. **3.** ►Accounts.

Bilanz (Ger.) ►Balance sheet.

bill ►Bill of Exchange, Commercial Bill, Treasury Bill.

bill broker A firm or individual that deals in ►Treasury bills and ►bills of exchange on the London ►money market.

bill leak (UK) A device for evading the UK ►supplementary special deposits scheme ('the corset') whereby ►bank bills were negotiated and held outside the banking system; i.e. a bank *accepted* (►acceptance) a bill drawn by a commercial client, which was then sold to another non-bank holder, the acceptance remaining only as a contingent liability on the bank's balance sheet and not therefore included in its ►interest-bearing eligible liabilities.

bill of exchange An order in writing addressed by one person to another and signed by the person giving it, requiring the person to whom it is addressed to pay, on demand or at a fixed date, a specified sum of money. The bill is made out by the signatory (the *drawer*) always with the consent of the person to whom it is addressed, who signs or *accepts* it (►acceptance); and mainly in relation to the sale of goods or produce. Bills are ►negotiable in the ►money market, so enabling drawers to obtain their money at once. Bills of exchange are divided into the categories of ►bank bills, ►trade bills, ►fine trade bills and ►finance bills.

billet de trésorerie (Fr.) ►Commercial paper.

billion Originally a term meaning one million million, now conventionally used to mean one thousand million.

BIMBO Buy-in ►management buy-out.

binding authority Authority given to an agent by an insurance institution to accept business on behalf of that institution, within prescribed limits.

BIPAR (Bureau International des Producteurs d'Assurance et de Réassurance) (Fr.) ►(under English title) International Federation of Insurance Intermediaries.

BIS ►Bank for International Settlements.

bit Binary digit, i.e. 0 or 1.

Black Monday The ►crash of world stock market prices on Monday 19 October 1987.

Black Tuesday (US) The Wall Street (►New York Stock Exchange) stock market ►crash on Tuesday 29 October 1929.

Black Wednesday ►Maastricht Treaty.

block (US) A large holding of ►shares or ►stock in one company. A block trade is usually considered to involve the sale or purchase of at least 10,000 shares.

block order exposure system (BLOX) (UK) Offers to buy or sell large ►blocks of ►shares carried on the ►Teletext Output of Price Information by Computer (TOPIC).

BLOX ►block order exposure system.

Blue Book (UK, US) 1. A familiar term for the review of ►monetary control options presented by the staff director for monetary policy reviews to members of the ►Federal Open Market Committee (FOMC) before each meeting (US) (►Beige Book; Green Book). 2. A familiar term for the UK *National Accounts*, an annual collection of the main macroeconomic statistics compiled by the Central Statistical Office (CSO) and published by HMSO.

blue chips ►Shares in leading ►quoted companies that can be easily bought and sold without influencing their price (►liquidity) and are regarded as low-risk ►investments.

blue month (UK) The most actively traded month of a ►derivative, decided by the ►London International Financial Futures Exchange (LIFFE) in the light of trading activity. Designated in order to facilitate price quotation.

blue-sky laws (US) State laws in the USA that require a ►security to be registered with a state before it can be traded there. ►National Market System stocks traded on the ►National Association of Securities Dealers Automated Quotation System (NASDAQ) are now exempt from these laws.

BM & F (Brazil) ►Bolsa de Mercadorias e Futuros.

Bobl An abbreviation used in English-speaking markets to denote a *Bundesobligation*, a German government five-year bond in which ►derivatives are also traded.

boiler room ►bucket shop.

bolsa (Sp.) ►Stock exchange.

Bolsa de Comercio de Santiago ►Chilean Stock Exchange.

Bolsa de Mercadorias e Futuros (BM & F) (Brazil) The São Paulo Commodities and Futures Exchange. The BM & F is the major ►commodities and ►futures exchange of Brazil. Founded in 1986, it was by 1996 the fourth largest futures exchange in the world. It has an office in New York.

Bolsa de Valores de Lisboa ➤Lisbon Stock Exchange.

Bolsa de Valores de São Paulo ➤São Paulo Stock Exchange.

Bolsa Mexicana de Valores ➤Mexican Stock Exchange.

Bombay Stock Exchange The oldest ➤stock exchange in India. There are also exchanges in Calcutta, Delhi and other cities. The exchanges are regulated by the Securities and Exchange Board of India (SEBI). ➤➤National Stock Exchange.

bon du trésor (Fr.) ➤Treasury bill or ➤bond.

bon marché (Fr.) Cheap.

bond A form of interest-bearing ➤security issued by central or local governments, companies, banks and other institutions. Bonds are usually a form of long-term security; but they do not always carry fixed interest (➤variable rate security), they may be irredeemable (➤redemption date) and they may be secured or unsecured. In the USA the term *bond* includes ➤debentures (➤bearer security; Eurobond). ➤➤deferred coupon note; straight bond.

bond washing ➤dividend stripping.

bonos Abbreviation used in English-speaking markets, derived from *bono*, a bond, to denote long-term Spanish government bonds.

bonus 1. A free share or *scrip* issue. ➤bonus issue. **2**. A distribution of life assurance company investment profits. ➤life assurance.

BONUS (borrower's option for notes and underwritten standby) An arrangement by which a borrower receives a loan package comprising mixed ➤commercial paper and ➤Euro-commercial paper liabilities, e.g. an ➤uncommitted (non-➤underwritten) ➤note issuance facility, a US commercial paper programme and a ➤standby credit.

bonus issue A term virtually synonymous with *scrip issue* and *capitalization issue* (US = *stock dividend* and *stock split*), describing ➤shares given without charge to existing shareholders in proportion to the shares already held. A scrip issue does not add to the ➤capital employed by the firm but is made where the capital employed has been increased by retaining profits and is therefore out of line with the ➤issued capital. Consequently it is a pure bookkeeping transaction. For example, ➤dividends will, after a scrip issue, be divided among a larger number of shares, so that the dividend per share will fall in proportion to the number of bonus shares issued. The motive for splitting shares in this way may be to capitalize retained profits or it may simply be to reduce the unit price of the shares (without altering the ➤yield) and so improve their marketability. ➤➤drip; heavy share.

borrow Of ➤commodity markets, to buy at current prices and simultaneously sell ➤forward.

borrowed reserves (US) The total of ➤adjustment credit and ➤seasonal borrowings from the ➤Federal Reserve held by US banks.

bors (Den.) ➤*drittmarkt*.

borsa (It.) ➤Stock exchange.

Borsa Valori (It.) The main ➤stock exchange in Milan. Unlisted shares are traded on the ➤*mercato ristretto* and the *terzo mercato*.

Börse (Ger.) ➤Stock exchange.

Börsenmakler (Ger.) ➤*freier Makler*.

Börsenumsatzsteuer (Ger.) An ➤*ad valorem* tax on transactions on the ➤German stock exchanges. Applies only to purchases and sales by residents.

Börsenvorstand (Ger.) The governing body of a German ➤stock exchange.

bottom fishing Buying shares in a declining market in the hope of profit when the market revives.

bottom-up ➤Investment approaches.

bought deal A term used in ➤venture capital where the financing company acquires a subsidiary from a large firm with a view to syndicating the acquisition later through a ➤management buy-out or other means (➤syndicate).

bought ledger The accounting record of purchases by an organization from its suppliers.

bourse (Fr.) French term for ➤stock exchange, also used in Belgium, Switzerland and other European countries. ➤Paris Bourse.

boutique ➤niche player.

BOVESPA (Bolsa de Valores de São Paulo) ➤São Paulo Stock Exchange.

box spread A combination of ➤options, namely a ➤long-call option held against a ➤short-*put* option with the same ➤exercise price, coupled with a short-call option held against a long-put option, both with the same exercise price.

Brady bonds Interest-bearing ➤securities issued in the early 1990s by Latin American borrowers (e.g. Argentina and Venezuela) as part of an arrangement to reschedule international bank debt. The bonds were denominated in US dollars and US government securities carrying no interest provided ➤collateral security. The plan was the idea of Nicholas Brady, the former US Treasury Secretary.

Several issuers, including Mexico and Brazil, have since bought back some of their Brady bonds and replaced them with unsecured debt.

Brady Commission Report (US) Report of the commission of inquiry chaired by Nicholas Brady into the October 1987 stock market ►crash. ►►circuit-breaker mechanism.

Brazilian stock exchanges ►São Paulo Stock Exchange.

break-even The point at which cumulative sales revenue is equal to total costs. At that point no profit or loss will have been incurred.

Bretton Woods A conference (official title: the United Nations Monetary and Financial Conference) held at Bretton Woods, New Hampshire, USA, in July 1944, called to consider the postwar organization of international monetary relations and resulting in the establishment of the ►International Bank for Reconstruction and Development (World Bank) and the ►International Monetary Fund (IMF).

bridge finance A short-term ►loan provided by a ►venture capital provider while a company is seeking alternative finance, e.g. by ►flotation.

bridging loan A short-term ►loan provided for an individual who has bought a new property before selling an existing one.

British Institute of Dealers in Securities (BIDS) (UK) A trade association of ►dealers in ►over-the-counter securities. Now defunct.

British Insurance and Investment Brokers Association (BIIBA) (UK) A body formed in 1977 to represent registered insurance brokers (►Insurance Brokers Registration Council (IBRC)) and investment intermediaries authorized under the ►Financial Services Act 1986 and members of the relevant self-regulating organization under that Act. There are some 3,000 members responsible for probably 80% of insurance placed by brokers in the UK. BIIBA co-ordinates the views of its members, makes these known to government and Parliament, to regulators and other key trade associations including the ►Association of British Insurers (ABI), and offers advice, assistance and training to members.

British Venture Capital Association (BVCA) An association representing all major suppliers of ►venture capital which invest principally in the UK. Its objects are: to provide information to those seeking venture capital; to represent members in discussions with government and other organizations; to provide a forum for the exchange of members' views; to provide education and training for members' employees; and to foster high standards of practice. The organization has some 100 full members, together with some 100 associate members.

broker An intermediary between a buyer and a seller in a highly organized market, e.g. a ►stockbroker, a commodity broker or a market operator working on their own account, such as an ►insurance broker, ►pawnbroker or ►bill broker.

On the ►London Stock Exchange a broker was an intermediary between the public and ►market makers or ►jobbers, but since the ►Big Bang many brokers have become ►broker-dealers (a firm of broker-dealers is known as a *brokerage house* in the USA), combining functions of the broker and the market maker. ►►commission broker.

broker-dealer A person or organization buying and selling ►securities, ►commodities and ►contracts, both on their own account (i.e. as ►principal) and as agent for clients. Prior to the ►Big Bang in the UK, ►brokers on the ►London Stock Exchange were not permitted to act in this dual capacity because of the possibility of conflicts of interest. ►►market maker.

broker pool A grouping of ►insurers for the purpose of contracting ►reinsurance through one ►broker.

brokerage The ►commission charged by a ►broker.

brokerage account (US) The record of purchases and sales of ►securities on behalf of a client kept by a ►stockbroker.

brokerage house (US) ►broker.

Brussels Stock Exchange With the closure of the ►bourse in Antwerp at the end of 1997, trading of local shares in Belgium is now concentrated in Brussels. That city, however, is also the home of the ►European Association of Securities Dealers Automated Quotations System (EASDAQ).

BTP ►*buono tesoro poliennali.*

brutto (Ger.) Gross.

Buba Abbreviation of ►Bundesbank.

bucket shop A term of US origin meaning an unregistered and illegal firm of ►stockbrokers, but now used to refer to any low-price sales operation. A 'boiler room' is a ►share-pushing operation selling dubious ►stock by telephone.

Budapest Stock Exchange ►Eastern Europe.

budget An estimate of income and expenditure for a future period, as opposed to an account, which records financial transactions after the event. In the UK the national budget sets out estimates of central government revenue and expenditure for the financial year and is presented to Parliament in the autumn by the Chancellor of the ►Exchequer. The fiscal year ends on 5 April in the UK. The US federal budget is prepared by the Office of Manpower and Budget (OMB) and reviewed and approved by the President for submission to Congress around January prior to the fiscal year, which runs from 1 July to 30 June.

Buenos Aires Stock Exchange The oldest ►stock exchange in Latin America, dating from 1872; called in Spanish El Mercado de Valores de Buenos Aires. There are four other exchanges in Argentina.

buffer stock A quantity of a ➤commodity, normally established under an ➤international commodity agreement, held by a designated common agency for the purpose of release into the market, or of accumulation by drawing from the market, in order to influence the market price.

Building Societies Act 1986 ➤building society.

building society (UK) A UK financial institution engaged in the provision of ➤mortgages, deriving its funds from ➤deposits by the general public. Building societies are non-profit-making bodies (➤mutual). Interest is paid on deposits at rates varying with amount and term of retention. By arrangement with the Inland Revenue a lump sum in respect of the income tax liability of depositors was until 1991 paid over by the building society and represented an advantageous settlement for the depositors. Interest payments are now subject to deduction of tax at the basic rate, with exemption for non-taxpayers. Interest on mortgages advanced attracts relief from the mortgagor's income tax liability on amounts paid on mortgages up to £30,000.

Under the UK Building Societies Act 1986 wider consumer services are permitted for building societies, including the provision of unsecured ➤personal loans, the management of ➤unit trusts, the operation of estate agencies, activity in insurance broking and the sale of ➤money purchase ➤personal pensions. These changes enabled the societies to compete on more equal terms with ➤commercial banks and other ➤financial institutions, competition from which reduced the societies' share of the new mortgage market from 75% in 1986 to 54% in 1987.

In 1994 further changes to the scope of operations of building societies were envisaged, including the provision of unsecured loans to small businesses, insurance services and higher limits on raising funds from ➤wholesale markets. Building societies are also to be made more accountable to members. The Building Societies Act 1997 *inter alia* reaffirmed the principle that the major business of building societies was the provision of mortgages on residential property. Equal voting rights were accorded to borrowers and lenders (depositors). The range of activities of building societies was widened in that any business, except certain forms of financial trading, was permissible provided it was set out in a society's memorandum. Recently a number of building societies have given up mutual status and become banks.

In mid-1997 the UK government announced that the building societies industry was to be placed under the supervision of the Financial Services Authority, rather than the Building Societies Commission (➤Financial Services Act).

➤➤Savings and Loan Associations.

Bulis (Ger.) Contraction of *Bundesliquiditätsschatzwechsel*, German government one-year Treasury bills introduced in early 1993 with the purpose of absorbing excess liquidity in the non-banking sector.

bull A speculator who buys ➤securities in the belief that prices will rise and that they will be able to sell them again later at a profit. The antonym of ➤bear. The market is said to be 'bullish' when it is generally anticipated that prices will rise.

bull call spread The purchase of a call ➤option combined with the sale of a call option of the same expiry date but with a higher ➤exercise price: the intention is to profit by a rise in the value of the underlying ➤asset.

bull market A period of time during which ➤stock market prices are rising. ➤➤bull. Antonym of ➤bear market.

bull position ➤position.

bull put spread The simultaneous purchase and sale of put options with the same expiry date, but with an ➤exercise price for the purchased ➤option lower than for the sold option. The operator expects a rise in the value of the underlying ➤asset.

bulldog bond (UK) A sterling bond in the UK capital market issued by a non-resident. ➤foreign bond.

bullet (US) Repayment of the whole of the ➤principal of a ➤loan at ➤maturity.

bulletin board ➤company bulletin board.

bullion ➤Gold, silver or other precious metal in bulk, i.e. in the form of ingots or bars rather than in coin. Gold bullion is used in international monetary transactions between ➤central banks and forms partial backing for many ➤currencies.

Bund Abbreviation used in English-speaking markets to refer to a *Bundesanleihe*, a long-term German government bond, in which ➤derivatives are also traded.

Bundesaufsichtsamt für das Kreditwesen (BAK) (Ger.) The Federal Supervisory Office for Credit. The institution is responsible for banking business and the regulation of investment activity by funds such as ➤unit trusts.

Bundesbank The ➤central bank of the Federal Republic of Germany (formerly West Germany), based in Frankfurt. Established in 1957 as a successor to the Bank Deutscher Länder, which was set up in 1948 after the Second World War, the Bundesbank (= 'federal bank') has an exceptional degree of independence from government in its role of safeguarding the ➤currency. The Deutsche Bundesbank, to give it its full name, co-ordinates the 11 regional or *Länder* banks (*Landeszentralbanken*) in former West Germany and from 1990 has been responsible for monetary policy in former East Germany. Changes in ➤Lombard and ➤discount rates are usually announced after the fortnightly meetings of the Bundesbank Central

Council, on which the presidents of the *Länder* banks are represented. ➤➤repurchase agreement.

Bundesobligation (Ger.) A federal ➤bond.

bundling The provision of more than one product or service to a customer at an inclusive price, e.g. 'free' life insurance with a loan.

buono tesoro poliennali (It.) Italian government bonds of 5–10-year maturities, mostly 10-year maturity.

burn rate The rate at which a company needs additional capital in order to stay in business, e.g. a biotechnology company carrying out R&D.

Business Expansion Scheme (BES) (UK) A scheme intended to encourage individuals to subscribe and hold on to ➤shares in a small ➤unlisted company raising funds to expand. Funds up to a specified limit invested in eligible BES companies were fully deductible for tax purposes (i.e. they could be deducted from taxable income at higher rates of ➤income tax). There were a number of conditions, notably that subscribers could not be directors or employees; nor could they own more than 30% of the ➤equity; nor could they dispose of the shares within five years without forfeiting tax relief. The BES was replaced by the ➤Enterprise Investment Scheme at the beginning of 1994.

business finance The provision of money for commercial use; when relating specifically to companies it may also be referred to as corporate finance. The short-term ➤capital of a business may come from ➤retained earnings or from ➤factoring, bank borrowings (➤banking), other borrowings, ➤bills of exchange, trade creditors (➤trade credit) and expense creditors. These are all sources of short-term capital that in theory should be used only for investment in relatively liquid ➤assets (➤➤liquidity), so that it is readily available to discharge the liability if necessary. Sources of long-term capital include ➤reserves and ➤depreciation provisions, ➤equity share capital and long-term loans such as ➤debentures and ➤term loans.

Business Start-Up Scheme (BSS) (UK) A scheme intended to encourage individuals to subscribe to ➤shares in an ➤unlisted company. Up to a certain limit, such purchases were deductible for tax purposes from taxable income at higher rates of ➤income tax. It was replaced in 1983 by the ➤Business Expansion Scheme.

butterfly The purchase and sale of two identical ➤options and the simultaneous purchase and sale of two options, one with a higher ➤exercise price and the other with a lower exercise price. All four options are for the same ➤asset, are of the same type and have the same expiry date.

buy-back 1. An agreement to repurchase something on certain conditions, e.g. an entrepreneur may agree to sell ➤shares in his business to a ➤venture capital company on the understanding that they may be bought back at a certain price if financial performance targets are achieved. **2.** A company may buy back its own shares and cancel them so as to reduce the number of shares at issue and improve ►earnings per share (EPS).

buy-out Purchase by the management of the shares of its company, so making it the owner; or purchase by a company of its shares held by the public, so making the company a private company. ►management buy-out.

buy-side ►investment analyst.

BUX Index The share price index of the Budapest Stock Exchange.

buying in shares ►incorporation.

BVCA ►British Venture Capital Association.

BV (Neth.) A private limited company. ►incorporation.

BVL 30 Index The main share price index of the ►Lisbon Stock Exchange.

bylaws ►memorandum of association.

byte A set of ►bits or binary digits, eight, sixteen or thirty-two in most computer systems, which is a unit of information representing a number or word or part of a word.

C

C-corporation ➤sub-chapter S corporation.

CAC 40 ➤Paris Bourse.

cage ➤back office.

caisses d'épargne (Fr.) ➤savings bank.

calendar spread The simultaneous purchase and sale, or vice versa, of an option of the same strike (➤striking price) but for different months.

call 1. The act of a company in requiring the surrender of its bonds for repayment. **2.** The repayment of a bond in the ➤Eurobond market, possible under the terms of the issue at pre-set dates before ➤maturity. **3.** A requirement by the director of a company for payment for issued capital not yet ➤paid up. **4.** The period in a ➤commodity market trading session in which business is conducted by the chair, as contrasted with ➤open outcry. In this session ➤futures prices are officially fixed for dissemination and use internationally. The session normally takes place several times a day. ➤➤call money; call-over; option (*call option*).

call money A bank loan repayable on demand, i.e. at call. Most notably used in the UK as a means for the commercial banks to place short-term funds with the ➤discount houses. This both provides a profitable outlet for the banks' liquid resources and furnishes the supply of funds with which the discount houses can conduct their transactions in ➤bills with the Bank of England. Under the arrangements for ➤monetary control brought in in 1981, the commercial banks guaranteed to keep aggregate call money with the discount houses at a level averaging 6% of their ➤eligible liabilities and not falling below 4% on any one day. Call money is very short term, normally day to day, and is always, when taken on the above basis, ➤secured. Until the abolition of the ➤reserve asset ratio in 1981, call money was an important ➤reserve asset of the commercial banks. Since then it has been recognized by the Bank of England, in its supervision of banks' *prudential* status (➤capital adequacy), as a high-quality liquid asset.

call option ➤option.

call-or-put option ➤as-you-like option.

call-over The practice in ➤commodity markets whereby the chair conducts the trading, as against trading by ➤open outcry.

call-over price Price arrived at by ➤call-over in a ➤commodity exchange, then adopted and published as the official price for the session and used for ➤physical trading generally.

call warrant A warrant giving the holder the right to buy the underlying asset at a predetermined date and price. Similar to a call ➤option, but used chiefly for ➤gold purchases.

cap 1. An abbreviation for ➤capitalization, as in ➤small cap stocks. **2.** A limit or ceiling, usually setting the maximum ➤interest that may be charged on a ➤loan. Where there is also a 'floor' or lower limit to protect the lender, the arrangement may be described as a 'collar' (➤➤adjustable rate preferred stock).

capacity Of insurance, the volume of insurance cover on offer at any particular time.

capital In general, the accumulated (i.e. unspent) wealth of a business or individual that is capable of generating income, but the term has no precise meaning out of context. Nominal share capital, for example, is the ➤par value of funds subscribed by ➤shareholders (➤➤capital employed; paid-up capital; shareholders' equity; undercapitalized). Capital may be in the form of money or of physical ➤assets.

capital, cost of The ➤rate of interest paid on the ➤capital employed in a business. Since capital will be drawn from a variety of sources, it will be an average cost derived from a ➤weighted average of the costs of each source, including ➤equity. The average cost of existing sources of capital may be higher or lower than the marginal cost, i.e. the cost of additional capital. ➤➤weighted average cost of capital.

capital account ➤balance of payments.

capital adequacy Various regulatory bodies set minimum ➤capital requirements for ➤financial institutions such as ➤unit trust managers. Until recently capital adequacy requirements were set only at a national level (➤e.g. Federal Reserve System; liquidity ratio). The increasing globalization of the world financial system now requires international agreement on capital adequacy standards. In December 1987, 11 countries and the then European Community (➤European Union) signed an international agreement for capital adequacy for ➤commercial banks under the auspices of the ➤Bank for International Settlements (the Basle Agreement). The agreement provided for common prudential ratios and a common definition of ➤risk-adjusted assets. ➤Banks operating in signatory countries now need to have capital (➤equity and long-term ➤debt) equal to 8% of risk-adjusted assets (➤➤liquidity ratio). The percentage adequacy requirement can vary with an individual bank's exposure to ➤foreign exchange risks and ➤derivatives. ➤➤Investment Services Directive.

capital allowances (UK) Reductions in tax (➤taxation) liability that are related to a firm's ➤capital expenditure. In most countries expenditure on new capital assets is encouraged by various kinds of allowances (though more recently there has been a tendency for those to be phased out), and annual ►depreciation is recognized as an expense of the business in calculating tax liability. The tax authorities' methods of depreciating an ►asset are standardized in most countries and not necessarily the same as those used by the company in published ►accounts. Where a company may claim depreciation for tax purposes at will, e.g. to write off the whole of the cost of an asset against tax in a single year, or to spread it over 20 years as it chooses, this is known as *free depreciation* or *depreciation at choice*. In the UK from 1972 until 1983/4, a business could obtain a first-year allowance or ►tax credit of 100% of the cost of plant and machinery. This was known as *accelerated depreciation*, since the depreciation rate was faster than justified by the life of the asset. The business now qualifies instead for a *writing-down allowance* or *annual depreciation allowance* (►depreciation). ►►investment allowances.

capital asset pricing model (CAPM) A model of the market in financial ►assets that assumes that, in equilibrium, asset prices will adjust to ensure that the return on an asset compensates investors for *systematic risk*, i.e. risk that cannot be eliminated by portfolio diversification. ►►portfolio theory.

capital duty (UK) A tax (►taxation) levied on ►companies on the proceeds of a ►new issue of ►shares. Abolished in 1988. ►►stamp duty.

capital employed The ►capital in use in a business. There is no universally agreed definition of the term. It is sometimes taken to mean ►net assets (i.e. fixed plus current assets minus current ►liabilities), but more usually ►bank loans and ►overdrafts are included and other adjustments made for the purposes of calculating the return on net capital employed (►rate of return), such as the exclusion of intangible assets and the revaluation of ►trade investments at market prices. ►►investment appraisal.

capital expenditure The purchase of fixed ►assets (e.g. plant and equipment), expenditure on ►trade investments or acquisitions of other businesses and expenditure on current assets (e.g. stocks).

capital formation ►investment.

capital gain A realized increase in the value of a capital ►asset, as when a ►share is sold for more than the price at which it was purchased. Strictly speaking the terms refers to ►capital appreciation outside the normal course of business. In the UK, capital gains are subject to ►capital gains tax (CGT). The tax does not cover gains arising from the sale of personal belongings, including cars or principal dwelling houses, but it does cover gains from the sale of ►stock exchange securities (with special treatment for ►gilt-edged securities). The tax for individuals is now the same as that for other income (►income tax), while incorporated businesses pay ►corporation tax on capital gains. ►Capital losses may be set against tax liability and the first £6,300 is exempt from income tax (1996–97). Capital gains arise from changes in the supply and demand for capital assets, but also from ➤inflation, and for assets disposed of after the beginning of the 1982 tax year the original cost may be increased by ➤indexation, i.e. the expenditure scaled up in proportion to the increase in the ➤retail price index between, in most cases, a year after the acquisition and the date of sale. Capital gains are taxed in some countries at lower rates for short-term gains, while a few do not tax capital gains at all.

capital gains tax (CGT) (UK) ➤capital gain.

capital gearing (UK) Bank borrowings and other ➤debt as a percentage of ➤net tangible assets. ➤gearing.

capital loss ➤capital gain.

capital market(s) The market for longer-term loanable funds as distinct from the ➤money market, which deals in short-term funds. There is no clear-cut distinction between the two markets, although in principle capital market loans are used by industry and commerce for fixed ➤investment and acquisitions. The capital market is an increasingly international one and in each country consists of all those institutions that canalize the supply of and demand for capital, including the ➤banking system, the ➤stock exchange, ➤insurance companies and other ➤financial intermediaries.

capital reserves Undistributable ➤reserves. Some items in the reserves of a company cannot be distributed because they are part of the equity capital of the business – e.g. sums received from the issue of new ➤shares at a price in excess of the ➤nominal value.

capital shares ➤investment trust.

capital structure The make-up of the ➤capital employed in a business or other organization. The most prominent characteristic of capital structure will be the relationship of ➤debt to ➤equity (➤gearing).

capital transfer tax (CTT) (UK) A tax on the transmission of wealth by gift, both during a person's lifetime and on their death. Introduced in 1975 and replaced by ➤inheritance tax with effect from 16 March 1986.

capitalization ➤market capitalization.

capitalization issue ➤bonus issue.

CAPM ➤capital asset pricing model.

capped floating rate note A ➤floating rate note (FRN), the ➤coupon of which is subject to a pre-agreed maximum.

captive A company providing ➤investment or other services that is owned by an institution offering related services; e.g. an ➤insurance company or ➤venture capital company owned by a ➤bank or a ➤hire-purchase firm owned by a car manufacturer. ➤➤captive insurer.

captive finance company ➤finance house.

captive insurer An ➤insurer established and wholly owned by an industrial or commercial company, or a group of such companies, for the purpose of underwriting all the insurance ➤risks of that company or those companies. The earliest captives were formed in the 1930s, but wide use of the vehicle did not occur until the 1950s and the name did not come into being until the 1960s. In 1996 the worldwide total of captive insurance companies was 3,795; total premiums amounted to $19bn, and total assets equalled $100bn.

carried interest A share in, or ➤option on ➤equity or in the value of, a ➤venture capital investment fund granted to the managers of that fund.

carry-over Of ➤commodity markets, inventories held at the start of the marketing year.

carrying market A ➤commodity market in which a commodity can be accepted on delivery in one month, then stored and redelivered in a later month. This is confined to commodities with durable life.

carte à mémoire (Fr.) ➤Smart card.

cash 1. Money in tangible form, namely coins and banknotes, in contrast to bank cheques and deposits. **2.** For purposes of ➤monetary control, notes and coin, together with deposits at the central bank held by a ➤commercial bank. **3.** Of agricultural produce, those forms grown for sale, normally to other countries, rather than for local consumption: cash crops. **4.** A ➤commodity sold on a ➤commodity market for immediate or very early delivery. ➤actual price; physical price; spot price.

cash and carry In ➤commodity markets, the practice of buying ➤spot with a view to selling later at a profit that, after meeting handling, storage and insurance charges, represents a higher rate of interest on dealers' money than they would obtain by investing in ➤fixed-interest securities.

cash crops ➤cash.

cash flow The movement of money into (cash inflow) and out of (cash outflow) a business. It is generally defined as net ➤profit plus ➤depreciation (net cash flow) but may be used more loosely to include all cash movements. ➤discounted cash flow.

cash limits (UK) A method of government expenditure control introduced in 1976 to constrain the existing system whereby expenditure planning was in volume terms only, i.e. in terms of fixed prices relating to a previous period, with accordingly an unrestrained outturn in current price terms. Certain government expenditures were subjected to a limit in a current price, or *cash* terms. In 1981 all planning reverted to cash terms, and cash limits became redundant.

cash price The price of a ►commodity immediately available for sale and delivery. Also known as *physical price* or *actual price*. ►►forward; futures; option.

cash ratio 1. The ratio of ►cash to ►deposits in the banking system, frequently set by the ►central bank in the interests of ►monetary policy. A cash ratio has always been required by the ►Federal Reserve authorities of the USA and it has formed an important part of ►monetary control in that country. A cash ratio of 8% was informally required by the Bank of England up to 1971 (►►credit control). The banks themselves customarily maintained a ratio of 5% to 7% thereafter, until 1981, when a cash ratio of 8% of ►eligible liabilities, to be held at the Bank of England, was set for all banks. The Bank of England stressed, however, that the cash holdings were for the purpose of providing income resources to itself and played no part in monetary control. 2. The ratio of ►liquid assets to the current ►liabilities of a business.

cash settlement The alternative in the ►derivatives market to ►physical delivery of the underlying instrument. The cash is the current market price of the security.

CATS ►Toronto Stock Exchange.

caveat emptor 'Let the buyer beware.' An expression conveying purchasers' obligation to assure themselves that the object of their purchase satisfies their requirements. This does not, however, exonerate sellers from various forms of ►liability for their product.

CBOE ►Chicago Board Options Exchange.

CBOT ►Chicago Board of Trade.

CBS Index The Amsterdam ►share index.

CCIFP ►Chambre de Compensation des Instruments Financiers de Paris.

CD ►certificate of deposit.

cedant (ceding insurer) An ►insurer initiating ►reinsurance. ►►facultative reinsurance; reinsurance treaty.

CEDEL ►Centrale de Livraison de Valeurs Mobilières.

ceding insurer ►cedant.

Census X-II (US) A computer program used by the ►Federal Reserve to apply seasonal adjustment to ►money supply totals.

central bank A bankers' bank at the centre of a country's monetary system (►monetary control). Central banks act as ►lenders of last resort, lead the interest rate structure, accept ►deposits, make ►loans to the ►commercial banks and in most countries supervise the ►banking system. The central bank also acts as the government's own bank, manages the ►national debt and controls the note issue (►banknote). Central banks deal with each other in conducting transfers of ►currency and ►bullion between countries and are heavily involved, with finance ministers, in international economic relations. ►Bank of England; Bank of Japan; Bundesbank; Federal Reserve System. ►►Bank for International Settlements.

Central Bank Advisory Board ►World Gold Council.

central bank discount rate The interest rate at which a ►central bank will ►discount eligible bills (in the UK), ►eligible paper (in the USA) and ►Treasury bills.

Central Fund A reserve fund of ►Lloyd's, financed by the members, maintained as a ►policy-holders' protection fund, to be invoked should members fail to meet their underwriting (►underwrite) ►liabilities.

central monetary institution ►central bank.

central parity ►European Monetary System (EMS).

Centrale de Livraison de Valeurs Mobilières (CEDEL) One of the two settlement systems for ►Eurobond trading, established in Luxembourg in 1970. CEDEL is both a clearing house and an agency for dividend collection. In collaboration with Citibank it provides capital to market dealers. It also collaborates with ►SWIFT in organizing settlements. Its owners are a number of international banks. ►►Euroclear.

CentreWrite A wholly owned ►subsidiary of ►Lloyd's, established in 1991 to offer ►reinsurance to close to syndicates in ►run-off, where, after some years, this appears practicable; and also to ►underwrite ►estate protection reinsurance.

certain annuity ►terminable annuity.

certificate 1. A document attesting ownership, usually one certifying a ►debt, thus used for most ►securities. Examples are ►certificate of deposit, ►share certificate, ►tax deposit certificate. **2.** ►certificate of quality.

certificate of deposit (CD) A ►negotiable claim issued by a bank in return for a term ►deposit. The document is normally a ►bearer security. The advantage of the CD to depositors is that the latter can place their money in a fixed-►term or long-►maturity deposit, so obtaining a higher rate of interest while knowing that they can sell the CD in the ►secondary market whenever they may need to recover the money. The advantage to purchasers in the secondary market is that they can invest in and divest the instrument at will. The advantage to the bank is that it can acquire deposits perhaps not otherwise forthcoming and can hold them. CDs can be sold and resold at a ➤discount, so varying the ➤yield.

CDs were first issued in the USA in 1961 and gained immediate favour. After the partial suspension in 1970, and final suspension in 1973, of the application to CDs of ➤Regulation Q, the market grew rapidly. CDs were issued in ➤Eurodollar form in London in 1966. Sterling CDs were issued in 1968. The market in CDs is made up by the ➤discount houses and the ➤interbank market in London and by the banks in the USA. ➤Special drawing right CDs have been issued in London, and a substantial yen CD market has developed in Japan, after introduction in 1979. In 1983 the US Tax Act required all dollar CDs to be registered (i.e. not in bearer form). ➤Futures contracts in CDs are traded in the USA and on the ➤London International Financial Futures Exchange (LIFFE). ➤➤parallel money markets.

certificate of quality (UK) A document attesting that a ➤commodity has passed the test of ➤grading, valid in the case of most ➤soft commodities for six months.

certificate of tax deposit ➤tax deposit certificate.

CFTC ➤Commodity Futures Trading Commission.

chaebol (S. Korea) A large South Korean family-run conglomerate, frequently with substantial subsidiary operations abroad.

chain-base indices ➤chain-linked index.

chain-linked index An ➤index number in which each change in a number is measured against the value of the number in the immediately preceding period instead of against a fixed base (➤base-weighted indices). Chain-linked indices are used where the composition of the different components alters frequently over time.

chakuchi (Jap.) ➤Forward trade in ➤bonds in the ➤*gensaki* market.

Chambre de Compensation des Instruments Financiers de Paris (CCIFP) (Fr.) The ➤clearing house for the ➤Marché à Terme des Instruments Financiers (MATIF), the French financial ➤futures exchange.

Chambre Syndicale des Agents de Change (Fr.) The governing body of the ➤Compagnie des Agents de Change. Members are elected for one year by the *compagnie*; the *chambre* is responsible for the application of the *compagnie*'s rules. The chairperson of the *chambre* has the title of *syndic*, and the members are known as *gouverneurs*.

CHAPS ➤clearing house.

Chapter 11 ➤bankruptcy.

charge 1. To ►debit to, or impose a price for a good or service, as in bank charges. **2.** To take a pledge, ►assignment mortgage or ►collateral against a ►loan.

charge account ►revolving credit.

charge card ►credit card.

charter(ed) 1. (UK) An organization or member of an organization authorized to trade by royal charter, such as a company, e.g. the East India Company, or a member of a chartered governing body of a profession, e.g. a chartered accountant who is a member of the Institute of Chartered Accountants in England and Wales. **2.** (US) A charter, which consists of the articles of incorporation (►memorandum of association) and a certificate of incorporation or registration issued by a state or federal regulatory body, thus a ►chartered bank. The term *charter* is also used in the general sense of 1., i.e. a contract between the government and a private body that confers privileges.

chartered bank (US and Can.) US and Canadian banks are authorized by charter. In the USA the charter may be granted either by the authorities of a state or by those of the federal government, in the latter case the Comptroller of the Currency. The banks are known alternatively as state-chartered or nationally chartered banks. The practice of chartering derives from that previously in existence in the UK where companies and banks were authorized by royal charters, a system replaced by authorization under the Companies and Banking Acts.

Chartered Institute of Loss Adjusters (CILA) (UK) A professional association, founded in 1942, to set standards and rules for, and provide information to, ►loss adjusters. Membership is on an individual basis and is international. There are some 2,800 members. Before admission to membership, individuals must hold an approved professional qualification, such as ►chartered insurer or chartered surveyor, must have reached the age of 25, must normally have completed five years with a qualified member of the institute and must have passed the Final Examination.

Chartered Insurance Institute (CII) (UK) A professional association for individuals engages in insurance. The objects of the institute are to promote efficiency in insurance, to foster improvement in insurance practice, and to provide information and education in insurance. On passing professional examinations, members can become associates (ACII) or fellows (FCII) of the institute. There are some 90 local institutes in the UK and 50 affiliated institutes from overseas.

chartered insurer A member of the ►Chartered Insurance Institute.

chartist A stock market analyst who predicts ►share price movements solely from the study of graphs of share prices and sometimes trading volumes. ►►technical analysis.

checkable (US) Of bank deposit accounts, one on which cheques (US = *checks*) may be drawn.

checking account (US) ➤current account.

cheque (UK) An order written by the drawer to a ➤commercial bank or ➤central bank to pay on demand a specified sum to a bearer or a named person or ➤company (US = *check*). A cheque may be open or crossed. Crossed, the cheque is payable only into the bank account of the payee. A cheque becomes ➤negotiable when endorsed by the payee.

cheque card (UK) A plastic card issued by a bank (➤banking) to its customers to guarantee, up to a specified limit, usually £50, cheques drawn on the customer's account. The recipient of the cheque notes the cheque card number on the back of the cheque, payment of which is then guaranteed by the bank.

Chicago Board of Trade (CBOT) A ➤commodity market, first established in 1848 as a trading centre for grain. The CBOT quickly became a centre for ➤futures dealing, instituting the first contract in 1851. The market deals also in ➤options. Trade is in maize, crude soya bean oil, soya beans, soya bean meal, oats, silver and gold. After the Second World War the CBOT became an important market for ➤financial futures, trading in contracts in GNMAs (➤Government National Mortgage Association), the major market index, US Treasury bonds and US Treasury notes. Total volume of sales in September 1993 was 13.8m contracts.

Chicago Board of Trade Clearing Corporation An independent organization guaranteeing trades by the ➤Chicago Board of Trade, so maintaining the latter's top credit rating. This function may be extended to the ➤Chicago Mercantile Exchange should a projected merger of the two exchanges take place.

Chicago Board Options Exchange (CBOE) Established in 1973 as an ➤options exchange; one of the major world markets in this instrument.

Chicago Mercantile Exchange (CME) Instituted in 1919 as a ➤commodity futures market, the CME developed in 1972 the ➤international monetary market in which ➤currency futures were initiated. These were the first ➤financial futures to be traded. The market deals in futures contracts in livestock (live cattle, feeder cattle, live hogs, pork bellies), in which it was a pioneer. The financial futures division is now the more active and comprises contracts in Swiss francs, Mexican pesos, D-marks, Canadian dollars, pounds sterling, yen, French francs, domestic ➤certificates of deposit (CDs), Eurodollars, time deposits and 90-day US Treasury bills. The index and ➤options division of the market also trades in futures and options in ➤Standard and Poor's stock index and in options in D-marks, live cattle and random-length lumber. The CME accounts for some 30% of all US futures trade; and with a nominal value of underlying assets at $85,000bn in 1993 it was the world's largest exchange, comparing with the ➤London International Financial

Futures Exchange (LIFFE) at $27,000bn, the ►Chicago Board of Trade at $13,000bn, and the $2,000bn nominal value of stock traded on the ►New York Stock Exchange.

Chicago School ►Friedman, Milton.

Chicago Stock Exchange ►Midwest Stock Exchange.

Chilean Stock Exchange The Bolsa de Comercio de Santiago is the only ►stock exchange in Chile. The exchange at Valparaiso closed in 1982.

China The Shanghai Securities Exchange reopened in 1990. There is a screen-based quotation system linking traders in Shanghai with various cities including Shenzhen in the Special Economic Zone adjacent to Hong Kong. The price indices (►share indices) are the Jingan Index for Shanghai and the Shenyen Stock Price Index. B shares, which are denominated in US dollars, are reserved for foreigners. The markets are regulated by the ►China Securities Regulatory Commission (CSRC).

China International Trust and Investment Corporation (CITIC) (China) A Chinese-government-owned entity issuing bonds to finance joint ventures in China. The main bond in circulation is the CITIC 10-year bond.

China Securities Regulatory Commission The securities market regulator for mainland China.

Chinese Gold and Silver Exchange Society A gold and silver market in Hong Kong set up in 1910.

Chinese National Nonferrous Metals Corporation (CNNC) (China) A major state organization, formed in 1983 and based in Beijing, managing a substantial portion of China's nonferrous metals imports and exports. The latter trade at the moment is conducted through a member company of the group, the Chinese National Import and Export Corporation (CNIEC); it is planned to integrate this company into the main group. The CNNC has many offices throughout China and abroad.

Chinese wall A communications barrier between members or departments of a financial institution intended to prevent the transfer of price-sensitive information. Chinese walls are imaginary but are taken seriously in an attempt to minimize conflicts of interest, e.g. between clients of a broking department of a ►merchant bank advised to buy ►shares that an investment department might wish to dispose of.

CHIPS Clearing House Interbank Payments System. ►clearing house.

chooser option ►as-you-like option.

churning Buying and selling ➤shares by a ➤broker on a ➤discretionary account, primarily for the purpose of generating ➤commission.

chusho shoken (Jap.) All ➤securities houses except the ➤Big Four.

CIBOR ➤Copenhagen interbank offered rate.

c.i.f. Including cost, insurance and freight as declared by the seller in export contracts. *Free on board* (FOB) is a similar abbreviation meaning that the seller pays for the insured cost of sending the goods to the port and loading them on board ship, leaving the buyer to meet the remaining costs.

CII ➤Chartered Insurance Institute.

CILA ➤Chartered Institute of Loss Adjusters.

circuit-breaker mechanism (US) Price change limits and trading halts intended to control excessive fluctuations in market prices recommended in the ➤Brady Commission Report. Following ➤Black Monday there were many calls for new restrictions of these kinds including the limitation of ➤programme trading.

CISCO ➤City Group for Smaller Companies.

CITIC ➤China International Trust and Investment Corporation.

City (UK) A popular term for the financial institutions located in the financial district to the east of St Paul's Cathedral in London. Also referred to as the Square Mile. The term is often used to refer to all financial institutions, wherever located.

city bank (Jap.) Each of the thirteen major ➤commercial banks based in the cities of Kobe, Nagoya, Osaka, Sapporo, Tokyo and Urawa, but with national branch networks (Japanese = *toshi guiko*). ➤➤regional bank. Not to be confused with Citibank, the US bank.

City Group for Smaller Companies (CISCO) A lobby group formed in December 1992 with wide membership among ➤venture capital companies, ➤institutional investors, ➤stockbrokers and others to further reform of the UK ➤equity markets following the announced closure of the ➤unlisted securities market.

claim 1. An entitlement to a financial ➤asset, frequently applied to the document evidencing such a claim. 2. In the ➤money market and ➤banking, the ➤assets of a financial institution, namely outstanding loans and holdings of ➤Treasury bills and ➤commercial bills, as against the institution's ➤liabilities. 3. In insurance, an application by a policy-holder for payment of a loss under the terms of the policy.

claims-made policy An insurance policy under which the ➤insurer is obliged to pay only those claims made during the policy period, regardless of the date of the loss.

claims outstanding reserve A fund set aside by an insurance company to meet

➤claims under its insurance policies that are still in the course of settlement.

classical corporation tax ➤corporation tax.

clausing An entry on a ➤bill of exchange of details of the parties to, and the nature of, the transaction underlying the bill.

clearing The offsetting of ➤liabilities or purchases and sales between two parties. ➤clearing house.

clearing banks (UK) Members of the London Bankers' Clearing House (➤clearing house). Now used synonymously with ➤commercial banks.

clearing fee The fee charged on market transactions by the ➤clearing house of a ➤commodity exchange.

clearing house Any institution that settles mutual indebtedness between a number of organizations. The UK banks, through the *Association of Payment Clearing Services* (APACS), have: *Bankers Automated Clearing System* (BACS), which provides inter-bank clearing; *Clearing House Automated Payments System* (CHAPS), which now provides instant clearing for electronic transfers through the *Real Time Gross Settlement System* (RTGS); and EFTPOS for ➤electronic funds transfer at point of sale. There are similar institutions in other countries, e.g. the *Clearing House Interbank Payment System* (CHIPS) in New York. There is also a global system for settling payments that flow through the foreign exchange markets: *CLS services* set up by the large banks. There are similar arrangements on the ➤commodity exchanges (➤International Commodities Clearing House), the ➤stock exchanges (➤Transfer Accounting, Lodgement for Investors, Stock Management for Jobbers, TALISMAN), the ➤futures markets and for payments in the ➤Euromarkets (➤Centrale de Livraison de Valeurs Mobilières; Euroclear). The clearing house is normally financed by membership subscriptions and other dues of the market.

Clearing House Automated Payments System (CHAPS) ➤clearing house.

Clearing House Interbank Payments System (CHIPS) ➤clearing house.

CLOB International Central Limit Order Book. ➤Singapore Stock Exchange.

close company (UK) A ➤company effectively controlled by not more than five shareholders. (US = *closed company*.)

close out An offsetting transaction in two or more ➤instruments leaving the investor in a net zero position, i.e. neither in credit nor in debt.

closed-end fund An investment company with a fixed capitalization. ➤investment trust.

closing prices Prices as they stand at the end of each day's trading session in the ►securities and ►commodity markets.

CLS services ►clearing house.

CME ►Chicago Mercantile Exchange.

CMO ►collateralized mortgage obligation.

CNIEC (China) Chinese National Import and Export Corporation. ►Chinese National Nonferrous Metals Corporation.

CNMV ►Madrid Stock Exchange.

CNNC (China) ►Chinese National Nonferrous Metals Corporation.

COB (Fr.) ►Commission des Opérations de Bourse.

Cocoa Association of London A company limited by guarantee, the Cocoa Association of London was founded in 1929, with the mandate to 'promote, protect and regulate the cocoa trade' and to 'protect the status and interests of all persons engaged therein'. In pursuit of these aims the association has formulated the rules and regulations for the conduct of trade by the ►London Cocoa Terminal Market Association, and provides arbitration and appeal facilities. The Cocoa Association has some 100 voting members, and some 30 non-voting and non-trading members, drawn from all parts of the world and representing the world's cocoa producers, the chocolate and cocoa butter industry, trading houses, shipping and insurance companies, superintendence companies and related international trade associations.

Code of Liberalization ►Organization for European Economic Co-operation (OEEC).

COFACE ►Compagnie Française pour l'Assurance du Commerce Extérieur.

Coffee, Sugar and Cocoa Exchange Inc. of New York A ►commodity market first established to deal in coffee in 1882, to which were added sugar in 1916 and cocoa in 1925; name changed to present style in 1971. It trades in ►futures contracts in these commodities as well as in ►options in sugar. Together with London, a main world market in cocoa.

Coffee Terminal Market Association of London Ltd A major world ►commodity market founded as the Coffee Trade Association in 1888 and reopened under its present name in 1958. The market is principally a ►futures market, trading chiefly in contracts for African coffee of the Robusta variety. An attempt was made in 1973 to install a contract for South American coffee of the Arabica variety, but this proved unsuccessful, and the contract was withdrawn in 1974. The market is a member of the ►International Commodities Clearing House.

collar An ➤instrument, on which interest is contained within a maximum and minimum bracket. ➤➤cap.

collateral Originally the US term for ➤security, now used more widely. The official US definition (under the US Commercial Code) includes goods, intangibles, paper (➤negotiable instruments and documents of titles) and proceeds.

collateral security A second ➤security (in addition to the personal security of the borrower) for a ➤loan.

collateralized mortgage obligation (CMO) (US) A ➤bond, the ➤security of which is a ➤portfolio of ➤mortgages issued by the Federal Home Loan Mortgage Corporation (➤Federal Home Loan Bank Board) offering certainty of redemption date.

collateralized mortgage security (US) A ➤bond, the ➤security of which is a ➤portfolio of ➤mortgages. The ➤yield and ➤redemption of the bond are paid out of the interest and capital repayments of the mortgagors, such payments being made through ➤pass-through arrangements.

Coloroll case ➤equalization of pensions.

COMEX ➤Commodity Exchange of New York. The name Comex is also often used to refer to the price of copper as fixed in New York.

Comisión Nacional del Mercado de Valores (Sp.) ➤Madrid Stock Exchange.

Comit Index (It.) The ➤share index for the ➤Milan Stock Exchange, published by the Banca Commerciale Italiana.

Comitato Direttivo degli Agenti di Cambio (It.) The association of ➤stock-brokers on the ➤stock exchange in Milan, having the task of supervising the conduct of business. Its rules have legal force, and it is subject to the ➤Commissione Nazionale per le Società e la Borsa.

commercial banks Privately owned banks (➤banking); otherwise referred to as ➤clearing banks (UK), national banks and state banks (US), joint-stock banks and, in Western Europe, credit banks, to distinguish them from ➤investment banks.

commercial bill Any bill other than a ➤Treasury bill. Commercial bills are ➤bank bills or ➤trade bills. ➤➤bill of exchange.

commercial credit company ➤finance house.

commercial loan selling The sale by one bank to another of a loan to a commercial company. The sale is normally from an originating bank, having access to a reputable borrower but not wishing for overhead cost reasons to keep the loan on its books, to another bank without access to the borrower but with the capacity to absorb the loan. As a result of the transaction, the originating bank makes a turn on the sale, the client borrows on more favourable terms, and the purchasing bank obtains a good asset not otherwise available. The practice began in the USA in 1986 and developed rapidly.

commercial paper (CP) An ►unsecured note issued by companies for short-term borrowing purposes. It differs from a ►bill of exchange in that it is *one-name* paper; a bill of exchange contains the names of the drawer and the drawee, both of whom are liable, whereas commercial paper has only the name of the issuer. Commercial paper has been in use in the USA for many years but was for long frowned on in the UK. In April 1986 sterling commercial paper was authorized by the ►Bank of England, subject to a number of conditions, in particular that maturities should be not less than seven days and not more than a year and that the right to issue should be restricted to companies having net assets of not less than £50m and that are listed on the ►stock exchange. Issues began in May 1986. CP is frequently sold by the issuer direct to the investor, the latter normally being institutions, namely ►money-market funds, ►insurance companies, corporations, bank trust departments and ►pension funds. CP is also placed by intermediary banks or securities dealers. Unlike ►acceptances, CP is not tied to a particular trade transaction.

CP has been introduced in recent years not only into the UK but also into Australia, Spain, Hong Kong, Sweden, Singapore, Norway, France and the Netherlands. In 1987 $359bn of CP was outstanding in all countries, but $323bn of this was accounted for by the USA. There were also £356bn of ►Euronote and ►Euro-commercial paper issues. In 1981 only $170bn of CP was outstanding and issued only in the USA, Canada and Australia.

Commercial paper issues in the USA are sometimes backed by a bank's *irrevocable* ►letter of credit. Most issues are ►rated by a ►rating agency, and to secure a good rating borrowers must maintain a committed credit facility equal to the value of the paper involved. In Canada issues are normally backed by a pledge of assets (e.g. ►receivables) and rated. In France issues may be made only by French-based companies, and issues are increasingly rated. There are legal requirements for disclosure of financial details, and all issues up to two years' ►maturity must be backed by a credit line equal to 75% of their value. CP in France is known as *billets de trésorerie*. There is a commercial paper clearing house in Australia, Austraclear, established in 1984, and many issues are rated and underwritten; letters of credit are used as backing for lesser-known borrowers. In Norway commercial paper, known as loan certificates, is one of the four classes of short-term negotiable paper authorized by the Ministry of Finance in December 1984; issues are restricted to Norwegian borrowers. The third largest CP market, after the USA and Canada, is Sweden, where back-up credit is not legally required; rating is not undertaken. ►►note (*promissory note*).

Commissão de Valores Mobiliaros ►São Paulo Stock Exchange.

commission Payment made to a salesperson or intermediary, e.g. a ►broker, in return for their services in promoting a transaction, usually a sale, usually determined as a percentage of the value of the transaction.

commission broker (US) A ►dealer on the ►stock exchange who executes orders to buy or sell securities for the public in return for a ►commission or fee.

Commission des Opérations de Bourse (COB) (Fr.) The official body for the supervision of the ►stock exchanges in France, established by legislation of 1967. Its specific tasks are to approve, on the advice of the ►Chambre Syndicale des Agents de Change, securities for official listing; to ensure full disclosure, under the law, of listed companies' affairs; to prevent ►insider dealing; and to transmit complaints on, and initiate new rules for, the conduct of business. There is a similar body with the same name in Belgium.

Commissione Nazionale per le Società e la Borsa (CONSOB) (It.) The official body for the supervision of the ►stock exchange in Italy, instituted in 1974; responsible for the approval of new *listings* (►listed security), fixing of brokers' commissions, invigilation of company finances, notification of abuses and the overview of company ownership.

commitment Of a ►note issuance facility (NIF), undertaking by a bank or ►syndicate of banks to ►underwrite or provide ►back-up credit.

commitment fee A fee charged by a bank in respect of an unused balance of a ►line of credit, designed to offset the bank's cost of keeping the funds available.

committed Of ►Euronote or ►Euro-commercial paper issue, guaranteed by a bank ►syndicate that either ►underwrites the issue or provides ►back-up credit.

committee of subscribers (UK) The elected body of ►London Metal Exchange members responsible for the administration of the exchange.

commodity 1. In economic theory, all subjects of production and exchange, i.e. all goods and services. 2. Raw materials, or primary products, used in manufacturing and industrial processing, consumed in their natural form. 3. Those commodities traded in ►commodity markets.

Commodity Exchange of New York (COMEX) A major ►commodity market in metals, established in 1870, dealing principally in ►futures contracts and sharing with the ►London Metal Exchange a dominant role in world metal trading. Trades are in copper, silver, gold and aluminium futures and in gold options. The term *Comex* is commonly used in the commodities market to mean the New York copper price.

Commodity Futures Trading Commission (CFTC) (US) A regulatory body with authority over all US ►commodity futures exchanges, established by the Commodity Futures Trading Act 1974. It consists of five members (commissioners) appointed by the US President. Originally set up to supervise trade in agricultural products, its remit has been continuously extended. In the early 1990s it was given powers to regulate dealings in ➤derivatives. Under new powers granted on its 1992 reauthorization, the commission exempted off-exchange swap, hybrid and energy contracts from its purview.

commodity market A market, or exchange, in which ➤commodities are bought and sold. Such commodities are those required to satisfy production, food and ornamentation needs, e.g. cotton, grain and precious metals. Commodities are traded in the light of their basic distinguishing characteristics: (a) physical properties, (b) time of availability and (c) place of availability. Characteristic (a) determines the initial desirability of the commodity; (b) and (c) influence the price. Commodity markets are no longer chiefly physical markets, where deals are made out of warehouses, but are places for the sale and purchase by contract of commodities available anywhere in the world and at any point in time. Contracts for the latter are known as ➤forward contracts and ➤futures; those for immediate delivery are known as ➤cash, ➤physical or ➤actual transactions. Major world commodity markets are in London, Chicago, Amsterdam, New York, Sydney and Singapore. Individual markets, with brief details of their history and characteristics, are to be found under the separate names.

Commodity Research Bureau (US) A research institution specializing in ➤commodity price trends, whose index of commodity prices is deemed an important indicator of future consumer price movements.

Common Market ➤European Union.

common stocks (US) Shares in the ➤equity capital of a business. ➤ordinary shares.

community charge ➤local taxation.

Compagnie des Agents de Change (CAC) (Fr.) The association of French ➤stockbrokers. All stockbrokers active on all French ➤stock exchanges are required to be members, and the CAC has official recognition and support from the government. The rules of the CAC, known as the Règlement Général de la Compagnie des Agents de Change, regulate the conduct of business on all stock exchanges and have the backing of the ministry. The CAC maintains close relations with the official ➤Commission des Opérations de Bourse (COB). The governing body of the CAC is the ➤Chambre Syndicale des Agents de Change. ➤➤Paris Bourse.

Compagnie Française pour l'Assurance du Commerce Extérieur (COFACE) (Fr.) The French export credit guarantee system, providing ➤insurance against political as well as commercial risks and also insuring foreign exchange risks where these cannot be ➤covered forward. COFACE's capital is supplied from public resources. COFACE is a world leader in private market export credit insurance.

Companies Acts ►incorporation.

company 1. An incorporated business. ►incorporation. **2.** More loosely, any business organization, which may be a ►sole proprietorship, a ►partnership or another form.

Company Bulletin Board A screen-based system for trading least liquid stocks (►liquidity), introduced on the ►London Stock Exchange in April 1992 and replaced by the ►Stock Exchange Alternative Trading Service in November of the same year.

Company Directors Disqualification Act ►bankruptcy.

company limited by guarantee A company (►incorporation) in which the ►liability of the ►shareholders is limited to the amount they guarantee to pay in the event of ►liquidation rather than by the amount of the ►equity.

competition and credit control (UK) ►credit control.

compliance department, officer All official ►stock exchanges and many large ►financial institutions have people responsible for ensuring that laws and ►regulations governing ►share dealing and ►investment are complied with. Compliance officers may be required to investigate transactions carried out by their colleagues. ►►Chinese wall.

composite company An insurance company transacting both ►general insurance and ►long-term business.

compound option An ►option to buy an option at a prescribed price and date.

comptant (Fr.) ►Cash, ►spot.

Comptroller of the Currency ►national bank.

concentration risk Exposure in securities trading to a high level of risk in any one ►instrument or in any one market sector.

Confederation of Coffee Producing Countries A grouping of South and Central American producers brought together in 1993 with the aim to limit exports in an effort to counteract the steep fall in world prices. The members were reckoned to produce more than two-thirds of world supplies. ►International Coffee Organization.

conflict of interest A situation where a financial institution is acting for the parties on both sides of a transaction, or where the institution itself has a financial interest in the outcome of the transaction; e.g. a ►merchant bank both placing ►shares on the ►stock exchange on behalf of a client company and recommending the purchase of those shares to an investor client whose ►portfolio it manages; or a ►securities house offering to an investor shares with which it is itself oversupplied and that it is under pressure to sell. ►►Chinese wall.

conglomerate (US) A business organization generally consisting of a ►holding company and a group of ►subsidiaries engaged in dissimilar activities. ►*konzern*; trust; *zaibatsu*.

conseil d'administration (Fr.) Board of directors.

consideration Something given in exchange for something else, i.e. the total amount of cash, goods or other property, or rights to cash or property, transferred from buyer to seller in settlement of a transaction. In ►securities trading, the amount paid for securities before ►commission and ►taxation. In the UK a transaction may not be legally binding until the consideration is paid.

CONSOB ►Commissione Nazionale per le Società e la Borsa.

consolidated accounts Financial statements that bring together the ►balance sheets and ►profit and loss accounts of parent and subsidiary companies so that the financial affairs of the group can be treated as a whole. Where the parent controls (i.e. owns more than 50% of the equity of) a subsidiary, the balance sheet may include the ►assets of the subsidiary at market value, with any premium paid for ►goodwill included in the parent's balance sheet and written off against earnings. This is called *acquisition accounting* (US = *purchase acquisition*) or *full consolidation*. Adjustments are made to eliminate the double counting of purchases and sales, borrowing and lending between subsidiaries. Where subsidiaries are not wholly owned, the profits and assets attributable to the minority shareholders (minority interests) have to be shown separately. Under merger accounting (US = *pooling of interests*), assets of acquired subsidiaries are put in at historic cost (►costs, historical); i.e. the balance sheets of parents and subsidiaries are added together line by line. Merger accounting gives a more favourable view, and this may be particularly desirable where the subsidiary has been acquired by an exchange of shares.

The term *subsidiary* is usually reserved for companies controlled by the parent. Companies in which the parent has between about 20% and 50% of the equity are *associate companies*, which it has influence over but does not control. The accounts of these associates may be partially consolidated by valuing them in the balance sheet at their investment cost plus the proportion of undistributed profits attributable to the parent. Companies in which the company has less than about 20% of the equity are referred to as *trade investments*.

The techniques of financial consolidation are complex, and practices differ between countries. Generally, consolidation of earnings is less usual in Japan and continental Europe than in the UK and the USA, and this may affect comparisons of ►yields.

The European Union's Seventh Directive harmonizes the requirements for the consolidated accounts of companies.

Consolidated Fund (UK) The UK government's main expenditure and income account, kept with the Bank of England.

consols (UK) Abbreviation for *consolidated stock*: irredeemable government stock, first issued in the 18th century and bearing a ➤nominal interest rate of $2\frac{1}{2}$%.

consorzio per investimenti (It.) ➤Investment trust.

constant-dollar plan ➤pound-cost averaging.

consumer credit Short-term ➤loans to the public for the purchase of specific goods. Consumer ➤credit takes the form of credit by shopkeepers and other suppliers, ➤credit accounts, ➤personal loans and ➤hire purchase.

Consumer Credit Act 1974 (UK) Legislation introducing a licensing system for all agencies involved in ➤consumer credit. The Act provides protection for the borrower in consumer ➤credit business. The Act applies to bank and ➤hire-purchase credit, to ➤credit sales, ➤credit cards, private loans and ➤mortgages, and also to debt collectors. The Act principally provides for full disclosure of cost information, including the ➤annual percentage rate (APR), for a ➤cooling-off period and for a written agreement, except in the case of ➤overdrafts.

consumer instalment loan (US) ➤hire purchase.

consumer price index ➤retail price index.

contango A situation in a ➤commodity market in which prices for future delivery are higher than those for immediate or very early delivery. Also known as *forwardation*.

contemporaneous reserve requirements (CRR) (US) The constitution by banks of reserves against deposits made simultaneously with the calculation of the level of deposits for the period in question.

contingent liability ➤provisions.

contract 1. Any agreement under law, including an agreement to buy or sell a ➤security (➤contract note). **2**. Traded ➤options and ➤futures are agreements to buy or sell a security or ➤commodity at a specified price and date and thus are referred to as contracts.

contract note (UK) A document sent by a ➤broker soon after a transaction, showing the price at which a ➤security was bought or sold, a note of any benefits attached or excluded (e.g. ➤ex-dividend), the broker's ➤commission, tax charge, the ➤consideration and the terms of payment.

contracting out (UK) The act of an occupational ➤pensions scheme in withdrawing from the State Earnings-Related Pension Scheme (SERPS), subject to a guarantee of equivalent benefit, and attracting a reduction in contributions to the state.

contractual savings ►savings.

contrarian ►investment approaches.

contratto a premi (It.) An ►option contract.

convergence The move towards common economic and financial conditions – the *criteria* – required of ►European Union members wishing to take part in ►Economic and Monetary Union (EMU). The criteria were set out in the ►Maastricht Treaty and were to be met by 1 July 1998. They are:

Government deficit: Not more than 3% of gross domestic product.
Government debt: Not more than 60% of gross domestic product.
Inflation: Over the previous year, not more than 1½ percentage points above that of the three best performing member states.
Interest rates: Over the previous year, an average nominal long-term interest rate not more than two percentage points above that of the three best performing member states in terms of price stability.
Exchange rate: Over the previous two years, maintenance without severe tensions of the normal fluctuation margins of the ►European Monetary System (EMS); and no devaluation, on the state's own initiative, of the rate against any other member state.

conversion 1. Transfer of one type of ►security into another, e.g. convertible loan stock or convertible bond, a fixed-interest security that on ►maturity or at a specified date or dates may be exchanged for ►equity at a fixed price. There may be an option to receive cash for those who do not wish to exercise their conversion rights. Convertibles usually carry a lower interest rate than similar fixed-interest securities, since the investor may make a ►capital gain if the price of the underlying equity rises above the conversion price. ►►conversion premium; warrant. 2. Change in legal form, e.g. conversion of a ►building society to a public limited company (plc; ►incorporation) under the Building Societies Act 1986.

conversion discount ►conversion premium.

conversion premium The difference between the current market price of a ►share and the price at which a convertible security (►conversion) or ►warrant can be exchanged for the share. Expressed as a percentage of the market price of the convertible security, this is the conversion premium or, if the difference is negative, the conversion discount.

convertible 1. A ►currency is said to be convertible when it can be bought or sold without restriction in exchange for other currencies. ►exchange control. 2. A ►security is convertible when it carries the right for the holder to exchange it at a fixed price for another form of security. ➤conversion. ➤➤adjustable rate preferred stock.

convertible adjustable rate preferred stock ➤adjustable rate preferred stock.

convertible bond A ➤bond that can be converted at a fixed price into the ➤shares of a company, usually within a given time period. ➤➤conversion.

convertible debenture ➤debentures.

convertible loan stock ➤conversion.

convertible revolving credit A ➤revolving credit convertible at the end of the ➤term, or earlier, into a fixed-term loan.

cooling-off period (UK) A period, provided under the UK Insurance Companies Act and the Consumer Credit Act 1974, during which a person having entered into a long-term ➤life assurance policy or a ➤hire-purchase agreement has the right to withdraw from the commitment. The period is of 10 days of effecting the life assurance policy and payment of the first premium; and five days of receipt of confirmation of the hire-purchase agreement. ➤➤Truth in Lending Act (US).

Copenhagen interbank offer rate (CIBOR) (Den.) The Danish equivalent of the ➤London interbank offered rate (LIBOR). The rate is available to banks and savings banks depositing three-month uncollateralized kroner with a prime bank.

Copenhagen Stock Exchange The exchange became a public limited company in 1995 and ceased, following implementation of the ➤Investment Services Directive, to have a monopoly. There is an electronic ➤order-driven system with arrangements for less liquid shares. ➤Settlement is T+ 3. ➤➤Nordquote.

core price index The retail price index from which items deemed unrepresentative of the true movement of prices have been removed. In the USA these items are those relating to food and energy; in the UK the item usually removed is mortgage interest payments; food and seasonal foods can also be removed.

CORES Computer-Assisted Order Routing and Execution System. ➤Tokyo Stock Exchange.

corporate finance ➤business finance.

corporate raider (US) An individual organization that makes hostile ➤take-over bids for ➤quoted companies. These bids may be financed by ➤junk bonds and involve *greenmail* in which the target company may avert the take-over by buying in at a premium the ➤share stake built up by the raider or a risk arbitrageur (➤arbitrage). The latter buys stakes in companies that are expected to be the subject of a contested bid (➤merger), selling the ➤stock of the acquiring company. In a take-over bid, the shares of the acquiring company usually fall on announcement of the bid, while those of the victim rise. The term *greenmail* derives from the colour of dollar bills and the implication of blackmail in some threatened take-over bids. ➤➤poison pill; white knight.

corporate venturing ➤Venture capital provided by non-financial companies. Large international companies sometimes acquire shares in smaller-growth companies, particularly in new technology-based industries, and may provide them with research and development or other support. This is done primarily to secure an interest in new technologies.

corporation ➤incorporation.

corporation tax A tax (➤taxation) levied on the assessable ➤profits of companies. Until 1997 the UK had a full *imputation* system. The company paid tax on its profits at the corporation tax rate before any distribution, while all shareholders were given a ➤tax credit in respect of the part of corporation tax paid on distributed profits. The total amount of the tax imputed to shareholders was remitted to the ➤Inland Revenue as *advance corporation tax* (ACT) and was deductible from liability for mainstream corporation tax. Some companies had insufficient tax liabilities against which to offset ACT; this was known as *unrelieved corporation tax* or *surplus ACT*, and arose where a high proportion of profits was earned overseas. From 1994, companies might opt to classify a ➤dividend as a *foreign income dividend* (FID), which was treated as having borne income tax at the lower rate. The purpose of these complex imputation arrangements was to ensure that shareholders were not taxed twice on their dividends, once by corporation tax and once by income tax.

In 1997 the government announced that although ACT payments would continue, the related tax credit would no longer be recoverable by companies and pension funds. FIDs were to be abolished.

Germany, France, Italy and Japan operate an imputation system. The Netherlands, Switzerland, the US and others use the *classical system of corporation tax* that treats the company as having a fiscal as well as a legal identity distinct from its shareholders; these countries tax company profits and also dividends in the hands of shareholders.

Several countries, including the US and the UK, have a lower rate of tax for smaller companies. In the UK, as in many other countries, companies are liable to a tax on ➤capital gains. ➤Unincorporated businesses are subject to business ➤income tax. ➤➤sub-chapter S corporations.

correspondent bank A ➤bank in one country that acts as an ➤agent for a bank in another country, e.g. in the transmission of funds.

corset ➤supplementary special deposit.

cost of capital ➤capital, cost of.

cost of funds (US) A term used to describe banks' setting of lending rates in relation to the rates paid by themselves for funds raised in the ►wholesale market. ►base rate.

cost of sales (UK) The cost of producing what is sold before making an allowance for contribution to general ►overheads, i.e. material costs, manufacturing wage costs and production overheads.

costanti (It.) A sale for ►cash.

costs, historical Actual costs at the time incurred. An ►asset in the ►balance sheet at historical cost is shown at the price paid for it, even though it may be worth more or cost more to replace (►inflation accounting).

cotation (Fr.) A ►stock exchange listing.

cote (Fr.) The official price of a ►security on the ►stock exchange.

cote officielle (Fr.) The full term for ►*cote*, also used to denote the ►stock market itself. The word *officielle* derives from the fact that the market was until 1962 divided into a market at official prices and the ►*coulisse* or market at unofficial prices.

coulisse (Fr.) The unofficial securities market in the ►Paris Bourse, the *coulisse* closed in 1962. ►*cote officielle*.

council tax ►local taxation.

counterparty risk The risk in securities trading that the counterparty to a purchase or sale may fail to discharge his obligation. If default occurs before settlement is due, the counterparty risk takes the form of *replacement risk*, i.e. the risk of incurring the cost of replacing the deal. Counterparty risk may also take the form of *settlement risk*, in which one side of the deal pays cash or delivers securities, but where the other side delays completing his part, causing illiquidity which may be serious.

countertrading Another term for barter, i.e. the exchange of goods or services without any monetary consideration.

country risk ►Sovereign risk.

coupon A counterfoil or tag that, when detached from a ►bond, serves as evidence of entitlement to interest. It is invariably used to refer to the rate of interest itself; and by extension is also used to refer to the rate of interest on most financial ►instruments, particularly ►notes.

coupon issue (US) ►coupon security.

coupon pass (US) The purchase outright of a ►security.

coupon security (US) US government ►securities that pay a rate of interest, or

➤coupon, as compared with those bought at a ➤discount. Coupon securities are ➤Treasury bonds and certain ➤Treasury notes or ➤bills.

coupure (Fr.) The total number of shares in an issue.

cours (Fr.) **1.** ➤Rate. **2.** Market price (of ➤securities or ➤commodities), i.e. in the sense of the going market price, as against *prix*, the price paid in a particular transaction.

Court of Auditors A panel of expert ➤auditors with the task of examining all revenues and expenditures of the ➤European Union and having the right to comment on these and, where requested, to offer advice on them. The Court of Auditors was set up in 1975 and is composed of 12 members, one from each member country, appointed each for a term of six years by the Council of Ministers, in consultation with the European Parliament.

courte échéance (Fr.) ➤Short term.

courtier (Fr.) A ➤broker on the French unofficial stock market or ➤*coulisse*, which closed in 1962.

cover 1. To ➤hedge. **2.** To obtain the ➤currency, ➤security or ➤commodity needed to honour a contracted sale. **3.** To insure. **4.** Of ➤dividends, the amount by which the *pay-out* is covered by the company's earnings (➤dividend cover).

cover note A temporary confirmation that an ➤insurance risk has been covered, issued pending the completion of a full insurance contract.

covered interest arbitrage Taking advantage of differences in ➤interest rates between two countries by borrowing in one ➤currency and investing the proceeds to earn the higher rate while covering the ➤exchange rate risk in the ➤forward market.

CP ➤commercial paper.

CPI Consumer price index. ➤retail price index.

crash A precipitate one-day fall in stock market prices.

crawling peg Revaluation or devaluation of an ➤exchange rate in small amounts spread over time and linked to a ➤moving average of past rates or a country's gold ➤reserves.

créance (Fr.) A ➤claim.

credit Granting the use or possession of goods and services without immediate payment. ➤bank credit; consumer credit; double-entry bookkeeping; trade credit.

credit availability theory (US) The theory that a modest increase in interest rates could lead to capital losses in banks' portfolios of ➤Treasury securities, so inducing the banks to restrict the availability of business loans for investment.

credit card A plastic, personal, magnetized card issued by an agency, bank or other institution against which purchases, up to a prescribed ceiling (*credit limit*), may be credited on signature of a voucher franked by the card. The vendor recovers the cash from the issuer of the card (less a percentage ➤commission), and the purchaser pays the issuer on receipt of a monthly statement. If desired, the purchaser has the option of paying a minimum amount and settling the account in instalments plus interest. Credit cards are sometimes available free to creditworthy users; other cards, known as *charge cards*, are paid for by an annual fee and do not offer the option of a loan. A *debit card* works in the same way as the credit card but debits the purchaser's bank account immediately. Credit cards may be used to withdraw cash from an ➤automatic teller machine, and the card may be magnetically inspected for authenticity. Credit cards are popularly referred to as 'plastic money'. ➤➤cheque card; smart card.

credit control (UK) The ➤regulation of bank and other forms of ➤credit in the interests of ➤monetary policy. Specifically the term applies to the arrangements for the control of bank credit announced in September 1971, to replace credit ceilings, entitled competition and credit control, which led to the introduction of the ➤minimum lending rate and were intended to stimulate competition in the ➤banking system. ➤➤monetary control.

credit guarantee A type of ➤insurance against default, provided by a credit guarantee association, government body or other institution, to a lending institution, to allow small firms that lack ➤collateral security, or are unable to obtain loans for other reasons, to obtain credit from banks. A government loan guarantee scheme of this type was introduced in the UK in 1980. Not to be confused with ➤deposit insurance.

credit line (US) ➤overdraft.

crédit mixte (Fr.) A combined package of bank ➤credit and official aid funds for financing an export transaction.

credit rating An assessment of the likelihood of an individual or business being able to meet its financial obligations. Credit ratings are provided by credit agencies or ➤rating agencies for sellers who wish to verify the financial strength of buyers, for lenders and for investors (ratings for specific ➤securities). Banks also provide confidential trade references.

credit sale A sale agreement under which payment is made in instalments, but with ownership of the object of the sale passing immediately to the purchaser.

credit union A non-profit organization accepting ➤deposits and making ➤loans, operated as a co-operative; a ➤mutual organization that is in effect a ➤savings bank. Similar credit associations exist in many countries, e.g. the *shinyo kinku* and the smaller *shinyo kumiai* credit co-operatives in Japan, which act as banks for small firms.

creditor One to whom money is due.

CREST Electronic share register (►registrar and ►settlement system) introduced to the London ►stock exchange in 1996. By recording title to shares electronically it will reduce the cost of the traditional system of ►share certificates sent through the post. Title will be recorded through ►nominee companies set up by ►stockbrokers and others. However, shareholders may continue to hold paper certificates if they wish. CREST is owned by Crestco, a company in which the ►London Stock Exchange has a minority holding along with other financial institutions. CREST will replace TALISMAN, the ►Transfer Accounting, Lodgement for Investors, Stock Management for Jobbers system.

crore (Indian) The Indian term for 10,000,000 rupees.

cross ►crossing.

cross-border listing ►Shares and other ►securities may be traded on official ►stock exchanges only where they are listed on an exchange. Residents in other countries may purchase or sell securities through their own ►broker, who will get a broker in the country of listing to trade the securities. The practice known as cross-border listing means securities being listed on exchanges in more than one country.

cross-currency interest rate swap An ►interest rate swap in which two different streams of interest, in two different currencies, are exchanged.

crossed (US) A situation where one ►market maker has a lower ►offer price than another's ►bid price. This is referred to as a locked or crossed market and in the UK sometimes as ►backwardation or backward price. On the ►London Stock Exchange, market makers are supposed not to take advantage of the opportunity presented to buy from one ►dealer and sell to another at a profit (►arbitrage), but should draw the dealers' attention to the discrepancy and allow them to change their ►quotation.

crossing The purchase and sale of a quantity of ►securities by the same ►broker. ►Stock exchange rules normally require such transactions to cross the market so as to ensure that the buyer or seller has the opportunity to get a better price if it is available. Where the two orders are for the same individual, or by another acting in collusion with them, a crossed sale is known in the USA as a ►wash sale.

crowding in The theory that a national budget deficit in periods of economic depression, involving higher public expenditure and monetary growth and offsetting increased government borrowing, can lead to higher economic activity and so to an increase in private investment.

crowding out The theory that excessive central government borrowing on ►capital markets will consume funds otherwise available for private ►investment.

CRS Computer-readable systems.

CSRC ►China Securities Regulatory Commission.

cum-dividend With-dividend; the purchaser of a security quoted cum-dividend is entitled to receive the next ►dividend when due. The term *cum* is used in a similar sense in relation to ►bonus issues, ►rights issues or ►interest attached to ►securities, etc.

cumulative preference shares (UK) ►preference shares.

Curb Exchange ►American Stock Exchange.

currency **1.** Notes and coin that are the *current* medium of exchange in a country. A *soft* currency is one where ►exchange rate is tending to fall because demand for it is weak. This may be the result of changes in capital movements, patterns of trade or speculation. A *hard* currency is one that is tending to rise against other currencies. **2.** In US and UK banking, all foreign currencies. **3.** In US ►money supply terminology, currency refers to ►cash.

currency board A national body charged with maintaining a fixed ►exchange rate by expanding or contracting the issue of domestic currency in line with holdings of foreign currency and other liquid assets. Unlike a ►central bank, a currency board cannot simply issue new domestic currency without one-to-one backing, or act as a ►lender of last resort. Currency boards link their domestic currency to a foreign currency as the exchange-rate peg to the US dollar maintained by the Hong Kong currency board.

currency future A form of ►financial future in which the contract is in respect of the exchange rate of a currency.

currency interest rate swap An ►interest rate swap consisting of the exchange of two streams of the same interest rate but in different currencies. These are sometimes termed *fixed-rate currency swaps*. In the case of trade in currency interest rate swaps, the ►principal may also change hands.

currency option ►option.

currency overlay manager (US) An investment manager concerned with devising programmes to ►hedge or enhance investment portfolios of foreign ►stocks (and more rarely ►bonds) against ►currency risks or opportunities. These managers have come into prominence as ►equities denominated in foreign currencies have become more important in the portfolios of ►institutional investors. Investors may wish their equity returns to offset the ►interest or ►capital gain returns irrespective of currency changes, or they may actually wish to enhance their exposure to foreign currencies.

currency risk The risk, attaching to securities deals denominated in foreign currencies, that unforeseen exchange-rate changes may affect balance-sheet value in the home currency (also known as *translation risk*), or income or expenditure amounts in the home currency (also known as *trading risk* or *transaction risk*).

currency swap ➤currency interest rate swap; swap.

currency translation exposure The effect of currency movements on a company's accounts when foreign sales are recorded in the domestic currency.

current account 1. The most common type of ➤bank account, on which ➤deposits do not necessarily earn ➤interest but can be withdrawn by ➤cheque at any time (US = *demand deposit*; *checking account*). ➤➤bank charges. 2. That part of the balance of payments recording current, i.e. non-capital, transactions.

current account deposit ➤sight deposit.

current assets ➤assets.

current cost accounting ➤inflation accounting.

current liabilities ➤liabilities.

current prices Prices adjusted for changes in the purchasing power of money.

current ratio ➤working capital.

current yield ➤yield.

cursor A marker on a computer screen showing where the next text entered on the keyboard will be displayed. In most programs it can be moved around the screen by arrows on the keyboard.

CUSIP number (US) A nine-digit identifier for securities traded in the United States. The letters-and-numbers identifier system was set up by the Committee on Uniform Securities Identification Procedures.

customer repurchase agreement (US) A ➤repurchase agreement arranged by the ➤Federal Reserve for foreign central bank customers.

customer RP ➤customer repurchase agreement.

customized option An ➤option, generally offered in ➤over-the-counter trade, allowing the holder various departures from the fixed terms, strike prices, and exercise and settlement dates required for instruments traded on options exchanges. ➤➤flex stock option.

Customs and Excise, HM ➤Inland Revenue.

CVM Commissão de Valores Mobiliaros. ➤São Paulo Stock Exchange.

cyclical stocks ➤Shares in companies which are expected to prosper particularly in times of economic boom while their share prices tend to fall most during recessions. Building companies and motor distributors, for example, are generally included as cyclicals while food retailers are regarded as *defensive stocks* least affected by the state of the economy.

cylinder option An ➤option with a specially reduced ➤premium.

D

DA ➤discretionary account.

DAC Development Assistance Committee. ➤Organization for Economic Co-operation and Development (OECD).

Dachgesellschaft (Ger.) ➤Holding company.

daimyo bond (Jap.) A ➤bearer security issued by the ➤International Bank for Reconstruction and Development on the Japanese ➤capital market and also in the ➤Eurobond market. ➤Market makers are permitted to take ➤short positions in these bonds, unlike the provisions for ➤samurai bonds.

Danish Futures and Options Market A market opened in 1988, supported by the ➤Guarantee Fund for Futures and Options. In 1993 the first money-market future, based on the three-month ➤Copenhagen interbank offer rate (CIBOR), was launched with a contract size of DKr5m. This complemented the existing range of futures instruments for government bonds, long-term mortgage bonds, and the KFX index of most traded shares. There were plans for options on CIBOR futures and possibly on other money-market securities.

Darlehen (Ger.) A ➤loan.

date d'échéance (Fr.) ➤Redemption date.

dated securities ➤Bonds, ➤bills of exchange or other ➤securities that have a stated date for redemption (repayment) of their nominal value. Short-dated securities are those for which the ➤redemption date is near; long-dated securities are those for which it is a long time ahead.

dawn raid (UK) The acquisition of a large ➤block of ➤shares on the ➤stock exchange, sometimes as a prelude to a ➤take-over bid. Usually purchases are carried out simultaneously by a number of ➤brokers first thing in the morning.

DAX ➤*Deutsche Aktienindex.*

day order An order placed in a ➤commodity market for execution in the same trading session, or in the same day, following which the order lapses.

day-to-day money ➤overnight money.

DCF ➤discounted cash flow.

de minimis ►*de minimis non curat lex.*

de minimis non curat lex 'The law is not concerned with trifles.' An expression meaning that a law or proceeding consecrating a general principle should not be overturned by a contrary detail. In taxation, refers to amounts too small to be worth inclusion in legislation. Generally quoted simply as 'de minimis'.

dead-cat bounce A short-lived rally in the course of a ►bear market.

dealer Someone who buys and sells on their own account. ►broker-dealer.

dealerboard A fast telecommunications package enabling almost instant contact between dealers at the touch of a button, e.g. a ►touch screen.

debentures, debenture stocks (UK) Fixed-interest ►securities issued by limited companies (►incorporation) in return for long-term ►loans. The former term is sometimes also used to refer to any title on a secured interest-bearing loan. Debentures are dated for redemption between 10 and 40 years ahead (►redemption date). Debentures are usually secured against specific ►assets of the company (*mortgage debentures*) or by a *floating charge* on the assets. Debenture interest must be paid whether the company makes a ►profit or not. In the event of non-payment, debenture holders can force ►liquidation, and they rank ahead of all ►shareholders in their claims on the company's assets. Convertible debentures carry an option at a fixed date to convert the ►stock into ►ordinary shares at a fixed price (►conversion).

debit ►double-entry bookkeeping.

debit card ►credit card.

debt A sum of money or other property owed by one person or organization to another. Debt comes into being through the granting of ►credit or through raising ►loan capital. Debt servicing consists of paying interest on a debt. The term *debt* is, by extension, used to refer to the total loan exposure of an enterprise or public authority, or to the choice of ►bonds rather than ►equity in raising funds – 'to issue debt'.

debt–equity swap ►debt swap.

debt instrument A medium for raising a ►loan, usually a ►short-term loan. ►instrument.

debt ratio ►capital gearing.

debt rescheduling ►moratorium.

debt swap A term used to describe the practice begun by banks in the late 1980s of disposing of their outstanding loans to Third World borrowers, chiefly governments, at large discounts to other banks. The swaps take three forms: debt–

debt exchanges, where a bank more willing to extend credit takes over a loan from another bank; debt–equity swaps, where a country's debt is converted into the bank's holding of ►equity in a domestic company; and debt–peso swaps, where nationals of the debtor country buy the debt and convert it into local currency. Debt may also be exchanged for equity in ►venture capital packages and in ►privatizations.

debtor One who owes money to another.

decile ►percentile.

declaration The act of exercising rights in an ►option. Buyers indicate, through their and the seller's broker, that they are implementing the option. This must be done by a specified time before the ►prompt date, failing which the option is deemed to have been abandoned.

deductible The portion of a loss that must be borne by the ►insured. The deductible has the effect, unlike the case of an ►excess, of reducing the total sum insured. Thus a deductible of £10m in a contract of £100m leaves the insurer under an obligation to pay a claim, if made, of £90m, whereas with an excess and contract value of the same amounts, the insured pays the first £10m, and the insurer pays the next £100m; in the latter case, the insurer gains if the loss is £10m or below.

deep discount bonds Low-interest or no-interest ►debt issued at a price well below ►par value. This means that on ►redemption at maturity, the holder will make a ►capital gain which may be advantageous for tax purposes even though the running ►yield is low.

default Usually a failure to make payments or repayments of ►interest or ►principal on the due date. A country may be declared in default if it ceases to service a ►loan from another government or an international agency such as the World Bank (►International Bank for Reconstruction and Development).

defensive stocks ►cyclical stocks.

deferred annuity An ►annuity whose commencement occurs on a specified date after purchase.

deferred coupon note A ►bond upon which ►interest is paid only after a specified date. US = *deferred interest bond; extended bond.*

deferred interest bond ►deferred coupon note.

deferred start option ►deferred strike option.

deferred strike option An ►option permitting the holder to postpone setting the ►striking price either indefinitely or to an agreed date. Also known as a deferred or forward start option.

defined benefits scheme Occupational ➤pensions schemes promising a definite pension, with the employers binding themselves to make up, for this purpose, any shortfall in the proceeds of contributions.

defined contributions scheme An occupational ➤pensions scheme in which the level of contributions is fixed, with no promise of a specific level of pension. In effect, a ➤money purchase scheme.

del credere The risk of non-payment; an amount added to a charge to cover this risk.

del credere **agent** An agent taking on themselves, in return for a higher ➤commission, the risk of non-payment of bills by the customer they introduce.

delivery month The month that is the subject of a ➤futures contract and in which physical delivery must be made; a specific date within the month is prescribed for this purpose in the contract. Also known as the terminal month.

delivery versus payment A concept in the ➤settlement of multi-➤currency deals, under which the transfer of one currency does not proceed unless the transfer of the other currency is simultaneously taking place. The concept is intended to avoid ➤Herstatt risk.

delta The amount by which the price of an ➤option changes in consequence of a change in the price of the underlying ➤asset.

delta stocks ➤alpha securities; stocks.

demand deposit ➤current account; sight deposit.

demurrage Damages due to a shipowner where the contracted completion of loading or unloading is delayed.

denomination 1. The value, as printed on its face, of a ➤security and the sum payable on ➤redemption. ➤face value. **2.** The specification in the ➤foreign exchange market, the international ➤money market and the ➤securities market of the ➤currency to be used; often employed to refer to the currency itself.

Department of Trade and Industry (DTI) UK government department responsible for promoting trade with other countries and overseeing UK business and finance.

déport (Fr.) ➤Backwardation.

deposit 1. A sum of money lodged with a ➤bank, ➤discount house or other financial institution. **2.** A sum of money proportionate to the total size of the transaction, lodged to secure a ➤forward, ➤futures or ➤option contract. Also termed a premium or a margin.

deposit account A bank account in which ➤deposits earn interest, and withdrawals from which require notice (US = *time deposit*). In France and other European countries deposit accounts are called savings accounts.

deposit insurance A form of ➤insurance providing compensation to lenders with ➤deposits with ➤financial institutions in the event of failure of the bank (➤banking) or other institution. The Deposit Protection Scheme was set up in the UK under the Banking Act 1979; under this scheme the Deposit Protection Fund guarantees up to 75% of the first £100,000 of a sterling deposit. In the USA the Federal Deposit Insurance Corporation (FDIC) provides protection for depositors with members of the ➤Federal Reserve System and other banks that choose to join.

Deposit Protection Fund, Scheme ➤deposit insurance.

deposit-taking institution A bank (➤banking) or another ➤financial intermediary that accepts ➤deposits.

Depository Institutions Deregulation and Monetary Decontrol Act 1980 (DIDMCA) (US) An Act that removed interest-rate ceilings from passbook savings accounts, thus allowing these ➤deposit rates and borrowing costs to rise to market levels. Part of a continuing process of *deregulation* (➤regulation) of the US ➤banking system, it led to difficulties for many ➤savings and loan associations.

depository receipt ➤Warehouse receipt.

Depository Trust Company (DTC) (US) The central depository for ➤stock exchange ➤securities in the USA.

depreciation 1. The reduction in the value of an ➤asset through wear and tear. An allowance for the depreciation on a company's assets is always made before the calculation of ➤profit, on the grounds that the consumption of ➤capital assets is one of the costs of earning the revenues of the business and is allowed as such according to special rules by the tax authorities. Annual depreciation provisions are normally calculated either by the *straight-line method*, where the estimated residual value of the asset (e.g. scrap) is deducted from its original cost and the balance divided by the number of years of estimated life to arrive at an annual depreciation expense; or by the *reducing balance method*, in which case the actual depreciation expense is set at a constant proportion of the cost of the asset, i.e. a diminishing annual absolute amount. In periods of rising prices, the replacement cost of an asset may be very much greater than its original cost. This problem may be dealt with by revaluing assets at intervals and adjusting depreciation charges accordingly. This is called *replacement-cost* as opposed to *historic-cost* depreciation (➤inflation accounting). 2. A reduction in the value of a ➤currency in terms of ➤gold or other currencies in a free market. Also used to refer to a reduction in the purchasing power of any form of currency.

depreciation at choice ➤capital allowances.

---

deregulation ➤regulation.

derivative A generic term for ➤futures, ➤options and ➤swaps, i.e. instruments derived from conventional direct dealings in securities, currencies and commodities. Trade in derivatives increased substantially in the 1990s, given their usefulness to company treasurers and fund managers as a ➤hedge against security price changes and currency fluctuations, particularly in the disturbed currency markets of the period. Between 1992 and 1993, for example, turnover on the ➤London International Financial Futures Exchange (LIFFE) and the ➤Marché à Terme des Instruments Financiers (MATIF) increased by 20% and 30% respectively. In the 10 years to 1993, 18 derivatives exchanges were created in Europe, trading 98 different contracts. The market, which had come to be dominated by trade in swaps and to be handled chiefly by a relatively small number of banks, was estimated to have reached a total value of some $4bn by 1992. This figure was questioned by some commentators, who held that the true measure was not the total value of the instruments traded but the level of risk involved, a figure around a tenth of the total value. Moreover, many, including the ➤Group of 30 in a report published in July 1993, pointed out that the derivatives market was small in comparison with total bond, equity or foreign exchange transactions ($900bn).

In the same report the Group of 30, while suggesting guidelines for the proper conduct of business, concluded that further regulation was unnecessary. However, central banks in particular remained unconvinced, noting that most business was ➤over the counter, that the instruments were complex and not universally understood, and that the potential for undercapitalization, faulty systems, inadequate supervision and human error was greater than in other markets.

dernier cours (Fr.) ➤Closing prices.

designated investment exchange (DIE) (UK) An overseas investment exchange recognized by the Financial Services Authority as having equivalent operating procedures to its own recognized investment exchanges (➤Financial Services Act).

designated market maker (UK) A ➤market maker receiving fee and publicity concessions from the ➤London International Financial Futures Exchange (LIFFE) in return for an undertaking to maintain two-way and up-to-date prices and to be physically present in the *pit* (➤pit trader) throughout trading.

designated order turnaround (DOT) (US) An electronic order-processing system on the ➤New York Stock Exchange that allows members to place, e.g., a limit ➤order for ➤stock that will be executed automatically.

desk (US) A familiar term for the ➤open market desk.

destination principle ➤value added tax (VAT).

Deutsche Aktienindex (DAX) (Ger.) A share price index (➤share indices) for

30 leading ►equity shares quoted on the Frankfurt ►stock exchange (►German stock exchanges). The DAX is recalculated minute by minute from the Frankfurt market share information system known as Kurs Information Service System (KISS).

Deutsche Börse AG ►German stock exchanges.

Deutsche Bundesbank ►Bundesbank.

Deutsche Kassenverein AG ►German stock exchanges.

Deutsche Terminborse (DTB) The German ►futures and ►options exchange, opened in Frankfurt in 1990 after various problems relating to German gambling law had been resolved.

deuxième marché ►Swiss stock exchanges.

developing country A country that has low income per head of the population and has not yet reached the stage of economic development characterized by the growth of industrialization. Also referred to as *Third World countries*.

Development Assistance Committee (DAC) ►Organization for Economic Co-operation and Development (OECD).

development capital Finance provided, usually by a specialized institution, in the form of ►equity and ►loans to an established business. It is distinct from, though often used synonymously with, ►venture capital.

Devisen (Ger.) ►Foreign exchange.

devises (Fr.) ►Foreign exchange.

dilution An increase in the number of ►shares in a company, e.g. by the ►exercise of ►warrants, which reduces ►earnings per share.

direct business Of ►insurance: **1.** A ►policy concluded between the ►insurer and the insured, without the intervention of an ►intermediary. **2.** Business between the insurer and the policy-holding public, as against ►reinsurance. Also known as *primary business*.

direct finance The provision of a financial service by telephone.

direct investment ►Investment in the foreign operations of a company, e.g. by a ►multinational company. Direct investment implies control, and managerial and perhaps technical input, and is generally preferred by the host country to ►portfolio investment. ►►balance of payments.

direct placement The sale of ►shares directly to ►financial institutions without recourse to ►underwriters or a public subscription (►offer for sale) in the ►stock market. ►►placing.

direct quotation In ➤foreign exchange, the quotation of a rate of exchange in terms of one unit of the domestic currency, i.e. £1 = $1.50, in the UK rather, than $1 = £0.67.

direct tax ➤taxation.

directive 1. Written instructions from the ➤Federal Open Market Committee to the Federal Reserve Bank of New York, regarding the conduct of open market operations. 2. A decision of the ➤European union, binding as to the result but optional as to the form and method of achieving the result.

directives of the EU Outline legislation prepared by the Commission of the European Communities (➤European Union), for enactment by member states when approved by the Council of Ministers. ➤Banking Directives; Fourth Directive; Insurance Accounts Directive; Investment Services Directive.

dirham The national ➤currency unit of Morocco.

dirty float Governments sometimes declare that the ➤exchange rate is fully floating, i.e. determined by free market forces, and then surreptitiously intervene directly to influence the rate upwards or downwards. This contrasts with an internationally agreed managed rate, as with the ➤Exchange Rate Mechanism (➤Maastricht Treaty).

disclosure Enforced or voluntary publication of information. Under company law and other aspects of ➤regulation, businesses are required to reveal information that they might otherwise wish to keep confidential; e.g. in the implementation of the ➤Financial Services Act, brokers are required to reveal rates of ➤commission on certain insurance policies. ➤➤Form 10-K; Fourth Directive.

discount 1. Reduction in the ➤face value of a financial ➤claim, such as a ➤bill of exchange or ➤Treasury bill, by the amount of money represented by the interest due on the claim during the remainder of its ➤maturity. The reduction involved is the discount. It also denotes the action of selling a claim at a discount, i.e. to discount. 2. The term is used to refer specifically to the purchase of bills at a discount by the central bank, although ➤rediscount is more accurate. It is also used to denote direct lending to the commercial banks by the central bank, although more exactly an interest rate is charged rather than a discount deducted. 3. The amount by which the future value of a ➤currency is less than its ➤spot value; opposite of ➤premium. 4. The amount by which a ➤security's price in the ➤secondary market is less than the ➤issue price. 5. The amount by which an ➤option trades below its ➤intrinsic value. 6. ➤discounting. 7. The amount (usually expressed as a percentage) by which the price of a share in an ➤investment trust is less than ➤net asset value.

discount factor ➤discounted cash flow.

discount house 1. A now defunct term for a ►bill broker in a variety of ►debt instruments in the ►money market. Discount houses acted as principals for the purchase of ►market instruments and of ►Treasury bills, financed chiefly by borrowing from the banks with the support of the ►Bank of England as ►lender of last resort. From March 1997 on a phased basis the term 'discount house' has ceased to be used and the institutions bearing that name have become ►banks or other financial intermediaries. Discount houses as separately capitalized and regulated institutions have, or will soon have, ceased to exist. These changes result from the new policy of the Bank of England to influence interest rates via ►gilt repos. **2**. A 'cut price' retail store selling goods at a ►discount.

discount market The ►money market. ►discount house.

discount rate The interest rate used in determining the ►discount on the ►sale of a financial ►instrument. The term is frequently used in relation to ►central banks. The discount rate of the ►Bank of England is the rate at which it will discount ►eligible bills. In the USA the term has a more special meaning; the discount rate of the ►Federal Reserve is the interest rate at which it will lend, as ►lender of last resort, to the commercial banks. It is thus the US equivalent of ►bank rate. ►►discount window.

discount window The supply of ►short-term funds by a ►central bank to the banking system, subject to commencement (*opening*) or termination (*closing*) at any time. The supply will be either by purchase of ►Treasury bills or by lending, against security, usually by discounting in the USA and by charging an interest rate in the UK; the term *discount* in the latter context is therefore a slight anomaly. In Germany the term refers to the suspension of normal ►Lombard rate and the substitution of ►special Lombard rate lending. In all cases the discount window is used to assist ►monetary policy. ►►bank rate; minimum lending rate; window.

discounted cash flow (DCF) A sophisticated set of methods for ►investment appraisal that take the time value of money fully into account. For example, £100 today is worth more than £100 in a year's time, risk apart, because if received today it could be invested for one year; so that, at an annual ►rate of interest or discount factor of 10%, we should receive £110 a year from now. For an investment to have a *present value* (PV) of £100 now, therefore, we should need to expect a return of £10 in a year's time from that investment, i.e. the *net present value* (NPV) of the investment – the total return minus the cost of the investment.

This principle can be used to calculate the NPVs of the ►cash flows arising from more complex industrial and commercial investment projects where cash inflows and outflows are lumpy and spread over long periods of time. For two such projects, the one with the highest NPV will add most to the wealth of the business. An alternative method is to calculate the rate of interest that will equate the PV of the net cash flows and the cost of the investment. This is the *internal rate of return* (IRR), which will be the discount factor at which the NPV is zero and can be compared with the firm's borrowing costs (➤capital, cost of). If the IRR is higher than the cost of capital, then the project is worth undertaking. There are circumstances where the IRR method and the NPV method do not give the same result; in these circumstances the NPV method is generally to be preferred. Investment appraisal is not straightforward, since cash inflows and even cash outflows will be subject to uncertainty. An allowance for this can be made by choosing a higher discount factor for risky projects. DCF techniques will not necessarily rank investment projects in the same order of attractiveness as conventional accounting methods, such as ➤payback or ➤return on investment, which do not allow for the timing of receipts and payments.

discounting 1. The application of a ➤discount or ➤rate of interest to a ➤capital sum. Calculations of present value (see ➤discounted cash flow) or the price of a bill before ➤maturity are made by discounting at the current appropriate rate of interest. 2. The future effects of an anticipated event, e.g. a decline in ➤profit, are said to be discounted if selling leads to an adjustment of present prices in line with expected future changes in these prices.

discretionary account (DA) Funds for investment placed with a ➤stockbroker, ➤commodity broker or other authorized investment manager, with either no, or only general, instructions as to how they should be invested. The broker decides upon the distribution of the investments and keeps the client informed of purchases, sales and the value of the ➤portfolio. An account in which a ➤broker or manager may trade without the prior assent of the ➤principal.

discretionary funds ➤discretionary account.

disintermediation Flows of funds between borrowers and lenders avoiding the direct use of ➤financial intermediaries whose normal role is to carry out the intermediation between the users of funds and the suppliers of funds. Disintermediation occurs, e.g., when companies withdraw funds from the banks and lend them directly to each other or issue bills guaranteed (accepted) by the banks but sold to non-banks. Disintermediation may make it more difficult to measure and control the ➤money supply and indeed is often motivated by a desire to avoid ➤credit controls.

dispersion, measures of The variation of the values of any variable from the ➤average or between the extremes. ➤standard deviation.

disponibilités monétaires (Fr.) The French term for the monetary aggregate *M1*. ➤money supply.

disponibilités quasi-monétaires (Fr.) The French term for the monetary aggregate *M3*. ➤money supply.

distributable profits, distributable reserves Current or net ➤retained earnings which are available to pay ►dividends. For public companies in particular, there are legal constraints on what is distributable. ►►capital reserves.

distributed earnings ►Profits paid to ►shareholders in the form of ►dividends, as distinct from ►retained earnings.

divergence indicator ►European Monetary System (EMS).

dividend The amount of a company's ►profit distributed to ordinary ►shareholders; usually expressed either as a percentage of the *nominal value* (►par value) of the ►ordinary share capital, or as an absolute amount per ►share. A dividend is the same as a ►yield only where the shares stand at their nominal value. The amount of the dividend is decided by the board of directors depending upon profitability and the need for ►retained earnings. Where profitability is poor, if the outlook is good, then the dividend may be maintained at the previous year's level or even increased out of ►reserves. The profits after tax from which dividends are paid are those after payments to holders of ►preference shares and ►debentures have been allowed for, the balance being split between dividends and reserves.

Dividends are paid to shareholders after deduction of ►income tax at the lower rate, ►corporation tax where applicable having already been paid out by the company. The larger ►quoted companies pay dividends quarterly or biannually (*interim dividends*). In these instances the last dividend declared in the ►financial year is known as the final dividend. ►►cum-dividend; ex-dividend.

dividend check ►dividend warrant.

dividend cover (UK) The number of times the net ►profits available for distribution exceed the ►dividend actually paid or declared. In US terminology the *pay-out ratio* is the dividend as a percentage of the profit available.

dividend mandate ►mandate.

dividend stripping Buying ►fixed-interest securities when they have gone ►ex-dividend and selling them before the next ►dividend is paid, so as to avoid receiving dividends that in some countries are taxed at a higher rate than ►capital gains. Also called *bond washing*.

dividend warrant The ►cheque by which companies pay ►dividends to ►shareholders. US = *dividend check*.

dividend yield ►yield.

Divisia monetary aggregates A theory of money measurement that assigns index numbers to money forms, based on rates of return, indicating the weighting to be used in adding them together. Named after the French economist.

DJIA (US) Dow Jones Industrial Average. ►Dow Jones indexes.

DKV ►German Stock Exchanges.

DM (Ger.) The German mark, unit of German ➤currency; an abbreviation of 'die deutsche Mark'. The two initials are generally used, or the form D-mark; otherwise problems with the inflection of the adjective *deutsche* would arise.

documentary credit ➤Credit advanced by a bank to a buyer of goods, under which the bank pays the seller immediately and receives payment from the buyer at the end of a specified period, subject to receiving a specified set of shipping documents.

dollar pool (UK) The pool of foreign currency (chiefly in dollars) available under UK ➤exchange control for the purchase by UK residents of foreign ➤securities and residential property. The pool was fed only by sales of existing securities and property, no currency being furnished by the ➤Bank of England for new acquisitions. Accordingly such currency became available only at a premium, which varied according to the level of demand. At one time the pool actually shrank in consequence of a ruling that 25% of the foreign currency value of such overseas property was to be surrendered, on sale, to the Bank of England. The system was disbanded on the abolition of exchange control in 1979. The dollar pool was also variously known as the *premium pool* and the *investment currency pool*.

domestic open market desk (US) ➤open market desk.

DOT ➤designated order turnaround.

double auction An auction in which both bids (➤bid price) and offers (➤offer price) are made competitively; the normal form of ➤open outcry trading in ➤commodity markets.

double-entry bookkeeping The accounting system in which every business transaction, whether a receipt or payment of money, sale or purchase of goods or services, gives rise to two entries, a debit and a corresponding credit, traditionally on opposite pages of a ledger. Since every debit entry has an equal and corresponding credit entry, it follows that the book will (or should) balance.

double option An ➤option conveying the right either to buy or to sell the underlying asset, equivalent to a combined *put* and ➤call option. Only one of the alternatives may be exercised. The ➤deposit is double that of a put or a call option.

double taxation The situation in which the same tax base, e.g. personal income, is taxed more than once. Double-taxation agreements are designed to avoid, e.g., incomes of non-residents being taxed both in the country where they live and in their country of origin. ➤➤tax credit.

Dow-Jones Composite ➤Dow-Jones indexes.

Dow-Jones indexes (US) Dow-Jones & Co. compiles daily indices of the closing prices of ➤securities quoted on the ➤New York Stock Exchange. The Dow-Jones Industrial Average (DJIA) measures changes in the unweighted arithmetic average of 30 leading industrial shares (using a variable divisor to clean out the effect of ►stock splits). There are similar indices for 15 public utility stocks (DJ Utility Average), 20 transportation stocks (DJ Transportation Average) and an average for all 65 stocks called the Dow-Jones Composite or 65 Stock Average. There is also a Dow-Jones 40 Bond Average, a municipal bond index and a commodity future index.

Dow-Jones Industrial Average ►Dow-Jones indexes.

down-and-in call/put option An ►option that is not valid until the price of the underlying security falls below a specified price.

down-and-out call/put option An ►option that becomes valueless when the underlying security falls below a specified price.

downstream (US) To take action anticipating a later stage in a chain of financial operations, e.g. the issue of ►commercial paper at market rates by a bank holding company for on-lending to the subsidiary bank, thus enabling the latter to accumulate ►liabilities in the face of official limits on the level of interest rates that may be offered to depositors.

dragon bond A ►foreign bond issued in the markets of Far Eastern countries. Most purchasers have been found in Hong Kong, with some also in Singapore and South Korea. ►►dragons.

dragons Second wave of *newly industrialized countries* (NICs) in Asia – Indonesia, Malaysia, the Philippines and Thailand – following the ►tigers.

drawdown The drawing of the funds available under a bank ►credit, usually a ►Eurocredit, the term normally being used where drawdown is in stages, e.g. *flexible drawdown*.

drawing rights The mechanism by which member countries of the ►International Monetary Fund (IMF) receive financial assistance from that body when in balance of payments difficulties. The drawing right is the right to borrow needed foreign currency from the IMF. The amount available is fixed in relation to the member's own contribution to the IMF's central funds, its ►quota. 25% of the quota is available automatically on demand; a further 25% may be obtained without great difficulty. Succeeding portions, or ►tranches, may be obtained only subject to conditions, chiefly in regard to economic policy, of increasing rigour. In 1970 a drawing right denominated in a group of currencies and intended as a new form of *international liquidity* (►liquidity) was created, known as ►special drawing rights (SDRs).

drip A ►dividend re-investment plan where a company uses a planned ►dividend to buy its own shares at the ►stock exchange instead of issuing new shares by a ►bonus issue. Shareholders pay dealing charges and ►stamp duty.

drittmarkt (Den.) The second-tier ►unlisted securities market at the Copenhagen ►stock exchange. Also called Bors III because the stock exchange formerly had two upper segments, Bors I and Bors II, which differentiated listed companies according to their ►market capitalization.

droit de timbre (Fr.) ►Stamp duty.

drop-lock A ►bond that earns a floating return but automatically switches to a fixed return if ►rates of interest fall below a predetermined level.

DTB ►Deutsche Terminborse.

DTC ►Depository Trust Company.

dual capacity The situation where a ►market maker can buy or sell shares to and from members of the public or other members of the ►stock exchange without the need for a ►broker. The market maker acts as both ►jobber and broker.

dual currency bond A Japanese ►bond denominated in yen but paying interest in higher-yielding currencies such as the US $ and Australian $.

due diligence The analysis and appraisal of a business in preparation for a ►flotation or ►venture capital investment. Investors have a right to expect that these investigations are carried out thoroughly.

durée (Fr.) ►Maturity.

DVP ►delivery versus payment.

dynamic risk Of insurance, a ►risk arising out of change caused by people, e.g. changes in economic policy, in technology, in competition.

E

EAGGF ➤European Agricultural Guidance and Guarantee Fund.

early stage investments Investment by ➤venture capital institutions in the provision of *seed capital* (funds to finance research and development before a business is operating) and start-up finance for new companies.

earmarking The assignment of moneys in the ➤central fund of ➤Lloyd's to cover a deficiency arising where a member's assets (➤funds at Lloyd's and ➤premium trust fund) do not equal their liabilities.

earn-out Tying the purchase price paid for a company to future earnings. If the company performs less well than expected, for example, a final instalment on the purchase price may not fall due. A *ratchet* is a similar arrangement sometimes used by ➤venture capital institutions to motivate the management of the companies they finance by giving them a large share in ➤equity if performance is better than expected.

earned income Income from wages, salaries and certain ➤pensions and social security benefits that are treated as earned income for tax purposes. In the UK in the past, and in many countries still, earned income was taxed on a more favourable basis than *unearned income*, which includes dividends, interest and other investment income.

earnings per share (EPS) The total ➤profits of a company after ➤taxation and ➤interest, divided by the number of ➤shares at issue. Earnings per share will usually be higher than the ➤dividend per share, because some earnings will be retained in the company and not distributed as dividends.

earnings yield ➤yield.

EASD ➤European Association of Securities Dealers.

East African Tea Trade Association A ➤commodity market set up in Nairobi in 1958, trading in black tea.

Eastern Europe ➤Capital markets, including ➤banking systems, ➤stock exchanges and ➤commodity markets, are developing rapidly in the Eastern European countries, which are in transition from centrally planned to market economies. The former Yugoslavia was the most advanced until civil war halted activity. The Budapest Stock Exchange opened in mid-1990, and the Warsaw Stock Exchange, for which the share index is the Wig Index, opened in April 1991. There are commodity markets in Sofia, Budapest, Moscow and elsewhere. ➤➤Moscow Central Stock Exchange.

EBRD ➤European Bank for Reconstruction and Development.

EBS ➤Electronic Broking Service.

EC ➤European Union.

écart (Fr.) ➤Spread.

ECGD (UK) ➤Export Credit Guarantee Department.

échéance (Fr.) ➤Maturity.

Echo An international system set up in 1995, for the netting of multilateral foreign exchange trades between banks. Echo acts as a clearing house settling with a single payment at the end of each day. Designed to minimize ➤Herstatt risk.

ECHO ➤Exchange Clearing House.

Economic and Monetary Union (EMU) ➤European Union (EU); Maastricht Treaty.

economic structural adjustment programme ➤International Bank for Reconstruction and Development.

economic value added (EVA) A method for evaluating companies by comparing the rate of ➤return on investment with the ➤weighted average cost of capital. Companies which are seen to be earning less than their cost of capital are said to be destroying value, while those that have a rate of return above their cost of capital are creating value. In these calculations ➤assets in the ➤balance sheet are increased by writing back expenditure on research and development and adjusted in other ways, while profit is defined as ➤operating profits after tax (though there are variations in these definitions). An alternative approach is *market value added* (*MVA*). In this approach ➤market capitalization is compared with economic value measured by the capital it is using as defined above.

Ecopetrol The state-owned oil company of Colombia.

ECP ➤Euro-commercial paper; Euro-Commercial Paper Programme.

ECSC European Coal and Steel Community. ➤European Union.

ECU European Currency Unit. ➤European Monetary System.

ECU deposit A ➤deposit made in European Currency Units (➤European Monetary System).

EDF ➤European Development Fund.

Edgar (US) Electronic ►disclosure system for the receipt, storage, retrieval and dissemination of public documents filed with the ►Securities and Exchange Commission.

Edge Act 1919 (US) Legislation that first permitted US banks to set up subsidiaries to engage in banking activities overseas.

EDI ►electronic data interchange.

EDSP (UK) ►exchange delivery settlement price.

EEC European Economic Community. ►European Union.

EEIG ►European Economic Interest Grouping.

EFAS European Financial Analysts' Society.

Effekten (Ger.) ►securities.

effets privés (Fr.) Generic term for ►private-sector money-market instruments.

efficient markets hypothesis (EMH) The idea that asset prices, for example ►share prices, reflect the present value of the expected future returns from the ►asset. It assumes that all available information is incorporated in prices and that traders will bid prices up or down until assets are correctly priced. If it were true, EMH would mean that no investor could 'beat the market' for long. In its crude form EMH is not true, since it has been shown that, historically, share prices have fluctuated much more than ►dividends, while ►crashes have seen stock market prices fall by as much as one-third in a week, as in 1987, without new information becoming available that could conceivably affect fundamental values to this extent.

EFL ►external financial limit.

EFMA European Financial Marketing Association.

EFP ►exchange for physical.

EFT ►electronic funds transfer.

EFTA ►European Free Trade Association.

EFTPOS ►electronic funds transfer at point of sale.

EIB ►European Investment Bank.

eigyo tokkin **funds** (Jap.) Funds illegally placed by companies with ►securities houses against a guaranteed rate of return (guarantees of rates are illegal).

Einheitskurs (Ger.) A method of trading on the ►stock exchange, under which each ►security is traded at a single price only once each day.

elastic currency (US) The doctrine that a domestic ►currency should meet the needs of trade, through a stable relationship between the expansion of business activity and the expansion of ►credit. Also known as the *real bills doctrine*.

electronic banking The automated facility to call up bank account details, give instructions for payments and make use of other services by means of a computer, ►modem and telephone line or ►viewdata system. Used by businesses; retail customers appear to prefer ►telephone banking.

Electronic Broking Service (EBS) An automated ►broking system for ►currency dealing, developed by a consortium of major exchange trading banks in conjunction with Quotron, a specialist informatics company, and introduced in 1993. The EBS is in competition with two similar systems: Reuters 2000-2, launched in 1992; and Minex, created by a consortium of Japanese banks, together with the Japanese telecom company KDD and Dow-Jones Telerate, and introduced in 1993.

electronic data interchange (EDI) Means by which organizations may send and receive data, e.g. on orders, insurance contracts for processing and invoices and payments.

electronic funds transfer at point of sale (EFTPOS) (UK) A system that allows the automatic transfer of money from a buyer to a seller of goods or services at the time of sale. In the UK, EFTPOS is now widespread, e.g. using Connect and Switch cards.

electronic funds transfer (EFT) system A system for the automatic transfer of funds from one account to another by electronic means, e.g. ►electronic funds transfer at point of sale.

electronic mail or e-mail A system for sending messages automatically between computers via mailbox numbers using telephone or private circuits. Also refers to the message itself.

Electronic Price Information Computer (EPIC) (UK) The original ►London Stock Exchange system for recording and transmitting price via TOPIC (►Stock Exchange Automated Quotation System).

eligible bill 1. A ►bank bill issued by a bank on the ►eligible list, which may be ►rediscounted at the Bank of England. **2.** Eligible paper (US).

eligible liabilities (ELs) (UK) A measure of the ►deposits of the UK commercial banks used in the exercise of ►monetary policy by the ►Bank of England. With a view to limiting the degree to which banks could lend out their deposit holdings, the Bank of England required them to place a certain proportion of their eligible liabilities with it, as ►special deposits and ►supplementary special deposits. Eligible liabilities were defined as: sterling deposits, up to two years' ►maturity, of UK residents; all net sterling deposits of banks; all net holdings of ►certificates of deposit; and net liabilities in non-sterling ➤currencies. ➤➤interest-bearing eligible liabilities; liquidity ratio.

eligible list (UK) A list of banks entitled to discount acceptances at the ➤Bank of England.

eligible paper (US) US ➤bankers' acceptances that may be ➤rediscounted at the ➤Federal Reserve. They broadly comprise acceptances in respect of foreign trade or documented home deliveries of less than six months' ➤maturity, and in respect of staple goods in receipted storage.

eligible reserves (US) Forms (➤vault cash plus balances at ➤Federal Reserve banks) in which banks' ➤required reserves must be held.

EMA ➤European Monetary Agreement.

EMCOF European Monetary Co-operation Fund. ➤European Monetary System.

emerging markets ➤Security markets in ➤newly industrialized countries, in ➤Eastern Europe and in other countries with ➤capital markets at an early stage of development.

Emerging Markets Traders Association (EMTA) An organization set up in the late 1980s in New York to set standards for trading in commercial bank loans to emerging countries; from 1990 also to trade in ➤Brady bonds and ➤Eurobonds issued by such countries.

EMH ➤efficient markets hypothesis.

émission (Fr.) ➤Issue.

Employee Retirement Income Security Act 1974 (ERISA) (US) Law regulating private ➤pensions plans. Provisions included the setting up of the Pension Benefit Guarantee Corporation (PBGC), which protects beneficiaries in corporate pension schemes from loss in the event of insolvency or premature termination of a pension scheme.

employees' buy-out The purchase of all the ➤shares of a ➤company by its employees. An example of such a buy-out was that of the National Freight Corporation on ➤privatization. ➤➤management buy-out.

employees stock ownership plan (ESOP) A scheme to allow employees to acquire shares in the company in which they work. In the UK, ESOPs are employee share ownership plans that differ from Inland Revenue-approved profit-sharing schemes in that employees are liable to income tax when the shares are transferred at less than their market value. However, the costs of ESOPs borne by employers are deductible for ➤corporation tax purposes.

emprunt (Fr.) ➤Loan, loan ➤stock.

EMS ➤European Monetary System.

EMTA ➤Emerging Market Traders Association.

EMU ➤Economic and Monetary Union.

endaka (Jap.) Literally 'high yen'. A term describing the yen's appreciation (➤appreciate) after the ➤Plaza Agreement of September 1985.

endowment life assurance ➤life assurance.

Enterprise Investment Scheme (EIS) (UK) A scheme providing 20% up-front ➤income tax relief on investments by private individuals in the shares of qualifying unquoted companies (➤unlisted company) and on ➤capital gains and tax relief on losses. Capital gains are tax free. Investors are allowed to become paid directors. This replaced the ➤Business Expansion Scheme in January 1994.

E&O, E&OE ➤errors and omissions.

EOE ➤European Options Exchange.

EPC ➤European political co-operation.

EPP ➤Estate protection policy.

EPS ➤earnings per share.

equalization of pensions Equal entitlement to ➤pensions for men and women. Three cases submitted to the European Court of Justice in 1990 – the Barber case, the Ten Oever case and the Coloroll case – questioned the unequal pension rights of men and women. These cases were based on Article 119 of the ➤Treaty of Rome, which requires equal pay for equal work. By 1993 the Court had ruled that pensions deriving from contributions made on or after 17 May 1990 should be equalized. However, problems remain, arising from the actuarial implications of women's greater longevity and from the fact that state pensions still have to be equalized.

Equitas ➤Lloyd's.

equity The residual value of a company's ➤assets after all ➤liabilities (other than those to holders of ➤ordinary shares) have been allowed for. The equity of a company is the property of the ordinary shareholders, hence these shares are popularly called equities (UK). In a ➤mortgage or ➤hire-purchase contract, equity is the amount left for the borrower if the asset concerned is sold and the lender repaid.

equity gearing (UK) The ratio of borrowings to ➤equity or risk capital. ➤➤capital gearing; gearing.

equity kicker ➤mezzanine.

ERDF ➤European Regional Development Fund.

ERISA ➤Employee Retirement Income Security Act.

ERM ➤Exchange Rate Mechanism.

Eröffnungskurs (Ger.) ➤Opening price.

errors and omissions (E&O) 1. 'Errors and omissions excepted' ('E&OE') used to be included on invoices in an attempt to protect the issuer against clerical mistakes. It had no legal validity, and the term *errors and omissions* (E&O) is now little used except in the sense of: **2**. A cause of faulty accounts or records, against which insurance is frequently taken out. In ➤Lloyd's, the E&O insurance of managing and members' agents, normally placed within the market, stands as the first source of finance for agents requiring to meet compensation claims from ➤action groups.

ESAP Economic structural adjustment programme. ➤International Bank for Reconstruction and Development.

escompte (Fr.) ➤Discount.

escrow, escrow account An escrow is a document of agreement held by a third party until one or both of the other two parties have fulfilled certain conditions. Thus funds on an escrow account will be released by a bank when agreed conditions are met.

ESOP ➤Employees Stock Ownership Plan.

estate duty ➤inheritance tax.

estate protection reinsurance Cover, in the event of death, for all outstanding underwriting ➤liabilities (➤➤underwrite) of a member of ➤Lloyd's.

estoppel The doctrine that forbids a person from denying a truth already admitted by them. In ➤insurance, the doctrine prohibits an insurer, having begun to deal with a claim known by them to be faulty, from refusing to continue.

étalon-or (Fr.) ➤Gold standard.

EU ➤European Union.

Euratom European Atomic Energy Community. ➤European Union.

euro The proposed European ➤currency to be used in European Monetary Union (➤Maastricht Treaty).

Euro-commercial paper (ECP) ➤Commercial paper (CP) issued in a Eurocurrency (➤Eurodollar). The Euro-commercial market can be said to have been established in 1985. There is no underwriting commitment by banks; the paper is normally issued direct or through dealers. The market is chiefly centred on London.

Some linkage both with the US domestic commercial paper market, often through ➤swing lines, and with other domestic CP markets has recently come about. Daily publication of interest rates by the Bank of England began in August 1987. In 1992 total issues outstanding were reckoned at $8.2bn, after some years of decline, attributed to overcapacity. In 1993 the French authorities decreed that *sociétés d'investissement à capital variable* (➤unit trusts) should not hold more than 10% of their assets in Euro-paper or other unregulated investments. ➤➤BONUS (borrower's option for notes and underwritten standby); non-underwritten; underwritten.

Euro-commercial paper programme (ECP) ➤non-underwritten.

Eurobond A ➤bond issued in a ➤currency other than that of the country or market in which it is issued; i.e. a bond composed of claims in a particular currency but held outside the country of that currency. Eurobonds are identical in principle to ➤Eurodollars or ➤Eurocurrencies and arose out of the Eurodollar and Eurocurrency market. Most Eurobonds are ➤bearer securities, and interest is paid without deduction of tax. Eurobonds are normally sold by international ➤syndicates of banks, are ➤medium term and ➤long term in nature, are usually issued by governments, international organizations and large public bodies and are bought for the main part by wealthy individuals and families. Eurobonds can be ➤convertible or ➤straight. There are two main settlement clearing houses, ➤Euroclear and ➤Central de Livraison de Valeurs Mobilières (CEDEL). ➤➤Euroequity; Eurosterling bond.

Euroclear One of the two settlement systems for ➤Eurobonds, formed by a number of banks and securities houses under the leadership of Morgan Guaranty and set up in Brussels in 1968. It provides clearing house, accounting and dividend collection services, as well as providing working capital to dealers through Morgan Guaranty. ➤➤Centrale de Livraison de Valeurs Mobilières (CEDEL).

Eurocredit A loan, generally at ➤medium term, made by a bank in a ➤Eurocurrency. The loan is always large, not less than $500,000, and is usually raised by ➤syndication. ➤➤Euronote facility.

Eurocurrency A ➤currency used in the ➤Euromarket. ➤Eurodollar.

Eurocurrency market ➤Eurodollar.

Eurodeposit ➤Eurodollar.

Eurodollar A deposit in dollars in a US bank held outside the USA, e.g. a credit account with a bank in New York held by a French bank in Paris. The characteristic of Eurodollars is that they are on-lent by the holders to other banks or individuals outside the USA. The practice was begun in the 1950s by Eastern European bank branches in the main Western European banking centres, specifically, it is said, by the Moscow Narodny Bank in London, which held unspent balances in the USA that they feared might be frozen. Accordingly they lent them to other Western

European parties. Other banks then followed suit, the practice being nourished by the continuance over decades of US ➤balance of payments deficits, which produced a flood of credit balances surplus to the requirements of their holders outside the USA.

The advantage to the holders of Eurodollar accounts, which at first had been that of the avoidance of exchange transactions and of a possible profit on interest rate ➤arbitrage, quickly became that of participation in a large international money market, into and out of which parties could move easily. The market was further advantaged by the fact that interest on the US deposit was free of withholding tax and also of ➤Regulation Q, and so was further enhanced by the movement into it of US companies and bank branches based abroad, anxious to share in these advantages. It was also enhanced by the US banks' willingness to create Eurodeposits, given their freedom in the setting of interest rates.

The Eurodollar market has been thought to bring about the continuous creation of ➤credit in accordance with the usual bank ➤multiplier, in that it produces a succession of bank deposits from which new advances can be generated. In the light of this, the absence of any control by national banking authorities causes some concern. There has, however, been much argument as to whether the total volume of credit has been enlarged, given that the inherent movement has been the onlending of the same deposit between banks outside the US banking system. The use of the deposit by non-banks for payment, thus leading to the creation of further deposits in the US banking system, does not in principle cause a multiplication of credits greater than would have occurred by the use of the same deposit by domestic US transactors. In short, it has been argued that the Eurodollar market has increased the ➤velocity, but not the ➤volume, of the US ➤money supply.

With the advent of ➤certificates of deposit the market was further enlarged. A further development was the emergence of the ➤Eurobond market, for longer-term loans. The Eurodollar technique was quickly adopted for other currencies, the market in these for some time being erroneously referred to as the Eurodollar market. These are now known under their respective names, the whole complex being referred to as the Eurocurrency market.

Termed *Euro*dollar because the first participants were in Europe, the market quickly cased to bear out that title, with dealing taking place in Japan and in most other parts of the world.

Euroequity An international equity issue made on ➤stock exchanges outside the country in which the company whose ➤stock is being issued is based and denominated in a foreign currency. Since ➤exchange rates fluctuate, the issue of equity in multiple currencies by established companies may create problems.

Euromarket The generic term for all transactions in ➤Eurocurrencies, namely bank lending in Eurocurrencies, ➤Eurobonds, ➤Euronotes, ➤Euro-commercial paper, ➤Euroequity.

EURO.NM A loose alliance of the ➤Brussels Stock Exchange, Le ➤Société du

Nouveau Marché, the ►German stock exchange and the ►Amsterdam Stock Exchange announced in 1996. The network aims to offer common regulation, a unified trading and information dissemination system, common marketing initiatives and representation of members interests while retaining the local character of the exchanges. The network is specifically aimed at ►equity trading in growth companies. ►Unlisted Securities Markets.

Euronote A ►note used in a ►Euronote facility issued in ►bearer form and ►negotiable. Euronotes are invariably ►short term. They have been issued chiefly in US dollars, but other currencies have been used, including ECUs (European Currency Units; ►European Union) and Singapore dollars. ►Non-banks have been increasing purchasers since 1983, with the result that the ►spread has come to be related more to the *London interbank bid rate* (LIBID) than to the ►London interbank offered rate (LIBOR).

Euronote facility A form of ►note issuance facility (NIF) for the issue of ►Euronotes managed by a group of banks, or ►syndicate, and guaranteed by the latter. A ►front-end fee and a ►commitment fee are charged by the syndicate to the issuer. Euronote facilities were first introduced in 1981. Where banks provide the underlying credit by buying the notes, this is done by inviting a tender panel of banks to subscribe. Otherwise the notes are sold by *placement* organized by a sole placing agent. In either event, the syndicate ►underwrites the issue by undertaking to buy any notes not taken up, or supplies ►back-up credit. The term *Euronote facility* is sometimes used, more loosely, to refer to ►Euro-commercial paper issues.

European Agricultural Guidance and Guarantee Fund (EAGGF) A fund, set up under the common agricultural policy of the ►European Union, whose function is to purchase all agricultural products, when offered to it, at a fixed minimum price and, in theory, to sell produce stocks when prices are high; also to finance the modernization of, and reduction of costs in, Union agriculture. The EAGGF has been heavily criticized for its substantial expenditure, which has amounted over most of the existence of the Union (and previously the European Community) to between 65% and 80% of the total budget.

European Association of Securities Dealers (EASD) Founded in 1995 to further the development of a pan-European ►stock exchange. (►European Association of Securities Dealers Automated Quotations (EASDAQ).

European Association of Securities Dealers Automated Quotation System (EASDAQ) A pan-European ►stock exchange for growth companies, especially technology companies, and modelled upon the ►National Association of Securities Dealers Automated Quotation System (NASDAQ) in the US. EASDAQ began operations in Brussels towards the end of 1996. Price quotations are disseminated on the TRAX system operated by the ►International Securities Market Association

(ISMA). The trading system computer is in London and the clearance and settlement system in Switzerland (*Intersettle*, which is owned by Swiss banks).

European Atomic Energy Community (Euratom) ►European Union (EU).

European Bank for Reconstruction and Development (EBRD) An intergovernmental financial institution founded in 1990 to finance industrial and economic development in the countries of Eastern Europe by means of loans, guarantees, equity investment and underwriting. The EBRD has a membership of 43 countries, comprising all member states of the ►European Union and of the ►Organization for Economic Co-operation and Development (OECD), virtually all Eastern European countries – including the separate states of the former Soviet Union – Mexico, a number of African and Middle Eastern countries, the European Commission and the European Investment Bank. The EBRD had initial capital of ECUs 10bn ($12.2bn), of which 51% was subscribed by the EC and its member countries, 10% by the USA and 8½% by Japan, with the remainder coming from other non-EC and non-OECD members and the countries of Eastern Europe itself. There was a board of 23 directors. Some disquiet was occasioned by the disclosure at the end of 1992 that the EBRD had spent some $300m on fitting out its headquarters, as against only $150m disbursed in financial aid; this led to the resignation of the bank's first president, Jacques Attali, and the institution of various reforms. M. Attali was succeeded by M. Jacque de Larosière, former managing director of the ►International Monetary Fund.

European Coal and Steel Community (ECSC) ►European Union (EU).

European Community (EC) ►European Union (EU).

European Currency Unit (ECU) ►European Monetary System (EMS).

European Development Fund (EDF) A fund set up by the European Community (►European Union) in 1976 for the provision of aid finance to developing countries associated with the then EC (now EU) through the Lomé Convention; to certain non-associated states; and to a number of developing countries in the Mediterranean Basin. The funds are dispensed under five-year programmes in the form of grants and loans on advantageous terms. Sixty-six countries benefit under the Lomé Convention, and a further 14 under the Mediterranean programme. The fund's capital is supplied by the member states and it is administered by the European Commission. Annual outlays are about £2bn.

European Economic Area ►European Free Trade Association (EFTA).

European Economic Community (EEC) ►European Union (EU).

European economic interest grouping (EEIG) A recognized form of grouping that allows companies incorporated in the ►European Union (EU) to establish joint ventures employing up to 500 people throughout the EC without ►capitalization and with the simplification of ►fiscal transparency.

European Free Trade Association (EFTA) A group of countries that have removed import duties (►tariffs) on imports from each other. EFTA was formed in 1959 by Austria, Denmark, Norway, Portugal, Sweden, Switzerland and the UK. Finland effectively joined in 1961 and Iceland in 1970. Denmark and the UK left in 1973 and Portugal in 1986 on joining the European Community (EC) (►European Union). After negotiations that began in 1984, EFTA and the EC reached agreement in 1992 for a European Economic Area that would include the member countries of both institutions.

European Investment Bank (EIB) An international bank formed in 1958 by the then European Community (►European Union) to provide loan finance for member countries and associated countries, for the purposes of regional development, projects of common interest to the EC and projects for modernization and conversion. The bank finances itself through its capital, contributed by member countries, and by loans at fine rates raised on the international ►capital market.

European Monetary Agreement (EMA) ►Organization for European Economic Co-operation (OEEC).

European Monetary Co-operation Fund (EMCOF) ►European Monetary System (EMS).

European Monetary System (EMS) Instituted by the then European Community (►European Union, EU) in 1979 with two main purposes: (i) to stabilize the currencies of member states; and (ii) to create a joint reserve fund and ultimately a common monetary system, including a common currency.

(i) An Exchange Rate Mechanism (ERM) was set up. A European monetary unit known as the European Currency Unit (ECU) was created as a composite of the member countries' currencies weighted in accordance with country shares in EC (now EU) output; so 1 ECU = DM0.719+ FFr1.310+ L140+ FL0.256+ FrB3.71+ FrLux0.14+ £stg0.0378+ £Ire0.00871+ DKr0.217+ Dr1.15. The ECU fluctuates as a whole in relation to non-EU currencies. Member countries maintain their national currencies in a strict relationship (a central parity) to the ECU, being allowed to depart from this parity only by a margin determined for each currency (a divergence indicator). The ERM was an integral part of the EMS, requiring close alignment of EC currencies. Under this mechanism, EC currencies were permitted to diverge from each other only by a fixed percentage, $\pm 2.25\%$ (Italy $\pm 6\%$). This was a resumption of an earlier version of the same mechanism, known as the Snake, which had operated fitfully in the 1970s. The UK entered the ERM only in 1990. In September 1992 severe turbulence in the foreign exchange market brought about the withdrawal of the UK and Italy from the mechanism, and forced general adjustments in the relative parities of the remaining members. In July/

August 1993 renewed turbulence led to the widening of the permitted divergence to ± 30%, and the future of the ERM remained uncertain. The ECU is used for the internal accounting of the European Union institutions. It has also been used in private syndicated loans, for bond issues and for money market deposits.

(ii) A European Monetary Co-operation Fund (EMCOF) has been established by crediting ECUs to member countries in exchange for their depositing 20% of their gold and foreign exchange ►reserves. The UK has participated in this arrangement. The fund serves as a clearing house for the ►central bank operations in maintaining national currency alignment in accordance with the EMS. In due course the fund is intended to be replaced by a European Monetary Fund, which would act as a central bank for a fully integrated Union monetary and currency system, i.e. with a single currency after European Monetary Union (►Maastricht Treaty). ►►intervention mechanism; medium term financial assistance (MTFA); short-term monetary support (STMS).

European Monetary Union (EMU) ►Maastricht Treaty.

European Options Exchange (EOE) A market for *traded options* (►option) founded in Amsterdam in 1978. The market operates within the Amsterdam Stock Exchange. Trade is in options in gold and silver and in certain ►currencies and ►securities. The exchange was merged with the ►Amsterdam Stock Exchange in January 1997 to form the ►Amsterdam Exchanges.

European Payments Union (EPU) ►Organization for European Economic Co-operation (OEEC).

European Political Co-operation ►European Union (EU).

European Recovery Programme ►Organization for European Economic Co-operation (OEEC).

European Regional Development Fund (ERDF) Established in 1975 by the European Community (►European Union), the ERDF makes grants, normally to the governments of member states, for the purpose of improving the infrastructure in regions showing particular need, e.g. the assisted areas of the UK and the Mezzogiorno of Italy. The grants can be made only in relation to investment programmes presented by member-state governments and are intended to supplement, rather than replace, money spent by the latter. Grants are usually made up to a quota established for each Union member.

European style An ►option which can only be ►exercised on expiry date.

European Union (EU) The European Union, until 1992 known as the European Community (EC), comprises three component communities: the European Coal and Steel Community (ECSC), founded in 1952 under the Treaty of Paris of 1951; the European Economic Community (EEC), founded in 1958 under the Treaty of Rome of 1957; and the European Atomic Energy Community (Euratom), also founded in 1958 under a separate Treaty of Rome of 1957. At the outset each Community had a separate Council, in which member-country ministers made policy decisions; a separate central administration, the High Authority in the case of the ESCS and the Commission in the case of the EEC and Euratom; separate provision for the industries for which they were responsible (coal and steel in the case of ECSC, atomic energy in that of Euratom and all others in that of the EEC); a separate court of justice; and separate financial resources, levied on member states.

Under the Treaty of Brussels of 1965 the institutions were amalgamated into a single Council, Commission, Court of Justice and Parliament, and common revenues were set up. However, policy and administrative decisions continued to be taken in line with the provisions of the individual treaties. In 1978 specific member-state contributions for the financing of the then Community were replaced by a system of own resources under which the Community claimed an automatic proportion of the import duty and value added tax (VAT) revenues arising in the member states.

The original membership of the European Community comprised Belgium, France, West Germany, Italy, Luxembourg and the Netherlands. In 1973 these were joined by the UK, Ireland and Denmark, in 1981 by Greece and in 1986 by Spain and Portugal.

The purposes of the Community were at the outset to achieve far-reaching integration of the member countries' economies and, less well defined, a single Western European economy and a cohesive, if not federal, political framework. These purposes were to be attained primarily through the principle of supranationality, i.e. through the paramountcy of Community legislation over national laws, and by majority rather than unanimous voting on policy decisions. These principles were to be translated into common policies for the free movement of goods, services, labour and capital throughout the Community.

Total elimination of national tariffs was achieved by 1961, as was the establishment of a common external commercial policy and a common agricultural policy. The planned introduction of majority voting met with French opposition in 1965 and was indefinitely postponed. Other policy objectives, such as common transport and energy policies, proved difficult to attain. Some progress in financial policies was achieved through the establishment in 1978 of the ➤European Monetary System (EMS) and the extensive alignment of Community exchange rates. In 1979 direct elections to the European Parliament were instituted, and further powers accrued to this body. By the 1980s a measure of consultation and common action on foreign affairs had been attained.

A major advance in EC integration was denoted by the Single European Act (SEA), signed in February 1986, and ratified in the following year. The SEA was in itself a document amending and expanding the three original treaties of the European Community so as to bring about its desired objectives. In signing, the member states stated their intention to be 'to transform relations . . . among their

States into a European Union'. Two basic changes in procedure were: (i) abolition of the right of veto, i.e. the substitution of majority voting for unanimous voting on proposed legislation, on all subjects except taxation, free movement of people and the 'rights and interests of employed persons' (essentially wages); and (ii) greater involvement of the European Parliament in the legislative process.

A major element of the Single Act was a commitment to complete the unification of the internal market: 'an area without internal frontiers in which the free movement of goods, persons, services and capital is ensured'. To this end, a programme of some 300 measures, to be incorporated in Community/Union law by 31 December 1992, was agreed. By the due date 95% of the programme had indeed been adopted, although it was estimated that only half of this had been 'transposed' – enacted into national law – by the member states. A number of articles built on the EMS to foreshadow an Economic and Monetary Union (EMU), and on this basis a project for a European central bank and an eventual common currency was elaborated. Some further articles were used as the basis for a 'social charter' enunciating the rights of workers, signed in 1989 by all member states except the UK. Other articles called for greater alignment of economic conditions in the regions of the Community; for various efforts in the fields of research and development and the environment; and for the further development of European Political Co-operation (EPC), particularly in foreign policy. The European Community was renamed the European Union following agreement of the ►Maastricht Treaty in 1992.

In July 1997 a document entitled 'Agenda 2000', presented by the European Commission to the European Parliament, proposed that negotiations for entry to EU membership should be initiated in 1998 with the East European countries Estonia, Poland, the Czech Republic, Slovenia and Hungary, with a view to likely entry in 2002.

Negotiations, according to Agenda 2000, might be possible in due course for the entry, subject to further economic and political progress, of five further states: Latvia, Lithuania, Slovakia, Romania and Bulgaria.

Enlargement of the union as proposed would call for constitutional reform, including in particular a streamlining of the membership of the commission and a rebalancing of member countries' voting rights.

Eurosterling bond A ►Eurobond denominated in British pounds.

EVA ►economic value added.

ex-coupon ►ex-dividend.

ex-dividend (xd) Without ►dividend. The purchaser of a ►security quoted ex-dividend does not have the right to the next dividend when due; this belongs to the seller. The prefix *ex-*, meaning 'excluding', is also used in a similar sense in several other ways, e.g. *ex-coupon* excludes the next interest payment on a fixed-interest ►security; *ex-rights* means that there is no entitlement to a ►rights issue; *ex-warrant* excludes rights to a forthcoming warrant issue; *ex-all* (US) excludes all impending benefits (➤bonus issue).

ex gratia Action taken, or payment made, in order to reach a settlement while denying formal liability.

ex-parte The action by one party to a matter where other parties are absent.

ex-rights ➤ex-dividend.

exceptional items ➤below the line.

excess 1. Of ➤shares, the quantity remaining unsold and available for other buyers after a ➤rights issue. 2. Of bank reserves (US), a level of cash higher than that required by law or conversion. As this impeded the ➤Federal Reserve's power to influence the bank's operations, authority to regulate cash levels was given to the Federal Reserve. 3. Of insurance, the amount of the ➤risk to be borne by the ➤policy-holder or, in the case of ➤reinsurance treaties, by the *ceding insurer* (➤cedant). ➤➤excess of loss treaty.

excess of loss ➤excess.

excess of loss reinsurance Excess of loss cover as for normal insurance, but with an upper limit on the cover. ➤excess.

excess of loss treaty A ➤non-proportional reinsurance treaty under which a reinsurer refunds to the insurer the amount of all claims paid by the latter over and above a predetermined limit.

excess reserves (US) Reserves held by banks and other financial institutions over and above ➤required reserves.

exchange 1. A market, e.g. a ➤commodity exchange or ➤commodity market. 2. Foreign currencies or ➤foreign exchange. 3. Any form of trade.

Exchange Clearing House (ECHO) A ➤clearing house for ➤foreign exchange ➤derivatives contracts, established by Barclays Bank, Commerzbank, Rabobank and Banque Nationale de Paris.

exchange control A method by which governments seek to control the ➤exchange rate of their national ➤currency and to preserve the national ➤reserves, consisting in the imposition of limitations or prohibitions on the movement of currency across national frontiers. Exchange control normally operates on payments to foreigners, since these place an immediate demand on foreign-currency holdings; receipts of foreign currency and of domestic currency originating from abroad are also frequently controlled. Exchange control in the main operated on the capital account of the ➤balance of payments, too great a restriction on the current account being likely to endanger the country's essential trade. Restrictions on the capital account may take the form of an outright ban on the use of foreign currency for portfolio investment, and restrictions on the type and conditions of direct investment that may be tolerated. Foreign currency for private travel is nearly always strictly constrained.

All industrialized countries have, over time, enforced exchange control, some forms still being maintained, e.g. by France and Italy. The UK operated comprehensive exchange control from the Second World War until 1979, when it was abolished. In the USA the ➤interest equalization tax, and in Germany the ➤*Bardepot*, had exchange control purposes. Many developing countries now maintain exchange control. The ➤International Monetary Fund, the ➤Organization for Economic Co-operation and Development and the ➤European Union have all striven for its elimination.

exchange delivery settlement price (UK) The price for delivery or ➤cash settlement of the instrument underlying a ➤derivative traded in the ➤London International Financial Futures Exchange (LIFFE).

exchange for physical A ➤swap of a ➤futures position in a currency for one in the ➤spot market, undertaken when delivery of a currency in a futures contract is desired before the expiry of that contract.

exchange rate The rate at which one ➤currency may be exchanged against another, i.e. the number of units of the currency deemed to be equal to one unit of another; e.g. 1.60 units of US$ have been at various times deemed equal to £1 sterling. Terms with a similar meaning are ➤parity and ➤par value. Exchange rates may be set by supply and demand for the currency (➤floating rate) or may be fixed, i.e. tied or linked to gold (➤gold standard) or to other currencies. ➤➤crawling peg.

Exchange Rate Mechanism (ERM) ➤European Union (EU); Maastricht Treaty.

Exchequer (UK) Historically, the financial accounts of the government. More exactly at present, the account kept at the ➤Bank of England, through which all government receipts and payments pass.

excise duty Taxes levied upon goods (e.g. alcoholic drinks and tobacco) produced for home consumption as distinct from customs duties or tariffs.

execution 1. Effecting a trade, as when a ➤broker buys or sells ➤securities in the execution of an ➤order. **2.** A legal term meaning that a ➤contract has been signed, witnessed if necessary and delivered to the respective parties.

execution only The provision of ➤security dealing services without advice, research or other services.

executive share options ➤profit-sharing scheme.

exercice (Fr.) ➤Financial year.

exercise 1. A ➤financial year. **2.** To implement a ➤contract. **3.** To put an ➤option into effect, i.e. to buy or sell the ➤security that is the subject of the option.

exercise date The date on which an ➤option can be ➤exercised; usually after three, six or nine months.

exercise notice A formal intimation that an ➤option will be ➤exercised.

exercise price The price at which the ➤security, the subject of an ➤option, is agreed to be bought or sold. Also known as the ➤striking price or ➤strike price.

Eximbank (US, Jap.) ➤Export–Import Bank.

exit The realization of an ➤investment, usually in the context of ➤venture capital, where an ➤equity investment in an ➤unlisted company may be realized by a trade sale (sold to a larger company or another venture capital company), by a ➤management buy-out or by ➤flotation.

Export Credit Guarantee Department (ECGD) (UK) Established in 1919, a government department for the provision of insurance cover against risks of default on export credit, and of cover against the risk of expropriation of assets invested abroad. Since the ECGD also covers against official payment and licensing restrictions for the foreign purchase of UK goods and services, it may be said to be the only significant insurer of long-term ➤sovereign risk. The ECGD's short-term credit insurance operations were privatized (➤privatization) in 1991.

Export–Import Bank (Eximbank) (US) Founded in 1934 by the US government, Eximbank provides loans direct to foreign importers of US goods and services, and guarantees and ➤refinances export credit granted by US banks. Through the associated ➤Foreign Credit Insurance Association, it offers insurance of foreign credits. Operating independently as a Washington, DC, registered bank, Eximbank's task is to operate at a profit. Lending limits are, however, fixed by Congress, and the five members of its board are appointed by the President and confirmed by the Senate.

Export–Import Bank of Japan (Jap.) An institution for the financing of export credit, established in 1950, based on capital supplied by the government, by borrowings from the Trust Fund Bureau and by foreign exchange borrowings from commercial banks.

extended credit (US) Borrowing from the ➤Federal Reserve by financial institutions in prolonged reserve shortage; the loans being charged at an interest rate normally above ➤discount rate. Since such institutions will not normally deal in the ➤Federal funds market, such loans are counted as ➤non-borrowed reserves.

external account ➤balance of payments.

external bond A ►bond issued in one country but denominated in the ►currency of another.

external financial limit (EFL) ►Cash limits imposed by the UK government on the borrowing of nationalized industries.

external member A member of ►Lloyd's providing capital to the market but not engaged in the actual performance of underwriting. As such members finance the operation, they are properly said also to be underwriting.

extraordinary items ►below the line.

F

FAC Food Aid Convention. ►International Grain Council (IGC).

face value ►par value.

facility A generic term denoting a bank loan in various forms, e.g. ►acceptance, ►Eurocredit, ►overdraft.

factor ►factoring.

factoring A business activity in which a company takes over responsibility for collecting the ►debts of another. Typically, the client debits all its sales to the factor and receives immediate payment from it less a charge of about 2% to 3% and ►interest for the period of ►trade credit given to the customer. There are a number of different types of factoring; the simplest is invoice discounting. In its most elaborate form the factor maintains the company's sales ledger and other accounting functions, and does not seek recourse to its client if unable to obtain payment from that client's customers (*non-recourse factoring*). The customer need not know that a factor is being used.

facultative reinsurance A ►reinsurance arrangement under which the reinsurer can opt to accept or not to accept any risk offered; contrast treaty reinsurance (►reinsurance treaty).

fair value The price of a ►derivative that is equivalent, after transaction costs, to that of the underlying instrument.

FAL ►funds at Lloyd's.

fallen angel (US) A ►bond, initially of US investment grade quality, subsequently declining below that standard, then sold at high ►yield.

Fälligheit (Ger.) ►Maturity.

Fannie Mae (US) ►Federal Home Loan Bank Board.

FASB ►Financial Accounting Standards Board.

FCIA (US) ►Foreign Credit Insurance Association.

FCII Fellow of the ►Chartered Insurance Institute.

FDI ►foreign direct investment.

FDIC ➤deposit insurance.

FECDBA ➤Foreign Exchange and Currency Deposit Brokers' Association.

Fed (US) ➤Federal Reserve System.

Fed funds (US) ➤Deposits made by ➤commercial banks in their local ➤Federal Reserve bank. Fed funds include cash balances in excess of the reserve requirement, which may be loaned to other banks overnight to enable them to meet their reserve requirement. ➤➤Federal funds rate; Federal Reserve System.

Federal Deposit Insurance Corporation ➤deposit insurance.

Federal funds (US) ➤Fed funds.

Federal funds rate (US) Rate of interest charged on ➤Fed funds loaned by and to ➤commercial banks. Owing to the large scale of Federal funds borrowing, the rate is regarded by the ➤Federal Reserve System regulatory authorities as an important determinant of bank ➤liquidity.

Federal funds rate band (US) The target range within which the ➤Federal Open Market Committee (FOMC) expects the ➤Federal funds rate to vary as specified in the FOMC minutes.

Federal home loan bank (US) Member of a system of 12 US banks established by the Federal Home Loan Act 1932 for the purpose of extending loan credit to institutions engaged in housing credit, such as ➤savings and loan associations, building and loan associations, savings banks and insurance companies. The bank's advances are secured by mortgages or by US government bonds. ➤➤Federal Home Loan Bank Board.

Federal Home Loan Bank Act ➤Federal Home Loan Bank Board.

Federal Home Loan Bank Board (FHLBB) (US) Regulatory body for the ➤savings and loan associations (S&Ls) set up in the 1930s. The Federal Home Loan Bank System provides credit reserves for ➤mortgage lending institutions through 12 regional Federal Home Loan banks and was established by the Federal Home Loan Bank Act 1932. In the following year the Home Owners Loan Act established the FHLBB, which now ➤charters federal S&Ls. The Federal Home Loan Bank System also holds the ➤stock of the Federal Home Loan Mortgage Corporation (FHLMC) on behalf of the S&Ls. The FHLMC, established in 1970 and referred to as Freddie Mac, purchases home mortgages from S&Ls and other ➤thrifts and securities under guarantees for sale in the secondary market. An older and government-sponsored, though publicly ➤quoted, organization, the Federal National Mortgage Association (FNMA or Fannie Mae), performs a similar function, especially for mortgages guaranteed by the Federal Housing Administration. The FNMA is the largest source of housing finance in the USA. ➤➤collateralized mortgage obligation.

Federal Home Loan Bank System ➤Federal Home Loan Bank Board.

Federal Home Loan Mortgage Corporation ➤Federal Home Loan Bank Board.

Federal National Mortgage Association ➤Federal Home Loan Bank Board.

Federal Open Market Committee (FOMC) The monetary policy body of the ➤Federal Reserve System. Composed of seven members of the board of governors and the 12 presidents of the regional Reserve Banks, it meets each month in Washington, DC, to review the economic situation and to decide on the policy to follow in the succeeding month with regard to the Federal Reserve's ➤open market operations. The policy decision is communicated as a guideline to the Reserve Bank of New York, the member bank of the system that handles open market operations on its behalf. In deciding policy, one vote is allotted to each of the seven members of the board and to the president of the Reserve Bank of New York. The presidents of the remaining Reserve banks share four votes between them in rotation. The deliberations of the FOMC are published after an interval of about a month.

Federal Reserve bank (US) ➤Federal Reserve System.

Federal Reserve bond (US) ➤Federal Reserve System.

Federal Reserve float (US) The effect of ➤float on the US banking system as a whole, i.e. where the overall timing of credits to and claims from banks, arising out of the ➤Federal Reserve's cheque-clearing function, leaves the system either liquid or illiquid (➤liquidity).

Federal Reserve System (Fed) (US) The central banking system of the USA, established by the Federal Reserve Act 1913 and organized on a regional basis, given the large area involved and the multiplicity of small and medium-sized banks. The system is composed of 12 regional *Reserve banks*, 25 branches and 11 offices under the control of a board of governors located in Washington, DC (the Federal Reserve Board). The board of governors consists of seven governors appointed by Congress on the nomination of the President, each serving for 14 years, with one reappointment falling due every two years. The regional Reserve banks are controlled by boards of nine directors, of whom three are commercial bankers, three represent local labour and commerce, and three are appointed by the board of governors; the president and vice-president of each Reserve bank are drawn from the last three. The chairman of the board of governors is the head of the Federal Reserve System, appointed for a term of four years.

The regional Reserve banks supervise banking practice and management, act as ➤lenders of last resort, provide common services in cheque clearing, statistics and research, and apply monetary policy at the instance of the board of governors. Monetary control is exercised chiefly through open market operations and is determined by the board of governors' ➤Federal Open Market Committee, day-to-day transactions in pursuance of this being handled by the Reserve Bank of New York. The board of governors' constitutional independence is guaranteed by the long-term appointment of the governors and by the fact that the system generates a surplus (mostly paid as a dividend to the Treasury), relieving it of financial dependence on Congress. The chairman, members and staff of the board frequently explain Federal Reserve policy to congressional committees and maintain close contact with the US administration, but retain final responsibility for their policy.

Since the Monetary Control Act 1980, all US banks are members of the Federal Reserve System. The system was modified by the Banking Act 1935. ➤➤Fed funds; Federal funds rate; Federal Deposit Insurance Corporation.

Fédération Internationale des Bourses de Valeurs Private international organization formed in 1961 for the exchange of views and information on ➤stock markets.

Fédération National des Sociétés d'Assurance (FNSA) (Fr.) The French national association of insurance companies.

Fédération National des Syndicats d'agents généraux d'Assurance (FNSAGA) (Fr.) The French national association of independent general insurance sales agents.

Fedwire (US) An electronic system used by the ➤Federal Reserve for large interbank ➤clearing.

FEOGA ➤Fond Européen d'Orientation et de Garantie Agriculturale.

Festverzinslich (Ger.) ➤Fixed interest.

FETCL (Jap.) ➤Foreign Exchange and Trade Central Law.

FHLBB ➤Federal Home Loan Bank Board.

FHLMC Federal Home Loan Mortgage Corporation. ➤Federal Home Loan Bank Board.

FIBOR The Frankfurt interbank offered rate; the German equivalent of ➤London interbank offered rate (LIBOR).

FID ➤corporation tax.

FIDS ➤corporation tax.

fiduciary A person or legal body acting on behalf of others who have a beneficial interest in investments or other property. An *executor*.

FII Foreign ➤institutional investors.

FIL (Jap.) ➤Foreign Investment Law.

file server ►local area network.

filiale (Fr.) Subsidiary company.

FIMBRA Financial Intermediaries', Managers' and Brokers' Regulatory Association. ►Financial Services Act.

final dividend ►dividend.

final salary scheme An alternative term for an occupational pension scheme (►pensions).

finance The provision of money when and where required. Finance may be short term (usually up to one year), medium term (one to seven years) or long term. Finance may be provided in the form of loan finance, i.e. ►debt, or ►equity, or as a grant. Finance may be required for consumption or for ►investment. When provided for the latter, it becomes ►capital. ►►business finance; consumer credit; public finance.

finance bill, finance paper A ►bill of exchange relating to the ►receivables of a ►finance house.

finance house (UK) A financial institution engaged in the provision of ►hire purchase and other forms of instalment credit for customers and business, sometimes known as *industrial banks*. (US = *small loan company* for ►consumer credit, and *commercial credit company* for business credit.) Some suppliers, e.g. motor manufacturers, have their own finance houses, known in the USA as *captive finance companies*.

finance house base rate (UK) The rate of interest charged by UK ►finance houses to their borrowers. Calculated (1986) by averaging the three-weekly average of three-month ►London interbank offered rate (LIBOR) and rounding to the nearest one-half % above, it was first published in 1970 and since published monthly.

finance house deposit (UK) A deposit placed by a bank or other large lender with a ►finance house; a method of recruiting funds much used by finance houses in the face of their lack of a branch network through which retail funds (►retail deposit) could be collected.

Financial Accounting Standards Board (FASB) (US) The non-governmental body which sets the accounting rules for US companies. Although formal responsibility for rule-setting lies with the ►Securities and Exchange Commission (SEC), the latter leaves the task in the hands of the FASB, rarely intervening.

financial asset ►asset.

financial future A ►future in a financial ►asset, i.e. a contract for the purchase of a specific standard quantity of a financial asset at a specific price on a specific future date. Dealing is through markets or exchanges, namely the ►Chicago Board of Trade and the ►London International Financial Futures Exchange (LIFFE). It differs from a ►forward contract in that futures contracts are in standard amounts intended to be traded, whereas forward contracts are once-only transactions. ►Currency futures were the earliest financial futures and were traded on the US ►International Commercial Exchange in 1970. ►Interest rate futures were first traded on the ►Chicago Board of Trade in 1975. Since then a number of other forms of financial futures have been devised (LIFFE). The advantage of financial futures contracts to a commercial company in comparison with borrowing, or ►spot, as against ►forward transactions, is that no ►assets or ►liabilities are created and thus they do not enter into the company's ►balance sheet; nor are the ►spreads of the forward exchange market incurred.

financial institutions The group of major commercial and public organizations engaged in exchanging, lending, borrowing and investing money. The term is often used as an alternative for ►financial intermediaries.

financial instrument ►instrument.

financial intermediaries Institutions that hold money balances of, or borrow from, individuals and other institutions, in order to make loans or other ►investments. Hence they serve the purpose of channelling funds from lenders to borrowers. ►Banks, ►building societies, ►hire-purchase companies, ►insurance companies, ►savings banks and ►investment trusts are financial intermediaries; but it is usual to distinguish between bank and non-bank financial intermediaries because of the role of the former in determining the ►money supply. In the ►Financial Services Act the term has a narrower meaning (►intermediary).

Financial Intermediaries', Managers' and Brokers' Regulatory Association (FIMBRA) ►Financial Services Act.

financial mechanism An arrangement made by the European Community (►European Union) in 1976 under which the UK's net contribution to the then EC's budget was reduced; it was amended in 1980 to permit a further reduction.

financial ratios 1. Measures of creditworthiness such as the current ratio (►working capital), ►gearing, ►dividend cover, ►interest cover and the ratio of long-term ►debt to ►net tangible assets. 2. Calculations based on company accounts and other sources to indicate the profitability or other financial aspects of a business. ►price-earnings ratio; return on investment.

Financial Reporting Review Panel (UK) A body set up to ensure compliance with accounting standards set by the UK Accounting Standards Board.

financial reporting standards (FRS) ►accounting standards.

Financial Services Act (FSA) (UK) Legislation enacted in November 1986 but coming into force on 29 April 1988 ('A' day) to regulate the investment business in the UK. The Act followed a report on investor protection commissioned in 1981 from Professor Jim Gower and completed in 1984. The Gower Report recommended that the new regulatory system should cover ►life assurance, ►unit trusts and other forms of investment business in addition to ►stock exchange investments. The Act set up a Securities and Investment Board (SIB), run and paid for by investment professionals, but with statutory powers and reporting to the Department of Trade and Industry. Investment businesses must be registered with the SIB directly or with one of four *self-regulating organizations* (SROs). The original SROs were: the Financial Intermediaries', Managers' and Brokers' Regulatory Association (FIMBRA), which covers independent intermediaries such as ►insurance brokers; the Securities Association (TSA), for ►securities dealing such as by market makers; the Association of Futures Brokers and Dealers (AFBD), for dealing in ►futures and ►options (these last two bodies were merged to form the Securities and Futures Authority Ltd (SFA) in 1991); the Investment Managers' Regulatory Organization (IMRO), for investment management such as pension funds; and the Life Assurance and Unit Trust Regulatory Organization (LAUTRO). FIMBRA and LAUTRO were replaced by the Personal Investment Authority in 1994.

The SIB maintains a central register of firms authorized by itself or the SROs. Certain investment markets also have to be approved by the SIB or via the appropriate SRO; these markets are *recognized investment exchanges* (RIEs), e.g. the *International Stock Exchange* (►London Stock Exchange) and the ►Baltic Exchange (►►designated investment exchange). Lawyers and accountants for whom the provision of investment advice is only a minor part of their business are self-regulated by their own professional bodies. *Recognized professional bodies* (RPBs) have been approved by the SIB, including the Institute of Chartered Accountants of England and Wales.

In mid-1997 the UK government announced that the three self-regulatory organizations, the Securities and Futures Authority, the Investment Managers Regulatory Organization and the Personal Investment Authority, would be absorbed into the Securities and Investment Board, which itself was re-named the Financial Services Authority.

At the same time it was announced that the Authority would take over the regulation of the ►insurance industry (until then regulated by the Department of Trade and Industry) the ►building societies industry (until then regulated by the Building Societies Commission) and also ►friendly societies, ►credit unions and industrial and provident societies.

It was also announced that the Authority would take over, from the ►Bank of England, the supervision of the banking system.

All the above changes would not be fully in place for some two years.

Financial Services Authority ►Financial Services Act.

Financial Statement and Budget Report (FSBR) (UK) A document published by the Chancellor of the Exchequer on Budget day, and supplementing the Chancellor's statement that day to the House of Commons, summarizing the objectives and main provisions of the Budget, the situation of public-sector finances and the general state of the economy. Familiarly known as the Red Book.

Financial Times share indices *FTO (Financial Times (Industrial) Ordinary)* or *FT 30 Share Index*, an unweighted (►weighted average) *geometric* ►average of 30 leading ►blue chips quoted on the ►London Stock Exchange, was introduced in 1935 and calculated hourly. The FT 30 has been superseded by the *FT/SE 100* [*'Footsie 100'*] *Index*, a ►market capitalization weighted average calculated minute by minute (real time). The ►base period for the FT 100 is 3 January 1984 = 1,000, and its constituents are the 100 largest quoted industrial and commercial companies by capitalization, reviewed quarterly (►investment trusts are excluded). The *FT/SE Mid-250 Index*, also calculated minute by minute, covers the next 250 companies, ranked by market value; and the *FT/SE/Actuaries 350 Index* includes all the constituents of the 100 and 250 indices. The 350 Index covers about 92% of total market value and the 100 Index about 72%. The *FT/Actuaries All-Share Index* has been published daily since 10 April 1962; it now covers some 800 shares and fixed interest ►stocks and covers some 98% of total market value, and has indices for industry *baskets* and subsections. The *FT/SE Small Cap Index*, introduced in 1993 and calculated daily, covers those shares within the FT/A All-Share Index but not within the 350. In 1987 the *FT/Actuaries World Share Index* was introduced, based on a weighted sample of 2,400 share prices, initially from 24 countries. *The FT/Actuaries Fixed Interest Indices* measure the prices and ►yields of UK ►gilts, index-linked (►indexation), ►debentures and ►loans. Total return figures are calculated for all the UK indices and published daily. These figures, which are gross of tax, take account of both price performance and income received from ►dividends. ►►index number.

financial year A 12-month period in respect of which financial accounts are kept. Years of account for financial purposes often do not coincide with calendar years and hence are referred to as financial years. A financial year 1993/4, for example, might run from 31 August 1993 to 1 September 1994. Government financial years are called *fiscal years*. ►►budget.

fine trade bill A ►trade bill, the drawer and drawee (►bill of exchange) of which are reputable parties, or good ►names, and that commands a fine rate of ►discount in the ►money market.

fineness The proportion of precious metal in an alloy expressed as parts in 1,000.

Finnish Options Exchange (FOEX) (Finland) The exchange trades in currency ►derivatives, Finnish government ►bonds, interest-rate options and ►futures based on the wood-pulp price index (PIX).

firm order An order to buy or sell a ➤security within a specified time limit that can be executed without further confirmation.

first notice day The first day on which notice can be given that physical delivery is intended, or expected, on a ➤futures contract.

fiscal agent 1. A function of the ➤Federal Reserve *vis-à-vis* the US Treasury: the Federal Reserve processes all payments to and from the government. **2.** An agent for the issuer of a ➤Eurobond, who delivers the interest and capital payments on the bond to the ➤paying agent and assists the borrower in other ways, such as by aiding in the receipt of the bond certificates on redemption.

fiscal transparency A ➤partnership, a ➤European economic interest grouping and a ➤sub-chapter S corporation are said to be fiscally transparent because in these business-legal forms (➤incorporation) the ➤liabilities for ➤taxation fall not upon the business as such but on the people who own it.

fiscal year ➤financial year.

Fitch Investors Service ➤Standard and Poor's Ratings.

fix To settle a price by trading, normally in the ➤commodity markets, including the ➤gold market.

fixed assets ➤asset.

fixed charge ➤mortgage.

fixed exchange rate ➤exchange rate.

fixed interest Generally, refers to ➤securities such as ➤bonds on which the holder receives a predetermined and unchanging rate of interest on the *nominal value* (➤par value); as opposed to the non-guaranteed, variable return on ➤equities. Specifically, refers to ➤debt instruments having a fixed rate of interest, such as ➤gilts, as against those with a variable rate, e.g. ➤floating rate notes.

fixed price offer for sale ➤offer for sale.

fixed rate currency swap ➤currency interest rate swap.

flat rate forward A ➤forward contract offering a constant ➤contango throughout the period of the contract.

flat yield ➤yield.

flex stock option An ➤option introduced by the ➤Chicago Board of Trade in the early 1990s, allowing clients the choice of terms, ➤striking prices and expiry dates.

flexible drawdown ➤drawdown.

flip-flop ►floating rate note.

float 1. (US) A situation where the cheque-clearing function of the ►Federal Reserve may have a timing gap between the posting of matching ►credits and ►debits to pairs of banks, thus artificially draining or bolstering those banks' reserves. ►Federal Reserve float. **2.** ►floating rate; variable rate security. **3.** Cash in hand at a bank, or funds in course of transfer between banks.

floater ►variable rate security.

floating capital Capital invested not in fixed ►assets, such as buildings, but in work in progress, wages paid, etc. ►working capital.

floating charge An assignment of the total ►assets of a company or individual as ►collateral security for a ►debt; as opposed to particular assets, when such an assignment is known as a fixed charge or ►mortgage.

floating policy A policy for the ►insurance of ships' cargoes covering a number of anticipated movements, each of which must be declared separately to the ►insurer. The policy is fixed in duration.

floating rate 1. A ►rate of interest that varies with the market, more particularly with an agreed reference standard, e.g. the ►London interbank offered rate (LIBOR) (►variable rate security). **2.** A ►rate of exchange that is not fixed by the national authorities but varies according to supply and demand for the currency.

floating rate certificate of deposit (FRCD) A ►certificate of deposit (CD) on which the issuing bank pays a variable ►coupon, or interest rate. FRCDs were first issued in the USA in 1975. Normally of one-year ►maturity, the FRCD carried a coupon adjusted every 90 days in line with that paid on 90-day CDs. The advantage to the depositor is that of partial protection against interest rate changes in the market. The advantage to the bank is that of attracting long-term funds. FRCDs were thereafter introduced on the London market, generally in ►Eurodollar form, the coupon being linked to the London interbank rate, usually by a ►spread over ►London interbank offered rate (LIBOR).

floating rate note (FRN) A ►note issued in the ►Euromarket, the ►coupon of which fluctuates according to interest rate changes. Floating rate notes are bonds, having a maturity of seven to 15 years, and came into being in face of the difficulties encountered in the 1970s in issuing fixed-interest bonds in conditions of high interest rates and high inflation. The first FRN was issued by the Italian concern ENEL in 1970, following a period of rapidly rising interest rates and at a time when bond buyers virtually refused any ►denomination higher than $25m. The floating rate transferred the risk from the lender to the borrower. The FRN does not have the option for flexible ►drawdown or interest payment timing offered under syndicated credits (►syndication). However, as time went on, the advantages to borrowers – particularly those of lesser credit rating, and most of all as a means for banks themselves of acquiring liquid funds – became apparent. Thus FRN issues rose from under $5bn in 1980 to $55bn in 1985; banks were reckoned to have accounted for half of these. Banks frequently also found FRNs preferable to ►certificates of deposit (CDs) owing to their longer maturities. Where ►subordinated to ►deposits, FRNs issued by banks have been recognized as bank capital in most major countries, except Germany, Japan and France. Most borrowing has taken place in the USA and the UK, and most issues have been denominated in US dollars, although issues have been made in Euro-sterling, Euro-D-marks, Euro-yen, Euro-Dutch-guilders and other currencies. FRNs have also been used as ►asset-backed securities.

FRNs are normally issued as ►negotiable bearer ►notes in denominations of at least $1,000, with a ►coupon related to three- or six-month ►London interbank offered rate (LIBOR), above which there is a ►spread. Since they are ►bonds, their issue must be accompanied by a ►prospectus.

Recent innovations have included: perpetual FRNs, on which there is no ►redemption; flip-flop FRNs, or perpetual FRNs convertible at one or two years' notice into lower-yielding four-year FRNs, which can themselves be converted back into perpetual FRNs; mismatch FRNs, where the coupon is paid monthly at a longer-term rate; and capped FRNs, where the coupon is subject to a predetermined ceiling. In 1986, owing to falling interest rates and some increase in credit risk in the loan portfolios of hitherto active US banks, there were indications of a decrease in the rate of FRN issues. By then the total market, including international fixed-rate bonds, amounted to $750bn. ►►variable rate security.

floor ►cap; collar.

floor broker (US) **1**. A member (or employee of a member firm) of the ►stock exchange who buys or sells ►securities on the ►trading floor on behalf of clients; as distinct from floor traders, who do so on their own account. **2**. The representative of a member of a ►commodity market, authorized to deal on the trading floor of the market. A full member of the market and thus also called a floor member.

floor member (US) ►floor broker.

floor official (US) An employee of the ►stock exchange who settles disputes arising on the ►trading floor.

floor trader (US) ►floor broker.

floppy disk A magnetic data-storage device that can be inserted into and read by a computer. Floppy because it is made of thin plastic sheet; the standard sizes are 3½ and 5¼ inches.

flotation The issue of shares in a company on a ►stock exchange or ►unlisted securities market for the first time. The method may be an ►introduction, an

➤intermediate offer, a ➤placing or an ➤offer for sale. When a private company (➤incorporation) becomes a public company and has its ➤shares listed in this way, the process is known as *going public*.

flow of funds ➤sources and uses of funds.

flow of funds account (US) Statistics kept by the ➤Federal Reserve of the total demand and supply of credit funds in the US market, broken down by type of borrower and lender and by type of borrowing instrument.

FNSAGA ➤Fédération Nationale des Syndicats d'agents généraux d'Assurance.

FNSA ➤Fédération Nationale des Sociétés d'Assurance.

FOB Free on board. ➤c.i.f.

FOEX ➤Finnish Options Exchange.

FOMC ➤Federal Open Market Committee; FOMC minutes.

FOMC minutes (US) The official, summary record of the deliberations of the ➤Federal Open Market Committee, together with the text of the ➤directive, published about a month after the FOMC meeting.

Fond Européen d'Orientation et de Garantie Agriculturale The ➤European Union's farm fund. ➤European Agricultural Guidance and Guarantee Fund (English title).

fonds (Fr.) **1.** ➤Funds. **2.** ➤Capital.

Fonds (Ger.) **1.** ➤Funds. **2.** ➤Capital. **3.** Estate.

fonds d'état (Fr.) Government ➤stocks.

fonds publics (Fr.) Government ➤stocks, ➤public bonds.

Food Aid Committee (FAC) A body established in the 1950s but since 1986 administering the Food Aid Convention forming part of the ➤International Wheat Agreement (IWA). The task of the Food Aid Committee is to ensure the annual supply to developing countries of at least 7.5m tonnes of grain or grain products promised by each of the member governments of the Food Aid Convention. There are 23 member governments, all of them, with the exception of Argentina, industrialized countries. The actual target is 10m tonnes, and this has normally been exceeded.

Food Aid Convention ➤Food Aid Committee; International Wheat Agreement.

Footsie ➤Financial Times share indices.

foreign bond A ➤bond held in one country, issued in another country and denominated in the currency of that country. In the UK known as a ➤bulldog bond, in the US as a ➤yankee bond.

Foreign Credit Insurance Association (FCIA) (US) Established in 1962 by some four dozen insurance companies to ➤underwrite the risk of default on export credit, particularly that ➤refinanced by the ➤Export–Import Bank, with which it is closely associated.

Foreign Desk (US) The section of the *Reserve Bank* of New York (➤Federal Reserve System) that carries out ➤exchange market operations at the direction of the US ➤Treasury.

foreign direct investment (FDI) ➤Investment in the foreign operations of a business. ➤balance of payments.

foreign exchange 1. All foreign ➤currencies. **2.** The activity of exchanging currencies through purchase and sale; hence *foreign exchange market.*

Foreign Exchange and Currency Deposit Brokers' Association (FECDBA) (UK) The professional body for ➤brokers dealing in ➤foreign exchange and foreign ➤currency deposits.

Foreign Exchange and Trade Central Law (Jap.) Legislation, introduced in 1949, setting a standard form of settlement of import invoices. The settlement must conform to the Japanese national interest, and if this requirement is satisfied an import licence is issued. In other cases a special permit must be obtained from the Ministry of International Trade and Industry (MITI). Modifications were made in the law following Japan's entry to the ➤Organization for Economic Co-operation and Development (OECD) and acceptance of that body's code of liberalization.

foreign income dividends (FIDs) ➤corporation tax.

Foreign Investment Law (Jap.) A law regulating foreign investment in Japan between 1950 and 1979.

forex A contraction of ➤'foreign exchange'.

forfaiting A form of export finance in which the forfaiter accepts, at a discount from the exporter, a ➤bill of exchange or *promissory note* (➤note) from the exporter's customer; the forfaiter in due course collects payment of the debt. The notes are normally guaranteed by the customer's bank. ➤Maturities are normally up to three years.

Form 10-K (US) An annual return made to the ➤Securities and Exchange Commission by companies listed on one of the national stock exchanges, giving financial and other information. A public document available on ➤Edgar. ➤➤Form 10-Q; Form 13-D.

Form 10-Q (US) A quarterly return made by US companies to the ►Securities and Exchange Commission.

Form 13-D (US) A form filed by an investor with more than 5% of the ►equity of a listed company each time ►shares in that company are bought or sold.

forward A prospective amount of a ►currency or a ►commodity obtained by a contract between a buyer and a seller. Under this, the seller undertakes to provide the client with a fixed amount of the currency or commodity on a fixed future date at a fixed rate of exchange, or price. This differs from a ►futures contract in that each forward contract is a once-only deal between the two parties, while futures contracts are in standard amounts traded on exchanges.

forward-forward 1. A transaction for the purchase, at a future date, of an ►instrument maturing at a further future date. **2.** Purchase ►forward of a currency for one term (e.g. three months) against sale forward of the same currency at another term (e.g. six months).

forward price ►forward.

forward rate agreement (FRA) An agreement whereby a currency is bought and sold at a future date at an agreed ►exchange rate. ►forward.

forward start option ►deferred strike option.

forwardation ►contango.

401 K (US) A savings scheme under which employees may have up to 10% of their salary deducted before ►taxation for investment in ►securities.

Fourth Directive The most prominent of a series of European Union directives (►directives of the EU) leading to the harmonization of company law in member states. The Fourth Directive introduced detailed schedules for the form and content of company accounts and was implemented in the UK in the 1981 Companies Act (►incorporation). ►►consolidated accounts.

FOX ►Futures and Options Exchange.

FRA ►forward rate agreement.

frais de cotation (Fr.) An annual ►listing fee.

franc fort (Fr.) A term ('strong franc') applied to the French government's policy throughout the 1980s of maintaining the foreign exchange value of the French franc, particularly against the German mark; the policy was seen to be in some doubt after the currency turbulence of August/September 1993. ►European Monetary System (EMS).

franchise The proportion of the value of goods under insurance required under the contract with the ►insurer to be covered by the ►insured.

Frankfurt Stock Exchange ➤German stock exchanges.

Freddie Mac ➤Federal Home Loan Bank Board.

free asset ratio The ratio of the market value of an ➤insurance company's ➤assets to the value of its ➤liabilities.

free capital (UK) That proportion of the ➤equity of a ➤company available for trading by the public on a stock market. (US = *free float*.) It excludes equities held by controlling shareholders.

free depreciation ➤capital allowances.

free float (US) ➤free capital.

free reserves 1. Those ➤reserves of a bank that exceed the level prescribed by the monetary authorities (➤monetary control; monetary policy). In the USA ➤excess reserves less ➤borrowed reserves, i.e. those reserves accumulated by the banks by reason of their own business that exceed the reserves that they are required by the ➤Federal Reserve to maintain, less the amounts they have borrowed from the Federal Reserve. 2. Those reserves of an insurance company that exceed the level prescribed by the relevant supervisory authorities.

free resources The excess of an insurance company's ➤assets over ➤liabilities. In the case of a ➤proprietary company equivalent to ➤paid-up capital plus ➤free reserves.

free stocks Of ➤commodity markets, inventories held in commercial hands, as against those still held by producers.

Free Trade Agreement (FTA) An agreement signed between the USA and Canada in 1988 and ratified in 1989, abolishing all tariffs between the two countries. ➤➤North American Free Trade Agreement (NAFTA).

freier Makler (Ger.) An independent dealer on the German ➤stock exchange authorized by the ➤*Börsenvorstand*, dealing chiefly in the unofficial market. Also known as a *Börsenmakler*.

Freiverkehr (Ger.) The unofficial or ➤unlisted securities market or ➤German stock exchanges.

Friedman, Milton (US) Professor of Economics at the University of Chicago, and most celebrated for his monetary theory, popularly known as monetarism, based on the quantum theory of money. The theory propounds, in brief, that variations in ➤money supply cause variations in the general price level and that therefore the growth in the stock of money should be maintained within stable dimensions consonant with the real growth of the economy. The theory had great influence on the financial policies of the major industrial countries during the 1970s and early 1980s, but difficulties encountered in the measurement and control of the money supply, and in demonstrating the link between this and the level of prices, led thereafter to a weakening of this influence.

friendly society (UK) A ►mutual organization, often an ►insurance association. There are several thousand friendly societies in Britain, including working men's clubs, set up voluntarily to provide benefits and assistance during sickness, unemployment, retirement or death. The tax advantages enjoyed by the friendly societies have been reduced in recent years.

FRN ►floating rate note.

front-end fee A fee charged by a bank or ►syndicate of banks at the outset of a loan, e.g. management fee, ►participation fee, ►underwriting fee. Most commonly occurring in the ►Euro-market and in the US securities market.

front-end loading Of insurance premiums, unit trust prices and loan interest, the incorporation of administration expenses into the first payment by the customer or borrower. ►loading.

front month The first month available for trading in a ►derivative. Also known as the *nearby month*.

FRS Financial reporting standards. ►accounting standards.

FSA 1. Financial Services Act. 2. Financial Services Authority. ►Financial Services Act.

FSBR ►Financial Statement and Budget Report.

FT/Actuaries World Share Index ►Financial Times share indices.

FTA ►Free Trade Agreement.

FTO ►Financial Times share indices.

FT/SE futures contract (UK) A standardized ►futures contract based upon the ►Financial Times share indices and traded on the ►London International Financial Futures Exchange (LIFFE).

FT/SE Index ►Financial Times share indices.

full consolidation ►consolidated accounts.

full listing (UK) The inclusion of a ►company in the ►official list of the ►London Stock Exchange.

fund A sum of money, as in an amount of savings, handed to a ►stockbroker for investment and management (►discretionary account), or subscribed to a savings scheme or invested by a ►life assurance company to meet the claims of policy-holders. Fund management consists in carrying out administration such as the receipt of ►dividends and ►interest, subscribing to ►rights issues and adjusting the ➤portfolio by purchases and sales with the objective of maximizing capital growth or income. The term is frequently used to denote the institution managing the fund, e.g. a pension fund (➤pensions). Also used generally to describe any investment vehicle such as a ➤unit trust or an ➤investment trust.

fund management ➤fund.

fund of funds ➤managed unit trust.

fundamental analysis ➤technical analysis.

funded debt Generally, short-term ➤debt that has been converted into long-term debt. ➤funding.

funded pension scheme ➤pensions.

funding The process of converting short-term to long-term ➤debt by the sale of long-term ➤securities and using the funds raised to repay short-term debt. In ➤public finance, *overfunding* occurs when the government is selling more debt to the non-bank sector than is necessary to meet the ➤public-sector borrowing requirement (PSBR), and *underfunding* when it is selling less than is necessary for that purpose. Under *full funding* purchases of government paper by the banks do not count towards the financing needs of the PSBR, which are fully met by sales to non-banks, that is, to other ➤financial intermediaries, and the personal and corporate sectors.

funds at Lloyd's (FAL) Funds held in trust at ➤Lloyd's to support a member's ➤underwriting activities, comprising their ➤Lloyd's deposit, their ➤personal reserve and their ➤special reserve.

funds broker (US) An intermediary for the arrangement of short-term lending between banks.

funds rate (US) ➤Federal funds rate.

funds statements ➤sources and uses of funds.

fungible A class of good or ➤security that has the property of being substitutable or interchangeable with another in the same class. ➤Bearer securities, ➤common stocks and money, such as £5 notes, are fungible because, if of the same denomination, one can be replaced by another without loss or gain. Fungibility is important because it allows the pooling and offsetting of classes of items without the need to identify them individually by serial numbers or other means.

futures A vehicle for the purchase and sale of ➤commodities and ➤financial instruments at a date in the futures. Futures take the form of a fixed and binding contract for a standard amount to be sold at a fixed price at a fixed future date. In the precise obligation involved, the future differs from an ➤option and a ➤forward transaction. A future is a ➤negotiable instrument. ➤➤financial futures.

Futures and Options Exchange (London FOX) (UK) The leading exchange in Europe for soft ►commodities (including cocoa, sugar, rubber, potatoes and grain). It was formed in 1987 as successor to the London Commodity Exchange, sharing a trading floor with the ►International Petroleum Exchange, and in 1991 took over the Baltic Futures Exchange (BFE), which itself had also been formed in 1987. In 1996 FOX was merged with the ►London International Financial Futures Exchange (LIFFE) as a separate department – LIFFE Commodity Products – its operations remaining unchanged.

Futures Industry Association (US) The central body representing US operators in the ►futures market.

futures market A market dealing in ►futures and ►options on ►shares, ►bonds, foreign currencies and ►commodities.

futures option An ►option to buy or sell a ►futures contract.

FXnet An international system, set up in 1984, for the netting of bilateral foreign exchange trades between banks. Designed to minimize ►Herstatt risk.

G

GAB ➤general arrangements to borrow.

GAFTA ➤Grain and Feed Trade Associations.

gai atsu (Jap.) The term describing foreign pressure for a change in Japanese financial and trade policies.

gaijin (Jap.) Literally, 'foreigner'. Used in Japanese stock market parlance to refer to a foreign investor.

gaimuin (Jap.) A ➤broker in a small ➤securities house.

gamma stocks ➤alpha securities, ➤stocks.

Garn–St Germain Act 1982 (US) An Act that removed restrictions on the ➤asset base of ➤savings and loan associations, allowing these organizations to compete in the commercial lending market. ➤Building societies in the UK have also been deregulated (➤regulation) but are still restricted to the provision of financial service for individuals.

GATT ➤General Agreement on Tariffs and Trade.

GDP ➤gross domestic product.

gearing (UK) The relative importance of ➤loans in the ➤capital structure (US = *leverage*). There are several ways of measuring gearing. The usual way is the ratio of fixed-interest ➤debt to shareholder interest plus the debt (➤net assets). A corporation may borrow ➤capital at fixed interest, and if it can earn more on that capital than it has to pay for it in interest, then the additional earnings accrue to the ➤equity shareholders. Thus a firm with high gearing will be able to pay higher ➤dividends per ➤share than a firm with lower gearing earning exactly the same return on its total capital, provided that return is higher than the rate it pays for ➤loan capital. However, the contrary is also true; so the higher the gearing the greater the risk to the equity shareholder. ➤➤capital gearing; equity gearing; gearing effect.

gearing effect (UK) **1.** The impact upon ➤earnings per share of ➤capital structure. ➤gearing. **2.** The multiplication of a change in the price of a ➤warrant compared with that of a ➤share that may be exchanged for it, or in the price of a share compared with an ➤option.

Geldmenge (Ger.) ➤Money supply.

Geldvolumen (Ger.) ➤Money supply.

GEMU ➤German Economic and Monetary Union.

General Agreement on Tariffs and Trade (GATT) A convention entered into by most nations of the non-communist world in 1947 for the liberalization of world trade and for the establishment of an international trade organization. Provisions for the liberalization of trade – comprising chiefly an extensive reduction of ➤tariffs and acceptance of the *most-favoured nation* principle (i.e. non-discrimination in the extension of tariff reductions) – and adoption of a code of fair trading – chiefly the disavowal of restrictive trade practices and non-tariff trade obstacles – proved well received; while those for the establishment of an international trade organization were not. Accordingly the tariff reductions were put into effect, and a secretariat was established in the United Nations European office in Geneva on 1 January 1948 to assist with the task of further implementing trade liberalization under the convention.

In course of time the secretariat and the convention signatories constituted themselves into an organization with the status of a specialized agency of the United Nations, and the title General Agreement on Tariffs and Trade, or GATT, became applicable both to the organization and to the convention itself.

The GATT has since greatly enlarged the scope of liberalization, notably through eight further negotiating rounds – two more at Geneva, one at Torquay and one at Annécy between 1947 and 1962; the Dillon round of 1967; a major round, the Kennedy round, ending in 1967; a major round between 1973 and 1979, denoted the Tokyo round; and an eighth round, the Uruguay round, beginning in 1986 and concluded at the end of 1993. Apart from further tariff cuts, reductions in non-tariff barriers and a long-lasting endeavour to reconcile French and US agricultural interests, the Uruguay round was distinguished by a proposal for a *Multilateral Trade Organization* (MTO) to enforce rules for international trade, itself a harking back to the International Trade Organization at the heart of the original convention of 1947, for which the GATT organization was only a substitute. As a result of these, world trade tariff barriers were reduced to a small proportion of their level in 1947.

As time went on, not only was the GATT joined in the work of liberalization by other bodies, such as the ➤Organization for Economic Co-operation and Development and the ➤European Union, but its own efforts focused more particularly on non-tariff hindrances, such as subsidies and incentives, government procurement, restrictive trade agreements, developing country problems, agriculture and trade in services. Membership in 1988 numbered 88 nations. GATT was replaced by the ➤World Trade Organization in 1995.

general agreements to borrow (GAB) ➤International Monetary Fund.

general average ➤average.

general government A term normally used in public accounting matters to refer to central and local government, taken together, in a particular country. Thus the term refers in the UK to the government at Westminster and to all local authorities, i.e. district, county and borough councils; in the USA, to the federal government in Washington together with state, local and territorial governments; in Japan, to the central government of Tokyo together with prefectures and city, town and village authorities; in Germany, to the central government in Bonn together with *Länder*, city states and municipalities; in France, to the central government in Paris together with regions, departments and communes.

general insurance Insurance against fire, accident, theft, etc., as distinct from life.

general undertaking (UK) A document signed by the directors of a ►company, setting out their obligations to the ►stock exchange in terms of the provision of information and issue of ►shares for companies on the ►unlisted securities market. The version of this document used by companies going for a ►full listing is called the *listing agreement*.

generally accepted accounting principles (GAAP) (US) Rules for ►accounting standards. The ►Securities and Exchange Commission requires audited accounts for ►quoted companies to comply with GAAP.

gensaki (Jap.) A ►bond sale with a ►repurchase agreement, the difference between the sale price and the agreed repurchase price establishing the ►yield, which is expressed at an annual rate.

geometric average ►average.

geometric mean ►average.

geregelter Freiverkehr (Ger.) Second-tier official ►unlisted securities markets operating at the ►stock exchanges in Germany. There is also an unregulated third tier called the *ungeregelter Freiverkehr*. Finally, there is an ►over-the-counter telephone market in which both listed and unlisted shares are dealt, the *Telefonverkehr* (literally, 'telephone traffic'). ►►*freier Makler*.

German Economic and Monetary Union (GEMU) The process of integrating economic and monetary conditions in former East and West Germany, following the unification of the two countries in 1990.

German Futures and Options Market ►Deutsche Terminbörse.

German stock exchanges The numerous ►stock exchanges in Germany are now grouped under *Deutsche Börse AG* and there is a Federal Securities Supervisory Office in Frankfurt. Frankfurt is by far the largest exchange, accounting for over 75% of volume. A new electronic ►order driven trading system, 'Xetra', went live in November 1997 and will replace ►IBIS, initially for institutional investors.

In March 1997 the ►Neuer Markt (New Market) for fast-growing smaller companies (►unlisted securities markets) was launched subject to the same regulatory standards as the ►*geregelter Freiverkehr*. A new mid-cap index, the *MDAX*, comprising 70 stocks not in the ►Deutsche Aktienindex, was launched in 1996. There are computerized ►futures and ►options markets in Frankfurt. ►Deutsche Kassenverein (DKV) accounts for much of ►settlement and clearing.

Other exchanges in Germany are trying to differentiate themselves more clearly. The Berlin exchange offers extensive trading in third segment foreign securities, and Bremen has a medium-sized corporate market. A large proportion of trading volume on German exchanges is accounted for by foreign investors, and the shares in German companies are ►heavy shares because there is a minimum ►par value of DM50.

Gesellschaft (Ger.) ►Company.

Gesellschaft mit beschränkter Haftung (GmbH) (Ger.) A private limited company. ►incorporation.

gesichert (Ger.) ►Secured.

Gewerbeertragesteuer (Ger.) ►local taxation.

Gewerbekapitalsteuer (Ger.) ►local taxation.

Gewinn (Ger.) **1**. Profit. **2**. Gain on a transaction, or a price.

gift tax (US) A levy on the ►value of certain property given away to others and paid by the donor. The gift tax is graduated and levied by the US Federal Government and also by some states. In Britain, prior to the introduction of capital transfer tax (►inheritance tax), there was no tax on gifts as such, although they were added back into the estate of the donor for duty purposes if made within seven years of the donor's death.

gilts, gilt-edged securities (UK) Fixed-interest UK ►government securities traded on the ►London Stock Exchange. They are called gilt-edged because it is certain that ►interest will be paid and that they will be redeemed (where appropriate) on the due date. Some gilts are ►dated securities, some are ►undated securities, and some are index-linked (►indexation). Gilts are not a risk-free investment, of course, because of fluctuations in their market value. Gilt-edged securities do not include ►Treasury bills. The prices of gilts, hitherto quoted in fractions of one pound, are now quoted in decimals in line with European practice. ►►gilt strip.

Ginnie Maes (US) A familiar term for mortgage-backed bonds issued by the ►Government National Mortgage Association.

gilt repos The market in agreed sales and repurchase of ►gilt-edged securities (►repo) introduced by the ►Bank of England in January 1996. Within two months of launch the open gilt repo market was already much larger than the ►bill market

(►money market), the restricted size of which has recently hampered ►open market operations. The gilt repo market was launched to increase the attractiveness of gilts to foreign investors and to reduce the cost of funding the government ►deficit, but may be used by the Bank of England for open market operations as repos are used by the ►Bundesbank and the ►Federal Reserve System.

gilt strip (UK) A form of gilt-edged stock issued by the ►Bank of England as from December 1997. No interest is paid, but the stock is issued at a discount to provide the equivalent of the interest when the bond is repaid at maturity. The bond is divided into a series of annual 'gilt strip' issues where the amount of discount is fixed in relation to the present value, in the year in question, of the interest due at maturity.

Girozentalen (Ger.) ►*Landesbank.*

Glass–Steagal Act 1933 (US) Legislation prohibiting ►commercial banks from acting as ►investment banks or owning a firm dealing in securities. The Act has been challenged by banks offering ►money market mutual funds and other investment services and is expected to be the subject of reform.

global bond A ►fixed-interest security issued simultaneously in the USA, Europe and Asia. Principal issuers are ►sovereign governments and international organizations such as the ►International Bank for Reconstruction and Development but also ►multinational companies.

global custody A service provided by ►investment banks and other ►financial intermediaries to local ►fund managers for cross-border ►settlement and administration.

Globex An overnight electronic trading system developed in 1992 jointly by the ►Chicago Mercantile Exchange, the ►Chicago Board of Trade and ►Reuters, and dealing in ►currency futures and options. By 1993 little participation outside the founding exchanges and the ►Marché à Terme des Instruments Financiers (MATIF) was evident.

GmbH ►*Gesellschaft mit beschränkter Haftung.*

GNMA (US) ►Government National Mortgage Association.

GNP Gross national product. ►gross domestic product.

GOFO ►gold forward offered rate.

going concern value ►goodwill.

going public ►flotation.

gold This precious metal ceased to have a significant monetary role in 1971 when the US abandoned its commitment to buy or sell gold at a fixed price. However, the non-monetary rise of gold, especially in jewellery, has expanded rapidly and gold also remains in demand as a store of value as well as a means of adornment. In the long run gold has retained its value in real terms, though recent sales by some ►central banks have depressed sentiment in favour of gold. ►►London Gold Futures Market Ltd.

gold and foreign currency reserves ►reserves.

Gold Demand Trends ►World Gold Council.

gold forward offered rate The rate at which dealers will lend ►gold on ►swap against US dollars.

gold standard A form of international ►exchange practised until the 1930s. Each country's national ►currency was linked by a fixed rate to ►gold and varied in volume with the amount of gold held. Thus a ►balance of payments surplus would lead to an increase in the ►money supply, thence to a rise in prices and so to a drop in exports and a rise in imports, eliminating the surplus. A balance of payments deficit acted in the opposite direction. Economic difficulties in the 1930s led to the abandonment of the gold standard.

gold warrant An instrument enabling the holder to buy or sell ►gold at a predetermined price and time, closely akin to call and put ►options. However, warrants are for periods of one year or more, are not subject to the ►margin requirements of ►futures and ►options exchanges and, having a close resemblance to conventional ►securities, are acceptable to portfolios unable to deal in other forms of ►derivatives.

golden share ►privatization.

Goldilocks economy Term applied to economies where rising share prices and strong economic growth combine with low consumer price inflation.

good till cancelled (GTC) An order for a ►commodity remaining open for execution so long as not specifically cancelled.

goodwill (UK) The value of a business to a purchaser over and above its ►net asset value (US = *going concern value*). It is normal practice to show goodwill in the ►balance sheet but to write it down for ►depreciation. ►►consolidated accounts.

government broker The firm handling ►new issues of ►gilts for the ►Bank of England. Superseded by a number of ►market makers in gilts after the stock exchange reorganization (►Big Bang) of 1986.

Government National Mortgage Association (GNMA) (US) A government agency that approves and guarantees mortgage-backed ►securities for the finance of low-cost housing. ►►collateralized mortgage securities.

government securities All government fixed-interest paper, including ►funded debt and ►Treasury bills. ►►gilts.

government stock A ►bond issued by government; a term most commonly used to refer to central government stock or, in the UK, ►gilts.

Gower Report ►FInancial Services Act.

grading The setting and checking of quality and type standards for ►commodities traded on a ►commodity exchange.

Grain and Feed Trade Association (GAFTA) The controlling body of the London Grain Futures Market, a commodity market for wheat and barley that trades on the floor of the ►Baltic Exchange. The market is managed by a GAFTA committee, the Grain Futures and Clearing House Committee; and prices are fixed by market members nominated each week by a panel of that committee. Deliveries of grain are from a store registered by the committee. GAFTA holds a reserve fund drawn from the income of the association and used for the settlement of claims against default. GAFTA has wide regulatory powers over market members.

Grain Market Report ►International Wheat Council.

Gramm–Rudman Act 1985 (US) An Act of Congress, sponsored by senators Gramm, Rudman and Hollings, that required the US federal government to balance its ►budget by 1991. Despite various efforts, this object was not achieved.

granter ►options.

Green Book 1. (UK) A handbook published by the ►London Stock Exchange, setting out the requirements for admission to the former ►unlisted securities market and for subsequent reporting. **2.** (US) A familiar term for the economic forecast presented by the staff of the ►Federal Reserve Board to each meeting of the ►Federal Open Market Committee. One of three such information documents. ►►Beige Book; Blue Book.

greenmail ►corporate raider.

grey market A term describing a market in a ►new issue of ►shares before the shares have been received by subscribers.

gross domestic product (GDP) The money value (at market prices) of the goods and services produced by the economy in a period of time, usually a year or a quarter. No allowance is made for expenditure on the replacement of capital assets. Only goods for final consumption or investment are included, since the value of intermediate goods, e.g. raw materials, is included in the prices of final goods. GDP is distinguished from *gross national product* (GNP) by the exclusion of income on investment abroad. These national accounts aggregates, as they are called, may be valued at ►current prices or in ►real terms.

gross margin ➤margin.

gross national product ➤gross domestic product.

gross premium Of insurance, a ➤premium less the amount paid in rebates or refunds, but before deductions for ➤commissions and ➤reinsurance.

Group of Five ➤Plaza Agreement.

Group of 10 ➤general agreements to borrow (GAB).

Group of 20 An organization of 20 leading international banks based in Europe, the USA, Canada and Japan, set up for the purpose of consultation on common issues. The chairman of the Group in 1997 was Mr Stephen Thieke of J. P. Morgan Bank.

Group of 30 (US) A 'think tank' originally sponsored by the Rockefeller Foundation composed of 30 high-level individuals drawn from central banks, commercial bank management, the economics profession and finance ministries in both developed and developing countries. The group was founded in 1979, with headquarters first in New York, then in Washington, DC. The group's purpose is to prepare and publish studies on the basic function of international and economic systems, using the expertise of members and where appropriate that of outside contributors. A number of studies have been produced on such topics as ➤foreign exchange movements, ➤exchange rate policy and the role of the ➤International Monetary Fund (IMF) and the World Bank (➤International Bank for Reconstruction and Development). In 1993 a much discussed study was produced on ➤derivatives. The chairman is Paul Volcker, former chairman of the US ➤Federal Reserve.

Group of 40 An international association of medium-sized banks formed to safeguard the common interests of the members.

growth stocks ➤Shares in companies, usually in expanding sectors in the economy, which are expected to enjoy high rates of growth in ➤earnings per share and therefore have high ➤price–earnings (P/E) ratios.

Grundkapital (Ger.) ➤Share capital.

Grundsteuer (Ger.) ➤local taxation.

GTC ➤good till cancelled.

Guarantee Fund for Futures and Options (Den.) A fund underpinning trade in the ➤Danish Futures and Options Market.

H

hammering (UK) The announcement, formerly with three blows of a hammer, of the bankruptcy of a member of the ►London Stock Exchange. In the USA the term means widespread selling short (►position) or hammering the market down when prices are thought to be too high.

Handel (Ger.) Trade.

Hang Seng Index ►Hong Kong stock exchanges.

harakiri swap (Jap.) A ►swap carrying no ►spread, made for the purpose of increasing the initiator's market share.

hard currency ►currency.

hard disk A magnetic computer-storage device capable of holding large volumes of data. In general it is permanently fixed inside the computer, in contrast to a ►floppy disk.

hard dollars ►soft dollars.

hausse (Fr.) A rise in price.

hazard That element of an insurance ►risk that in the view of the insurer is capable of aggravating the loss.

head and shoulders A pattern seen in a graph of ►share prices against time which ►chartists claim can provide signals of a significant downturn in price.

heavy share (UK) A ►share that has a high unit price in relation to the average price of shares in the market. On the ►London Stock Exchange many shares are priced around £4, but a few are priced at £20 or more. For companies with similar earnings and prospects the ►yield may be the same but the price may be very different. In the UK investors seem to prefer to buy large numbers of shares at low prices, but in the US average unit prices are much higher. For this reason, to improve the marketability of its shares, a company that has experienced a rapid growth in the earnings may decide to make a ►bonus issue to reduce the price of its shares. ►►penny share.

hedge A transaction tending to the opposite effect of another transaction, engaged in to minimize a potential loss on the latter. Hedging usually relates to ►commodity, ►currency and financial transactions. Thus an anticipated liability in a currency can be covered, where a rise in its price is apprehended, by a ➤forward purchase of the same currency at a fixed price. Commodity and ➤security transactions can be hedged by ➤futures and ➤options contracts, sometimes *put* and *call* simultaneously. In the commodities markets hedging is generally effected by taking a position in the futures market opposite to that held in the ➤physical market. The word is used also to denote the instrument used to hedge.

'held covered' clause A clause in a marine ➤insurance contract exonerating the ➤insured from accidental misdescriptions of the goods, against an addition to the ➤premium.

Herstatt risk The risk of loss in the capital value of a ➤currency transaction, where one side of the bargain is completed, but completion on the other side is delayed. Named after the Herstatt Bank of Germany, which suffered loss in 1974 having settled the D-mark side of a transaction before closing for the night, leaving the dollar side unpaid in North America. ➤➤delivery versus payment.

Hex The Helsinki Stock Exchange ➤share index.

High Premiums Group A group of ➤Names investing substantially in ➤Lloyd's of London and established to safeguard the interests of its members during the period of 'Reconstruction and Renewal' and after.

high yield bond ➤junk bond.

hire purchase (UK) A form of ➤consumer credit in which the purchaser of a good or service pays the ➤principal and interest in regular instalments over a period of six months to two years or more; usually an initial deposit is required, and full ownership passes to the purchaser at the end of the period. US = *instalment credit*. ➤➤finance house.

historic cost ➤costs, historical.

historic-cost depreciation ➤depreciation.

hoekmen ➤Amsterdam Stock Exchange.

holder Of a ➤derivative, the buyer. ➤writer.

holding company A company (➤incorporation) that controls one or more other companies, normally by holding a majority of the ➤shares of these ➤subsidiaries. It is possible for a holding company to control a large number of companies with a combined ➤capital very much greater than its own, since it needs to hold only half or even less of the shares of its subsidiaries. This is known as *pyramiding*. ➤➤consolidated accounts.

home banking ➤viewdata.

home service ➤industrial branch.

Hong Kong Commodities Exchange Ltd Founded in 1977, the market deals in cotton, sugar, soya bean and gold ►futures.

Hong Kong stock exchanges The four ►stock exchanges in Hong Kong were modernized and unified in 1986, to become the Stock Exchange of Hong Kong (SEHK). They are regulated by the Securities and Futures Commission. Structural reforms including independence for the commission were recommended in a report by Ian Hay Davison following the October 1987 market crash and implemented. The Hang Seng Index of 33 leading stocks provides the basis for ►options and ►futures contracts on the futures exchange. There is also a more broadly based index, the Hong Kong Stock Index. A second-tier market has also been proposed.

horizontal spread A combination of ►options, namely a ►long-call option combined with a ►short-call option, or the same combination of *put* options, both with different expiry dates.

hot money Funds which flow into a country to take advantage of favourable ►rates of interest and shift elsewhere when relative rates favour such a move.

HPG ►High Premiums Group.

Hypo-Bank (Ger.) ►*Hypothekenbank.*

Hypothekenbank (Ger.) ►Mortgage bank.

I

IASC ➤International Accounting Standards Committee.

IBBR ➤London interbank offered rate.

IBELs ➤interest-bearing eligible liabilities.

IBEX-35 ➤Madrid Stock Exchange.

IBIS (Ger.) Interbank Information System. A screen-based securities quotation system.

IBMBR ➤London interbank offered rate.

IBNR ➤incurred but not reported.

IBNR claims reserve A fund (usually the ➤claims outstanding reserve) set aside by an insurance company to meet ➤claims that have arisen but not yet been presented to the company, i.e. ➤incurred but not reported (IBNR). ➤➤technical reserves.

IBRC ➤Insurance Brokers Registration Council.

IBRD ➤International Bank for Reconstruction and Development.

ICCH ➤International Commodities Clearing House.

ichibu (Jap.) The *first section* of the ➤stock exchange, dealing in prime ➤securities.

IDA International Development Association. ➤International Bank for Reconstruction and Development.

IET ➤interest equalization tax.

IFA ➤independent financial adviser.

IFAA ➤Independent Financial Advisers Association.

IFC International Finance Corporation. ➤International Bank for Reconstruction and Development.

IFOX (Ire.) Irish Futures and Options Exchange.

IFS (UK) ➤Institute for Fiscal Studies.

IGA International Grains Agreement. ➤International Grains Council (IGC).

IGC ➤Intergovernmental Conference. ➤➤International Grains Council.

IIB ➤Institute of Insurance Brokers.

ILU ➤Institute of London Underwriters.

IMF ➤International Monetary Fund.

IMKB Index (Turkey) The share price index (➤share indices) of the Istanbul Stock Exchange (➤Istanbul Menkul Kiymetter Borsasi).

immediate annuity An ➤annuity commencing immediately on purchase.

impact loan (Jap.) A loan made in foreign ➤currencies, provided by an ➤authorized foreign exchange bank, the use of which is unregulated.

impôt (Fr.) Tax.

imputation system ➤corporation tax.

IMRO ➤Investment Managers Regulatory Organization; Financial Services Act.

in camera In closed session of a law court.

in the money Of call ➤options, where the ➤strike price is less than the price of the underlying asset; of put options, where the strike price is greater than the underlying asset value. ➤intrinsic value.

inchoate instrument A money ➤instrument, e.g. a ➤cheque, ➤bill of exchange or *promissory note* (➤note), that is incomplete in all its particulars. A drawer of such an instrument can give authority to another party to insert the missing particulars, e.g. a drawer of a bill of exchange can leave the name of the drawee blank, authorizing a third party to find a drawee and add that person's name.

income gearing A measure of ability to service ➤debt. It is calculated by dividing ➤profit before ➤interest by total interest costs. Also referred to as *times covered*, i.e. the number of times profits exceed interest payments.

income shares ➤investment trust.

income statement (US) ➤profit and loss account.

income tax A compulsory transfer of a proportion of employment and investment income to the state. Gifts are taxed separately (➤inheritance tax). Income for income tax purposes consists of wages, salaries, bonuses from employment, unincorporated business profits, ➤pensions, rent, ➤interest and ➤dividends. In some countries the last three sources of income may be taxed under a different system; there may be a distinction made between earned income from employment and unearned income from rents and other investments. Some countries provide ➤tax allowances or ➤tax credits for ➤investment (e.g. the ➤Enterprise Investment Scheme) or investment income, and most do this also for pension provisions.

➤Capital gains may be taxed under separate systems, while employee fringe benefits may also be taxed. In most countries income tax is progressive on successive slices of income, and allowances are given for dependants, etc. There is an international trend towards a reduction in the number of income tax bands and rates, though the UK added one in 1992/3, and an additional 10% rate is under consideration. There are three rates of tax on successive bands of taxable income in the UK: a lower rate of 20%, a basic rate of 23% and a higher rate of 40% (1997/98). Some forms of investment income, e.g. ➤bank deposit interest and ➤dividends, have income tax deducted at source. People in employment are taxed under the Pay As You Earn (PAYE) system under schedule E. Under the PAYE system the employer deducts income tax by the use of code numbers that ensure that taxpayers receive the allowances to which they are entitled. The self-employed, including ➤partnerships, are taxed under schedule D. ➤Tax Reform Act. In 1996/97 a *self-assessment* system was introduced to enable taxpayers to assess their own income and ➤capital gains liabilities if they wish. Only a minority of taxpayers will be affected – those with more complex affairs. The US has a more comprehensive system of self-assessment which affects all taxpayers.

incorporation The act of forming a company by carrying out the necessary legal formalities (➤memorandum of association). A company is a legal person separate and distinct from the people who own it, usually with ➤limited liability. In the UK under the Companies Act 1985 there are three classes of company: (i) limited and (ii) unlimited private companies and (iii) *public limited companies* (plcs). All companies are obliged to file certain information for public inspection and to circulate accounts to their shareholders, though these ➤disclosure requirements are less onerous for smaller private companies (➤abbreviated accounts). A plc may have an unlimited number of shareholders and may offer ➤shares for public subscription (➤offer for sale). Only plcs may qualify for listing on the ➤London Stock Exchange or the unlisted securities market. Private companies may place certain restrictions on the transfer of shares but may not offer shares to the public (➤close company). The ➤European Union's *Twelfth Directive* providing for single-member limited liability companies is now implemented in the UK. Company law sets out other provisions dealing with the powers, appointment and terms of directors, the protection of investors, including *minority interests* (➤consolidated accounts), ownership and control, the regulation of shares, the disclosure of interests in shares, accounts, winding up (➤bankruptcy; liquidation) and other matters. The 1981 Companies Act allowed companies to acquire their own shares under certain circumstances, a practice known as buying in shares, which may be carried out to improve the dividend ➤yield.

The broad outline of company law is similar in most countries, though there are important differences in detail; e.g. in Germany, public companies are required to have two-tiered boards. In the USA, the term for an incorporated business is corporation (Inc.), but there are not separate *legal forms* for private companies and public companies. Other business-legal forms include the ►partnership, ►sole proprietorship and ►company limited by guarantee. ►►*Aktiengesellschaft Bv*; *Gesellschaft mit beschränkter Haftung (GmbH)*; *naamloze vennootschap*; *sociedad anónima*; *società per azioni*; *société à responsabilité limitée*; *société anonyme*.

incurred but not reported (IBNR) Losses believed by an insurer to be covered by a policy they have issued but not yet reported to them by the policy-holder, and not yet the subject of a claim. This can in particular be the case for ►long tail business. Insurers are legally required to constitute reserves in respect of IBNR.

indemnity The sum in compensation paid by an ►insurance company in the event of loss or damage under the contract.

independent financial adviser (IFA) A firm licensed under the ►Financial Services Act to advise on and to transact investment business on behalf of clients, acting on a wholly independent basis with no commitment to any producer of investment products. IFAs are legally obliged to give 'best advice', i.e. to offer the product best suited to the circumstances of their client. Relevant investment products include ►life assurance, ►pensions, ►unit trusts, investment management and investment advice.

Independent Financial Advisers Association (IFAA) (UK) An association formed in 1994 to represent British ►independent financial advisers (IFAs). Membership is open to all firms regulated by the ►Financial Services Act 1986 and who have at least one full-time adviser. Some 2,000 firms are members. The objects of the association are to represent the interests of members to government, the regulators, product providers and other interested parties; to promote high standards of performances; and to provide information and advice to members.

independent intermediary An independent insurance broker owing no allegiance to any insurance company, defined as a broker selling the products of more than one life company and of more than six general insurers, and legally bound to give 'best advice' to prospective policy-holders. None the less, the independent intermediary relies for their income on commissions paid by insurance companies on sales of policies. ►►independent financial adviser.

index fund ►indexing.

index-linking ►indexation.

index number An ►average of a group of observations of a price or some other variable, expressed as a percentage of the average of the same variable in the base year against which the comparison is being made. In price indices the variables may be unweighted averages or ►weighted averages. ►►retail price index; share indices.

indexation The indexation or automatic linkage between monetary obligations and the price level. ➤Securities may be index-linked. The UK government introduced an index-linked security in 1981 for financial institutions and has subsequently issued others for private investors as well as institutions, e.g. the 2½% *index-linked* Treasury stock 2011 in which both the interest and the ➤principal are adjusted in line with changes in the ➤retail price index. Some ➤National Savings certificates are also index-linked (US = *inflation proofing*). General indexation, including the index-linking of bank and other loans, has been used in some countries, e.g. Brazil, to help control inflation in the past. In the UK the amount of ➤capital gains and losses for tax purposes was subject to indexation, but in the November 1993 Budget the creation of losses by indexation was abolished. ➤➤indexing.

indexing Weighting a ➤portfolio in the same proportions as the components of a ➤share index such as ➤Standard and Poor's 500. The performance of a fund consisting of company shares weighted in this way will mirror that of the index, thus ensuring that an index fund will not perform worse (or better) than the market as a whole. Not to be confused with ➤indexation.

Indian Opportunities Fund An *offshore* (➤tax haven) ➤open-ended fund established to provide international investors with access to the Indian stock market free of ➤capital gains tax or ➤withholding tax.

Indian stock exchanges ➤Bombay Stock Exchange.

indice (Fr.) **1.** Index, ➤index number. **2.** Stock exchange index.

indirect tax ➤taxation.

individual retirement account (IRA) (US) A pension plan (➤pensions) under which employed people not covered by another retirement plan and whose income is below a specified minimum make tax-deductible contributions to a fund invested in ➤securities and other forms of investments. Contributions are subject to a limit of $2,000 a year for an individual, more for married couples, and withdrawals before age 59½ are subject to a penalty. ➤➤personal pension.

individual savings account (ISA) A new tax shelter for personal savings which the UK government proposes to introduce in April 1999. ISAs, like the ➤personal equity plan (PEP) and tax exempt savings account (TESSA), which they will replace, will be exempt from ➤income tax and ➤capital gains tax. There will be an overall ceiling of £50,000 on contributions to an ISA and annual limits on what may be invested in them (e.g. £5,000 in ➤stocks and ➤shares). PEPs can be rolled over into ISAs but only within the £50,000 ceiling. PEPs with an accumulated value in excess of the ceiling will not lose tax relief on the excess. TESSAs and PEPs open prior to their replacement by ISAs will be allowed to run their course. The plans for ISAs have been controversial and may be subject to change.

industrial bank ➤finance house.

industrial branch Life insurance business conducted through the collection of ►premiums at the ►policy-holder's home, also known as home service business. Now declining in relative importance.

inflation A fall in the purchasing power of money, reflected in a persistent increase in the general level of prices as measured by the ►retail price index.

inflation accounting Methods of keeping a record of financial transactions and analysing them in a way that allows for changes in the purchasing power of money over time. In periods of rapidly rising prices, with accounts maintained on a historical cost basis (►costs, historical), the replacement cost of assets may be much higher than their recorded costs, and ►depreciation provisions may be inadequate and ►profit overstated. *Current cost accounting* (CCA) is a form of replacement cost accounting that involves revaluing assets from historic costs to current costs.

inflation proofing ►indexation.

Inhaber (Ger.) Owner.

Inhaberaktie (Ger.) A bearer share. ►bearer security.

Inhabereffekten (Ger.) Bearer securities.

Inhaberobligation (Ger.) A bearer bond. ►bearer security.

Inhaberpapier (Ger.) A ►bearer security.

inheritance tax (UK) A tax on the transmission of wealth on death and on gifts made in the seven years before death. Cumulative transfers in excess of £215,000 (1997/98) are taxed at a flat rate of 40%, with tapering relief on gifts made between three and seven years of death. All transfers to a spouse living in Britain are exempt. Business property qualifies for relief of up to 50%. This tax is not a true inheritance tax because it is levied on the donor or his estate, not on the recipient. The tax replaced ►capital transfer tax in 1986, which in turn replaced *estate duty*, first introduced in 1894. Death taxes in the US are levied by states and include estate and inheritance taxes.

initial charge ►unit trust.

initial public offering (IPO) (US) The offering of the ►shares in the ►equity of a company to the public for the first time. ►►new issue.

initial yield ►yield.

Inland Revenue (UK) The government department responsible for the collection and administration of ►income tax, ►corporation tax, ►capital gains tax, ►inheritance tax, ►stamp duty and petroleum revenue tax. (Similar functions in the USA are carried out by the *Internal Revenue Service* (IRS).) In the UK ►value added tax, ►excise duty and other taxes including customs duties (►tariffs) are the responsibility of another department, HM Customs and Excise. ►►taxation.

innocent capacity ►reinsurance activity undertaken by an obscure or newly established operator, neither familiar with nor expert in the workings of the market. Used chiefly in respect of the new operators drawn into the reinsurance market in the late 1970s and early 1980s in response to overcapacity in the ►direct business market.

INRA International Natural Rubber Agreement. ►International Natural Rubber Organization.

INRO ►International Natural Rubber Organization.

insider dealing The buying and selling of ►shares while in possession of price-sensitive information obtained unlawfully, e.g. through employment in the company whose shares are being dealt with (US = *insider trading*). Insider dealing is illegal in the UK, the USA, France and other countries.

insider trading ►insider dealing.

insolvency ►bankruptcy.

instalment credit ►hire purchase.

Instinet An electronic broking service for ►equities with direct access via membership of the London, Paris, Stockholm and Frankfurt exchanges. Owned by ►Reuters.

Institute for Fiscal Studies (IFS) (UK) An organization set up in 1969 to conduct research in, and publish papers on, taxation and related issues. Best known to the general public for its 'Green Budget', a forecast each year of the actual UK ►budget.

Institute of Insurance Brokers (IIB) (UK) An association of independent insurance brokers founded in 1987. Primarily owing to the efforts of the IIB the ►Insurance Brokers Registrations Council (IBRC) was made a Recognized Professional Body (RPB) under the ►Financial Services Act (FSA), thus saving broker members of the IBRC from the need for dual registration with, and regulation by, the Securities and Investment Board under the FSA and the IBRC. Thenceforward registration with, and regulation by, the IBRC alone was necessary. Membership of the IIB is some 1,400 insurance broking practices in the UK, representing over £4bn general insurance premium income.

Institute of London Underwriters (ILU) Founded in 1884, and with an international membership (confined, however, to those underwriting (►underwriting) in the London market), the ILU is responsible for the standard clauses in marine and air cargo insurance; it services ►Lloyd's of London and non-Lloyd's marine committees, and it is a forum for professional discussion. Total membership stands at 55.

institutional investor An organization, as opposed to an individual, that invests funds arising from its receipts from the sale of ➤securities, from ➤deposits and from other sources; i.e. ➤insurance companies, ➤investment trusts, ➤unit trusts, ➤pensions funds and trustees (➤trust). Institutional investors probably own over 70% of the ➤shares of quoted UK companies.

instrument A term used to denote any form of financing medium, most usually those for the purpose of borrowing in the ➤money market, e.g. ➤bills of exchange, ➤bonds, ➤certificates of deposit, ➤Treasury bills and *promissory notes* (➤notes). Normally used to denote the document itself. ➤Financial instruments are acquired, or bought, by payment to the existing owner of the ➤face value of the instrument, normally less a ➤discount. By the same token, the owner transferring the instrument is the seller. On original sale, or ➤issue, the instrument is a means of raising a loan and thus of acquiring an ➤asset. The term also applies to ➤derivatives.

insurable interest A legal term referring to the value in the subject of ➤insurance directly attributable to the ➤insured; such value must normally exist both at the time of contracting the insurance and at the time of any ➤claim, if the contract is to be valid.

insurance A method of compensation for financial loss in the case of death, illness, injury, accident, theft, destruction or damage through fire and other hazards, claims for negligence or incompetence, and other eventualities. The method is the creation of a fund out of payments, or ➤premiums, by those exposed to the risk, out of which compensation is paid to those to whom the eventuality actually occurs. By the ➤law of large numbers, the total of the premiums collected can be made to equal at least the total compensation paid out.

Insurance business is broadly divided between *general insurance* and *life insurance* (or life *assurance*, as it is often deemed to be more properly termed). Life assurance consists in provision for compensation against an inevitable occurrence, that of death, and in this respect differs from other insurance, which offers compensation against an eventuality that may or may not occur. Life assurance thus relies heavily on ➤actuaries' computation of ➤mortality. Deaths from accident and other non-natural causes of course occur, but this category constitutes so small a fraction of all deaths, and also can be so reduced by exclusion of people engaged in hazardous activities, that calculation of appropriate premiums by actuarial methods can be most precise.

Central to the financing of insurance is the investment of the fund generated by premiums. Insurance companies constitute one of the biggest ➤portfolio holders on the ➤stock exchange. The practice of general insurance dates back to earliest times. Life assurance did not take on its modern proportions until the theory of probability had been developed and combined with the principle of compound interest, in the early 18th century. General insurance contracts or policies are normally for a risk of a specified monetary value and for a specified period of time. Life assurance policies are for a specified monetary amount and are necessarily indeterminate in time; however, life policies may also be taken out for a specified period of years, in which case they are known as term policies. ►Financial Services Act; general insurance; life assurance; reinsurance.

Insurance Accounts Directive A directive of the EU adopted by the Council of the ►European Union requiring consistent presentation of insurance company accounts in the Union.

Insurance Brokers' Registration Council (IBRC) (UK) A body created by the Insurance Brokers Registration Act 1977 to regulate the insurance broking industry. Only those admitted to registration under the IBRC are allowed to call themselves 'insurance broker'. Requirements for registration include possession of a recognized qualification (associate or fellow of the ►Chartered Insurance Institute), relevant employment for a stipulated period, and suitable work experience. The IBRC operates a code of conduct to which all registered members are subject. ►►Institute of Insurance Brokers (IIB).

insurance premium tax (UK) A tax of 3% on premiums for general insurance policies (i.e. including household and motor insurance but not life insurance, reinsurance, ships, aircraft or other commercial policies), introduced with effect from 1 October 1994. The rate was increased to 4% by the budget of November 1996.

insured The short term used to refer to the party to benefit under an ►insurance contract.

insurer An entity, either a company or a ►mutual society, engaged in the business of insurance.

intangible asset ►asset.

integrated data feeds An ►on-line information system in which several services, e.g. NASDAQ (►National Association of Securities Dealers Automated Quotation System) and ►Reuters, are available on one screen.

Inter-Africa Coffee Organization An association of 25 African coffee-producing countries, responsible for approximately one-fifth (some 1m tonnes) of world output, formed after the suspension in 1989 of the stabilization measures incorporated in the International Coffee Agreements (►International Coffee Organization). In 1993 the organization, along with Latin American growers, reached an agreement to withhold 20% of output until a target price was attained.

inter-dealer broker (IDB) (UK) A ►broker who buys and sells ►gilts only from and to ►market makers.

inter vivos Between living persons.

interbank market The ►money market in which banks (►banking) borrow or lend money among themselves either to accommodate short-term ►liquidity problems or for the lending on of surplus funds. These loans may be arranged either direct or through ►money brokers. ►London interbank offered rate (LIBOR).

Intercomalum An organization set up to promote and defend the aluminium industry of the former states of the Soviet Union. In 1993 a first contact with the then European Community (►European Union) arose out of a demand by European producers for strict quotas on imports from the states in question. ►►London Metal Exchange.

interest 1. Payment for a ►loan. ►►rate of interest. **2**. A share in ownership; e.g. company A may have an interest (own ►shares in) company B.

interest-bearing eligible liabilities (IBELs) That proportion of commercial bank deposits defined as ►eligible liabilities that carry a rate of interest.

interest cover The number of times the interest payments made by a company to service its ►loan capital are exceeded by the income of the business.

interest equalization tax (IET) (US) A tax introduced in 1963, with the effect of raising the cost to US citizens of investing in issues by foreigners on the domestic US capital market, US market interest ratios being at that time lower than in most foreign markets. The tax, introduced for the purpose of defending the US balance of payments, duly discouraged foreign borrowers and also encouraged US borrowers to resort to foreign capital markets. The IET is generally regarded as one of the contributory factors leading to the emergence of the ►Eurodollar market. It was withdrawn in 1974.

interest rate ►rate of interest.

interest rate future A form of ►financial future in which the contract is in respect of the interest rate on the underlying ►asset.

interest rate margin 1. The difference between a bank's lending and deposit interests. **2**. The difference between the interest rate paid on a debt security and a reference interest rate. Most commonly used in the ►Euromarket for ►floating rate notes (►note issuance facility). Also termed ►spread. The reference rate is invariably the ►London interbank offered rate (LIBOR) and also the *London interbank bid rate* (LIBID) and ►LIMEAN (London interbank mean rate).

interest rate option ►option.

interest rate swap A transaction under which two streams of interest rate payments are exchanged. The object is to enable a lower-class borrower to benefit from the better interest rate available to a higher-class borrower; the latter takes a small profit on the transaction. Interest rate swaps quickly came to be traded as ►negotiable instruments in their own right, the ►principal not in fact changing hands, and this trade now forms the bulk of the market. Dealing is done chiefly by banks and securities houses. Trade in interest rate swaps began in 1982, and the market grew rapidly thereafter. By the end of 1985 some $200bn of swaps were reckoned to be outstanding. Standardized terms were introduced in 1985 by the International Swap Dealers' Association and the British Bankers' Association. In 1985 the asset-based swap was introduced, i.e. a swap of the interest on an ►asset, rather than a ►liability of the party concerned, namely the swap of an interest stream due to the party, rather than the stream payable by that party. ►►cross-currency interest rate swap; currency interest rate swap; swap.

interest sensitive Economic and financial activities strongly influenced by movements in interest rates, e.g. house buying, hire purchasing, corporate borrowing.

interest yield ►yield.

Intergovernmental Conference (IGC) A conference of the ►European Union member governments called for the purpose of making changes in the ►Treaty of Rome. An IGC was convened for the adoption of the ►Maastricht Treaty and for its successor, the ►Amsterdam Treaty.

interim dividend A ►dividend paid during the year instead of at the end of the year. Some large companies pay dividends quarterly.

interim financial statement A summary financial statement issued part-way through a ►financial year.

intermarket spread swap A ►swap of securities made in the expectation of a change in the ►spread between the ►yields of the securities.

Intermarket Trading System (ITS) ►National Market System.

intermediary A person or firm, other than the insurance company itself, engaged in the selling of insurance; e.g. an agent, an insurance ►broker, a bank, an accountant, a solicitor, a financial adviser or an estate agent. ►financial intermediary.

intermediate offer A ►new issue of ►shares in which shares are placed with financial ►intermediaries (►placing). Private investors may apply for these shares through a ►stockbroker. ►offer for sale.

intermediation ►disintermediation.

internal rate of return ►discounted cash flow.

internal repurchase agreement pool (US) The total of short-term investment balances, arising out of ►repurchase agreements, held by the ►Federal Reserve in the name of foreign ►central banks and international organizations.

Internal Revenue Service (IRS) (US) ➤Inland Revenue.

internal Rp pool ➤internal repurchase agreement pool.

international accounting standards (IAS) Rules for the preparation of company accounts. Developed by the ➤International Accounting Standards Committee, the IAS conform to the Fourth and Seventh EU Company Law Directives (➤Fourth Directive).

International Accounting Standards Committee (IASC) A London-based body working to reach agreement on world-wide ➤accounting standards. Publishes *International Accounting Standards*. The Committee works with accounting brokers in all the major countries and its standards have been adopted by the ➤London Stock Exchange but not as yet by the regulatory authorities in Canada, Japan and the US.

International Bank for Reconstruction and Development (IBRD; World Bank) Founded, together with the ➤International Monetary Fund, by the ➤Bretton Woods Conference of 1944 as an international bank to finance the reconstruction and development of member countries. Operations started in 1946. The bank is financed partly by contributions paid by member countries, partly by bond issues. The national contributions constitute the bank's capital and relate to the individual countries' share of world trade. The bond issues finance the lending operations of the bank. Operational revenues have come to be supplemented over the course of time by receipts of interest on, and repayment of the capital of, loans. In financing the economic needs of member countries, the IBRD complements the IMF, which finances temporary balance of payments difficulties. Loans are made to governments or government-guaranteed entities. At first devoted to the reconstruction needs of industrial countries, the World Bank by the 1950s had focused its attention on the developing world.

In 1956 the IBRD formed the *International Finance Corporation* (IFC), the purpose of which was to promote growth in the private sector of ➤developing countries and to mobilize domestic and foreign capital for this purpose. In 1960 the IBRD formed the *International Development Association* (IDA) in order to assist the poorer developing countries. The IBRD's strategy since the 1960s has been to ensure that its aid reaches the broad masses of the people; this to be done by investments encouraging productivity and integrating the broad masses of the people as active partners into the development process. In 1995, the bank had an authorized capital of $184bn. In 1995, there were 179 member countries and gross disbursements of the bank were $12.7bn.

International Cocoa Agreement A series of intergovernmental agreements for the stabilization of the world cocoa market. The most recent, signed in September 1993 under the auspices of the United Nations, and replacing that of 1986, relies on production limits and consumption promotion measures; it is said to be the first

United Nations commodity pact to make production management its cornerstone. A production committee has the task of fixing 'indicative figures for annual levels of global production necessary to achieve and maintain equilibrium' in the cocoa market. A consumption committee seeks action by signatories 'to remove or reduce substantially' domestic taxes and import tariffs that deter consumption. The 40 signatories, both producing and consuming countries, account for three-quarters of world output and consumption. However, Malaysia, accounting for 10% of world production, and the USA, accounting for 25% of world use, did not sign.

International Coffee Council ➤International Coffee Organization.

International Coffee Organization An intergovernmental body established to administer a series of International Coffee Agreements, the first of which was negotiated in 1962 under the auspices of the United Nations and the remainder of which were negotiated at the headquarters of the organization in London. The latest of these, dating from 1983, has been successively extended to September 1994. The agreements for some time provided for stabilization of the market through production quotas, import controls, stock verification and a fund for the promotion of consumption. In 1973 these market stabilization measures were suspended, to be partly reinstated in 1976 and fully reinstated in 1983. However, in 1989 the measures were again withdrawn, not subsequently to be revived. The organization continues with its efforts, in force since the beginning, to further international co-operation between coffee-exporting and -importing countries in order to achieve a reasonable balance between supply and demand that will ensure adequate supplies of coffee at fair prices to consumers and at remunerative prices to producers; and to act as a centre for studies and research on the production, distribution and consumption of coffee. There are 67 member governments: 47 from exporting countries accounting for over 97% of world production, the remainder from importing countries accounting for over 80% of world consumption. The organization consists of a council, an executive board and an executive director with appropriate staff.

International Commercial Exchange (US) The pioneer in ➤financial futures, having first traded in these in 1970.

International Commodities Clearing House (ICCH) (UK) The major ➤clearing house for ➤futures dealings in the London ➤commodity market in most ➤soft commodities (except wheat and barley) and most metals, and also for ➤options in certain soft commodities. First began operating in 1888, as the London Produce Clearing House, changing to its present functions and name in 1973. All members of the ICCH are members of the individual exchanges, and all transactions in the latter must be conducted through a member of the ICCH.

international commodity agreement An international agreement, normally concluded between governments, intended to influence the price of a ►commodity. The need for such price influence is seen to lie in the fact that commodities, particularly ►primary commodities, have in many cases long production cycles, responding poorly to demand fluctuations and thus causing price volatility, and that earnings on commodity sales constitute a major proportion of the export revenues of developing countries. Commodity agreements have been concluded in respect of, among other things, coffee, sugar, wheat, tin, cocoa, natural rubber and textiles. Agreements are normally implemented through ►buffer stocks, production controls and purchase guarantees.

International Development Association (IDA) ►International Bank for Reconstruction and Development.

International Federation of Insurance Intermediaries (BIPAR) A body composed of 47 national ►broker associations established in 1996 and based in Brussels. BIPAR co-ordinates member views on common interests and collects statistics on market trends in member countries.

International Finance Corporation (IFC) ►International Bank for Reconstruction and Development.

International Grains Council (IGC) An intergovernmental consultative body assisting governments in the implementation of the International Grains Agreement (IGA) for fair and stable conditions in the world market for wheat and coarse grains and their products; and in the implementation of the Food Aid Convention (FAC) ensuring minimum annual aid, in the form of grains, to developing countries. Membership of the IGC comprises grain exporting and importing countries and totals 8 exporters, plus members of the ►European Union, and 20 importers, plus members of the Russian Federation.

The IGC, IGA and FAC are the most recent in a long history of similar agreements and institutions, dating back essentially to the International Wheat Agreement of 1934, the International Wheat Council established in 1942 and the Food Aid Convention of 1967.

international liquidity ►liquidity.

International Monetary Fund (IMF) Established by the ►Bretton Woods Conference in 1947, the purpose of the International Monetary Fund is to foster international monetary co-operation through the stabilization of exchange rates, the removal of ►foreign exchange restrictions and the facilitation of international payments and of *international* ►liquidity. At the outset member nations declared their ►exchange rates, or ►par values, to which, within a margin of 1% in either direction, they held their currencies. The par values were quoted in terms of the US dollar, which was itself valued in terms of ►gold. However, following the breaking of the dollar's link with gold in 1971 and the abandonment of national fixed parities from 1972 onwards, the IMF rule was abolished in 1976.

The major function of the IMF has been lending in support of countries in ►balance of payments difficulties. For this purpose the IMF has been funded by contributions, or ►quotas, from member countries. Countries in difficulties obtain foreign currencies in exchange for their own, which they must repay within three to five years. Members in severe balance of payments difficulties are obliged to consult with the IMF on remedial domestic policies, as a condition of further assistance. The funds of the IMF have been progressively increased over the years. A major increase occurred in 1962 under the *General Arrangements to Borrow* (GAB). A further large increase occurred through the creation, in 1970, of ►special drawing rights (SDRs).

In 1976 the use of gold as a constituent of the IMF's funds and as a ►unit of account was discontinued, and the IMF was authorized to sell its gold holdings. The IMF seeks the removal of restrictions on international monetary movements and publishes an annual record of these restrictions.

international monetary market ►Chicago Mercantile Exchange.

International Natural Rubber Agreement ►International Natural Rubber Organization.

International Natural Rubber Organization (INRO) An intergovernmental organization comprising six producer and 10 consumer members (the European Union being counted as one consumer country), based in Kuala Lumpur and formed to administer the International Natural Rubber Agreements. The object of the agreements has been to provide market stability, ensuring fair prices for both consumers and producers in the face of wide fluctuations in demand. This has been achieved by counter-cyclical buying and selling into and from a central buffer stock. Total natural rubber output and consumption in 1992 were some 5.6m tonnes, comparing with consumption of synthetic rubber of some 9m tonnes.

International Organization of Securities Commissions (IOSC) An association of the world's leading stock market regulators.

International Petroleum Exchange (IPE) (UK) A ►commodity market for petroleum; it instituted a ►futures contract for gas oil in 1981, following the dispersal of petroleum sales from the major world oil companies and following the success of a heating oil ►futures contract introduced by the ►New York Mercantile Exchange in 1958. The exchange also offers physical and futures contracts in natural gas. The IPE is a member of the ►International Commodities Clearing House.

International Primary Aluminium Institute (IPAI) An international industry association founded in 1972. The IPAI has some 36 member companies based in 24 countries, all engaged in the production of primary aluminium. The purposes of the IPAI include: the collection and publication of statistics; the study of environmental, health, energy, safety and other matters of concern to the industry;

the provision of a forum for the discussion of developments affecting the industry; and the promotion of understanding of the industry's activities and the broader use of its products.

International Securities Market Association (ISMA) A Zurich-based organization for participants in the ►Eurobond markets. Formerly the Association of International Bond Dealers (AIBD). Founded in 1969, ISMA also regulates trade in ►convertibles, medium-term ►notes and ►warrants. The association comprises 820 members from 51 countries. Its purpose is to oversee the orderly functioning of the market and to represent the interests of its members in issues affecting the market.

International Securities Regulatory Organization ►Securities Association.

International Stock Exchange ►London Stock Exchange.

International Sugar Organization A successor to the International Sugar Council of prewar origin, the International Sugar Organization is an intergovernmental body comprising 26 sugar-producing and sugar-importing member countries, established under the auspices of the United Nations Conference on Trade and Development (UNCTAD). Until 1984, under successive International Sugar Agreements, the member states sought to stabilize world sugar prices through quotas and the holding of stocks. These efforts were discontinued in 1984; the aims of the organization since then have been to 'ensure and enhance international co-operation' in world sugar matters, to 'facilitate trade by collecting and providing information on the world sugar market' and to 'encourage and increase the demand for sugar'. In particular, the organization disseminates daily information on sugar market prices.

International Swap Dealers' Association ►interest rate swaps.

International Swaps and Derivatives Association (ISDA) A global trade association, established in 1985, representing participants in the privately negotiated ►derivatives industry, i.e. the business including interest rates, currency, commodity and equity ►swaps as well as related ►caps, ►collars, ►floors and ►swaptions. Total international membership totals over 200, comprising most of the world's major institutions which deal in, or are leading end-users of, private negotiated derivatives. The association's primary purpose is to encourage the prudent and efficient development of privately negotiated derivatives business. It represents members in regulatory and legislative matters. It has produced the ISDA Master Agreement, a widely used and authoritative document for which legal backing has been obtained in a number of countries.

International Trade Organization (ITO) ►General Agreement on Tariffs and Trade (GATT).

International Union of Credit and Investment Insurers ►Berne Union.

International Wheat Agreement (IWA) ➤International Grains Council.

International Wheat Council (IWC) ➤International Grains Council.

Intersettle ➤European Association of Securities Dealers Automated Quotation System (EASDAQ).

intervention mechanism A term used to describe the methods used by the ➤European Monetary System (EMS) to maintain agreed ➤exchange rate relationships. This is done in the first place by a very ➤short-term financing ➤facility under which the central bank of a country under exchange rate pressure may borrow from other central banks for 75 days, extendable under certain conditions up to three months. Further possibilities are ➤short-term monetary support (STMS) and ➤medium-term financial assistance (MTFA).

Intex ➤Automated screen trading system software marketed by ➤Telerate.

intrinsic value 1. The value believed by some to attach inherently to a natural object, e.g. a precious metal, regardless of its price at any given time. In economics, value is determined only by demand and is denoted by price; hence intrinsic value is inapplicable. **2.** In the ➤options market, the amount by which the ➤striking price differs from the current price of the underlying asset; i.e. in a *call option* the intrinsic value is an amount in excess of the current price; in a *put option* it is an amount below that price. ➤time value.

introduction (UK) A means of initial entry to a stock market for companies whose shares are already widely held but, until the introduction is effected, are not quoted or listed. ➤offer for sale; placing.

inventories A term for stocks of raw materials, work in progress and finished goods.

investment 1. The act of placing monetary resources into the creation of ➤assets, in the manufacturing and services sectors of the economy. Only real *capital formation*, such as the production of machinery, adds to the stock of investment goods. **2.** The act of placing monetary resources into financial assets, namely the purchase of ➤shares or ➤bonds. Shifting money from a bank account to ➤securities in this way simply moves ➤savings from one form to another. **3.** The sum of money itself so invested, or the total of financial assets so acquired.

investment allowances, investment incentives Government assistance designed to encourage firms to invest in physical ➤assets in total, in particular industries or in particular locations. Incentives may take the form of ➤capital allowances for tax relief, cash payments or low interest rates.

investment analyst Someone who studies companies and financial ➤securities and makes recommendations to buy and sell ➤shares and other securities. Analysts work not only in investment banks and stockbroking firms (the *sell-side*), but also in the financial institutions such as pension funds (the *buy-side*), which own the majority of stocks and shares. ➤investment approaches.

investment appraisal ➤discounted cash flow.

investment approaches The approaches of investors, i.e. *asset allocation*, to the selection of ➤stocks and ➤shares in a portfolio, are referred to by a number of terms. *Bottom-up* refers to the selection of companies considered promising according to various criteria (e.g. ➤PEG), but without much regard to geographical or sectoral origin. *Top-down* refers to the selection of countries and industries which are believed to offer good prospects. A portfolio manager is said to be *underweight* or *overweight* in a stock or a market if the share of the ➤market capitalization of the stock or market in his portfolio is less or more than its share in total market capitalization. In practice, of course, both these approaches are generally used, but one may be emphasized over the other. *Contrarian* refers to the practice of buying shares when their prices have fallen to lows by historical standards, while *momentum investing* involves buying shares whose prices are rising. *Value investing* is an approach in which shares are sought whose price is below ➤net asset value or where there are unexploited or undervalued assets. ➤cyclical stocks; efficient market hypothesis; pound cost averaging; technical analysis.

investment balances ➤money supply.

investment bank (US) A ➤financial intermediary that purchases new issues and places them in smaller parcels among investors. In the UK, a ➤merchant bank or ➤issuing house.

investment credit (US) A ➤tax credit equivalent to 10% of the purchase price of investment goods by businesses. Intended to encourage investment in fixed ➤assets, the investment credit was abolished in the ➤Tax Reform Act 1986. (UK = ➤capital allowances.)

investment currency pool (UK) ➤dollar pool.

investment grade ➤Standard and Poor's ratings.

Investment Managers' Regulatory Organization ➤Financial Services Act.

investment multiplier ➤multiplier.

Investment Services Directive (ISD) ➤Banking Directives.

investment trust A company whose sole object is to invest its ➤capital in a wide range of ➤securities, i.e. a ➤closed-end fund. An investment trust issues shares and uses its capital to buy securities and ➤shares in other companies. A ➤unit trust, in contrast, issues units that represent holdings of shares. Unit holders thus do not share in the ➤profits of the company managing the trust. Investment trusts can also raise part of their capital by issuing fixed-interest securities, and the yield on the ►ordinary shares of the trust can thus benefit from ►gearing. The trust deed (►trust) may provide for the holdings of the investment trust to be sold at a certain date (for which there may be provisions for extension) and the proceeds distributed to shareholders; this is an investment trust with a limited life. In some investment trusts with a limited life there are two types of shares: *income shares* and *capital shares*. Holders of income shares receive all or most of the income from the ►assets of the trust, while holders of capital shares receive all or most of the capital value of the assets of the trust on ►liquidation. Such trusts are known as *split-level trusts* and allow shareholders to choose to receive their returns in the form of income or ►capital gains. Stepped ►preference shares in split-level trusts offer a predetermined growth in both capital and income. The price of a share in an investment trust may be above (►premium) or below (►discount) the value of the underlying shares and other assets, i.e. the ►net asset value per share.

investor base The expected category of buyers of a ►security issue. Normally used in relation to ►short-term issues in the international market.

Investors Compensation Scheme (UK) Provides for payment of up to £48,000 to private investors if a firm authorized under the ►Financial Services Act goes into ►default.

invisible balance ►balance of payments.

IOSC ►International Organization of Securities Commissions.

IPAI ►International Primary Aluminium Institute.

IPC Index *Indice de Precios y Cotizaciones.* ►Mexican Stock Exchange.

IPE ►International Petroleum Exchange.

IPO ►initial public offering.

IRA ►individual retirement account.

IRR Internal rate of return. ►discounted cash flow.

irredeemable security ►redemption date.

irrevocable letter of credit ►letter of credit.

IRS (US) Internal Revenue Service. ►Inland Revenue.

ISA ►individual savings account.

ISDA ►International Swaps and Derivatives Association.

ISE International Stock Exchange. ►London Stock Exchange.

ISE Composite Index ►Istanbul Menkul Kiymetter Borsasi.

ISE/Nikkei 50 Index A ►share index based on the prices of 50 Japanese ►equities traded both on the International Stock Exchange (►London Stock Exchange) and on the ►Tokyo Stock Exchange. The index reflects prices of the shares during the trading hours in Tokyo and London and is given on TOPIC (►Teletext Output of Price Information by Computer). ►►Nikkei Stock Average.

ISMA ►International Securities Market Association.

ISRO ►Securities Association.

issue Initial sale of a ►security.

issue date The base date for calculating ►interest accrued on a ►security.

issue price The price, gross of any commissions, for any issue of ►securities, i.e. the price at which a ►new issue is offered.

issued capital The part of a company's ►capital that has been subscribed by shareholders. It may or may not be paid up (►paid-up capital).

issuing house (UK) A ►merchant bank, ►stockbroker or other ►financial institution that organizes a ►new issue of ►securities. The issuing house or securities house in conjunction with the issuing ►broker will advise the client on the timing and form of the issue and in return for a ►commission will ►underwrite or arrange underwriting for all or part of the issue. The issuing house is nowadays often referred to as a sponsor because it lends its reputation to the issue.

Istanbul Menkul Kiymetter Borsasi The ►stock exchange in Turkey, in its present form dating only from 1986. The principal ►share index is the ►ISE Composite Index.

itayose (Jap.) A method of ►stock exchange dealing under which all orders entering prior to the official start of business are treated as having arrived at the same time.

ITO International Trade Organization. ►General Agreement on Tariffs and Trade (GATT).

ITS Intermarket Trading System. ►National Market System.

IWA ►International Wheat Agreement.

IWC ►International Wheat Council.

J

Jahresabschluss (Ger.) **1**. Year end. **2**. Annual account.

Jahresbericht (Ger.) Annual report.

Jahrgang (Ger.) A year; the period of a year.

Jakarta Stock Exchange In its present form dates from 1977 but has its origins dating back to the Dutch colonial era. Regulated (➤regulation) by the Capital Market Executive Agency (BAPEPAM).

JASDAQ (Jap.) The Japanese equivalent of the US ➤National Association of Securities Dealers Automated Quotation System (NASDAQ).

JGB Japanese Government Bond.

jikihone **bill** (Jap.) An ➤acceptance under which an importer uses the yen counterpart of the ➤foreign currency value of an import invoice.

Jingen Index ➤China.

jobber (UK) A dealer in ➤securities who will buy and sell specific securities at all times, a ➤market maker. Prior to the ➤Big Bang, jobbers were one of two distinct classes of members of the ➤London Stock Exchange who were permitted to deal only with ➤brokers and not with the general public. The term is now obsolete.

jobber's turn ➤spread.

Johannesburg Stock Exchange (JSE) Established in 1886, the JSE is the only sizeable ➤stock exchange in Africa. There are exchanges in Kenya, Nigeria and Zimbabwe, but the development of all these markets has been restricted until recently by ➤exchange controls as well as by the relatively small size of the modern sectors of their economies.

joint and several liability A ➤liability that falls at the same time on each one of two or more parties, and on all together. A plaintiff can choose to sue one or more of the parties (severally), or all together (jointly).

joint-stock bank ➤commercial banks.

jouissance (Fr.) The date of the start of ➤interest payments.

jour de règlement (Fr.) ➤Settlement day.

JSE ➤Johannesburg Stock Exchange.

JSE/Actuaries Index ➤Share index for the ➤Johannesburg Stock Exchange.

junior debt ➤subordinated.

junk bond (US) Company bonds of low-quality ➤security backing sold with high ➤coupons, rated below investment grade by the two US rating agencies, ➤Standard and Poor's and Moody's, and giving a ➤yield of at least 200 to 250 ➤basis points above the yield on Treasury bonds. Junk bonds were pioneered in the mid-1970s by the New York house Drexel Burnham Lambert, and total issues in 1986 were estimated to amount to $32.4bn. However, this was a revival of a market dating back to at least the 1920s. ➤leveraged buy-out. Junk bonds are also known as *high-yield bonds*.

jusen (Jap.) A housing loan company.

K

kabushiki kaisha (Jap.) A joint-stock (►stock) company.

Kaffirs Shares in South African ►gold mining companies quoted on the London ►stock exchange.

kaishime (Jap.) ►Ramping.

kamikaze pricing (Jap.) Deliberate low pricing of ►securities in order to secure a greater share of the securities market.

Kansas City Board of Trade A ►commodity market for grain, sharing with those in Chicago and Minneapolis a dominant influence, through their ►futures trading, on world prices. The market was established in 1856 and began trading in wheat futures in 1876, in value line stock index futures in 1982 and in wheat options in 1984.

Kapitalanlage (Ger.) ►Investment.

Kapitalertragsteuer (Ger.) ►Withholding tax.

Kapitalgewinn (Ger.) ►Capital gain.

Kassa (Ger.) For ►cash.

Kassenobligation (Ger.) A public-sector medium-term ►note issued by government as a security at a time of government borrowing; used in Germany and Switzerland.

Kassenverein (Ger.) The German ►securities clearing house.

Keidenran (Jap.) The federation of Japanese company associations. Equivalent to the UK Confederation of British Industry, the French Patronat and the German Bundesverband der Deutschen Industrien.

keiretsu (Jap.) A Japanese company group formed by interlocking shareholdings. *Keiretsu* normally contain a bank. They differ from *zaibatsu* in that the bank is not the group holding company, legislation having reduced a bank's permitted shareholding in a company to 5%.

Keogh plan (US) A pension plan (►pensions) under which contributions by unincorporated businesses or self-employed people are tax-deductible, and appreciation in the fund is tax free, but withdrawals are taxed as income. Originally established by the Self-Employment Individuals Retirement Act 1982.

kerb trading (UK) Trading that occurs after the close of the official market. In the USA the ►American Stock Exchange is sometimes referred to as the Curb Exchange.

key pad A small keyboard used to enter data into a computer.

keyman insurance Insurance providing compensation for the loss to a business caused by the death or disability of key personnel.

***kingaishin* fund** (Jap.) Funds, part of the ►*tokkin* fund system, placed with ►trust banks.

KIO ►Kuwait Investment Office.

KISS Kurs Information Service System. ►Deutsche Aktienindex.

KLCE ►Kuala Lumpur Commodity Exchange.

KLOFFE ►Kuala Lumpur Options & Financial Futures Exchange.

KLSE ►Kuala Lumpur Stock Exchange.

knock-for-knock A practice whereby motor insurers agree, in the event of an accident, each to repair their own insured vehicles, so saving administrative and possibly legal expense. The insured's no-claim bonus is normally not affected.

knock-out An ►option which is automatically terminated whenever the price of the underlying ►asset reaches a predetermined level.

koko (Jap.) A public corporation engaged in the financing of a particular economic sector, e.g. housing. Funds derive from the Industrial Investment Special Account and from borrowing from the Trust Fund Bureau and from the Post Office life insurance and annuity accounts.

Kommunalobligation (Ger.) A loan to local authorities by a ►*Hypothekenbank*.

Kontrahent (Ger.) A contracting party.

Konzern (Ger.) A German company grouping of considerable size, the nucleus of which is a holding company having outright ownership, or a majority shareholding, of the remaining members of the group. Featured largely in German industry before the Second World War, subsequent legislation having disbanded many groups in pursuit of decartelization policy.

Korea Stock Exchange (KSE) Established in its present form in Seoul in 1956, with antecedents back to 1911. It is one of the largest and most modern ►stock exchanges in the Far East, recently second only to the Japanese and Hong Kong exchanges in ►equity market ►capitalization. Share indices include the *Korea Composite Stock Price Index* (KOSPI).

koruna The national ►currency unit of the Czech Republic.

KOSPI ►Korea Stock Exchange.

krona The national ►currency unit of Sweden.

Kruggerand A ►gold coin minted in South Africa for investment purposes.

KSE 100 The main share index of the Karachi Stock Exchange, the principal ►stock exchange of Pakistan.

Kuala Lumpur Commodity Exchange (KLCE) A ►commodity market set up in 1980 for trade in rubber and crude palm oil. A major world market for ►hedging in RSS 1 (Ribbed Smoked Sheet No. 1) quality, a long-established grade of natural rubber.

Kuala Lumpur Options & Financial Futures Exchange (KLOFFE) The Malaysian ►derivatives exchange. Trades are in a variety of instruments, including stock index ►options, stock index ►futures and individual stock options. Trades are screen-based in an open-market auction system. There are two classes of members: trading members – companies, trading both for themselves and for clients; local members – individuals, trading only on their own behalf. The exchange is regulated by the Ministry of Finance and the Securities Commission.

Kuala Lumpur Stock Exchange (KLSE) Dates from 1973 with the ending of the joint ►stock exchange of Malaysia and Singapore, which had been established in 1964. There is also an ►unlisted securities market.

Kuala Lumpur Tin Market A ►commodity market set up in 1984, dealing only in ►physical transactions in tin.

Kuponsteuer (Ger.) A tax on interest receipts of foreign holders of German ►bonds.

Kurs (Ger.) The official ►stock exchange price of a ►security.

Kurs Information Service System ►Deutsche Aktienindex.

Kursmakler (Ger.) An official ►broker in the German ►stock market, acting as intermediary between banks, admitted to deal on the exchange, but not acting for members of the public; also responsible for fixing prices.

kurzfristig (Ger.) ►Short term.

Kuwait Investment Office (KIO) A state-owned Kuwaiti company based in London carrying on substantial international investment.

L

ladder option An ►option during the life of which the holder can incorporate gains in the underlying security price. Also known as a *step-lock option*.

lagged reserve requirement (LRR) (US) A system in which banks are required to hold reserves with retrospective effect, i.e. in relation to the level of deposits in a recent past period. The maintenance period, normally of one week, is usually in respect of the preceding two weeks.

lakh (Indian) The Indian term for 100,000 rupees.

LAN ►local area network.

Land, Länder (Ger.) The eight major territorial subdivisions, or states, into which West Germany was divided after the Second World War, having wide powers of self-government and conforming closely to the pre-1914 principalities, kingdoms and city-states. On German reunification in 1990, the five *Länder* of former East Germany were added. To these must be added the self-governing 'city-states' of Berlin, Bremen and Hamburg.

Landesbank (Ger.) A regional bank providing services to ►savings banks including foreign exchange business, ►giro (hence the full name *Landesbanken/Girozentralen*) and the investment of surplus funds. The *Landesbanken* were originally the house banks for the formerly independent German states (or *Länder*) but now increasingly compete with the ►commercial banks.

Landeszentralbanken (Ger.) ►Bundesbank.

langfristig (Ger.) ►Long term.

LAPR ►Life assurance premium relief. ►►unit-linked life assurance.

last trading day The last day on which ►futures trading can be done for a particular ►delivery month. After that day physical delivery is mandatory.

laundering The conversion of money obtained illegally (e.g. from drugs) into apparently legitimate bank accounts or businesses. There are now elaborate regulations obliging banks to determine the origin of funds deposited with them.

LAUTRO Life Assurance and Unit Trust Regulatory Organization. ►Financial Services Act.

law of large numbers The mathematical law that states that the larger the number of times that several possible outcomes occur, the greater the likelihood that the frequency of occurrence of each particular outcome will coincide with the average frequency that can be established by theoretical calculation. Used in the calculation of ➤risk in insurance.

LBMA ➤London Bullion Market Association.

LBO ➤leveraged buy-out.

LDP ➤London daily prices.

lead manager A ➤bank, ➤venture capital company or other financial institution which co-ordinates a *syndicated loan* or the underwriting (➤underwrite) of ➤securities. The institutions share in the provision of funds for a syndicated loan, but the lead manager does much of the work and receives a larger fee than the others. Once completed, syndicated loans or ➤new issues are announced for the record in the press. The advertisement is called a *tombstone.* ➤➤syndication.

leaning into the wind (US) An expression used to describe the policy of the ➤Federal Reserve, practised particularly in the 1950s and 1960s, of lowering interest rates at times of low economic demand and raising them at times of high demand.

lease-back A contractual arrangement in which an ➤asset is sold and immediately leased back (➤leasing) to the seller. It is a means of raising ➤finance from an institution such as an insurance company and then renting it back on a long lease.

leasing An agreement between the owner of property (lessor) to grant use of it to another party (lessee) for a specified period at a specified rent. Leasing of business equipment, for example, may have tax advantages because the leasing company may receive tax relief on ➤depreciation or ➤investment allowances that it can pass on to the lessee. Leasing may in effect be a form of ➤hire purchase, because ownership of the ➤asset may be transferred to the lessee for a small sum at the end of the lease, and the distinction between the two becomes blurred. Leasing is also a form of ➤off-balance-sheet finance.

legal person ➤incorporation.

legal tender That which must be accepted in legal settlement of a money ➤debt. In Britain, pound notes or coins are legal tender up to any amount but there are limitations on the use of smaller denominations.

légume (Fr.) An edible vegetable ➤commodity (e.g. peas and beans).

lender of last resort An institution, normally a ➤central bank, that stands ready to lend to the commercial banking system when the latter is in overall shortage of funds. The latter position will arise when extra large payments out of the banking system, such as seasonal tax payments (e.g. periodic ➤corporation tax payments by companies), reduce the banking system's holdings below the level appropriate to its ➤reserves. The central bank will, in such cases, lend at short term to the banking system until such time as funds return through normal depositors. Lenders of last resort in the USA and the UK are the ➤Federal Reserve and the ➤Bank of England respectively. The Federal Reserve normally lends through ➤repurchase agreements. As part of its function as a regulator of ➤credit and ➤money supply a central bank will, on occasion, induce a shortage in the commercial banking system so as to force the system into resort to it ('into the bank') and to require commercial banks to borrow from it at high rates of interest, so bringing about a general rise of interest rates and discouraging subsequent lending.

letter of credit A non-negotiable (➤negotiable) order from a bank to a bank abroad, authorizing payment to a named person of a particular sum of money or up to a limit of a certain sum. Letters of credit are often required by exporters who wish to have proof that they will be paid before they ship goods, or who wish to minimize delay in payment for the goods. A confirmed letter of credit is one that has been recognized by the paying bank. Letters of credit may be irrevocable or revocable, depending on whether or not they can be cancelled at any time.

leverage (US) See ➤gearing.

leveraged buy-out (US) The acquisition of one company by another, financed mainly by bank loans and ➤bonds. ➤Corporate raiders in the USA launched ➤take-overs using ➤junk bonds and bank loans on many occasions in the 1980s.

levy A duty applied to imports into the ➤European Union of agricultural produce from third countries, the effect of which is to raise the price of such produce to a level consistent with that of prices of the same product sold within the Union.

LIA ➤Life Insurance Association.

liability 1. An obligation to make a financial payment, namely repayment of a bank loan, redemption of *loan stock* (➤stock), payment of a ➤commercial bill, payment of a business invoice. It may be either direct or implicit, i.e. the implicit obligation of a bank to repay the ➤deposits held with it. The liabilities of a company include its ➤bank loans and ➤overdraft, its short-term ➤debts for goods and services received (*current liabilities*) and its ➤loan capital and the ➤capital subscribed by ➤shareholders. Antithesis of ➤asset. Most frequently used in ➤money markets, ➤banking and business accounting. **2.** Of insurance, the insurance of the risk of claims in respect of misjudgment and incompetence to which employers and the professions (e.g. doctors and accountants) are exposed. The term also used to denote such exposure.

liability management The management of the ➤liability side of a bank's balance sheet i.e. of its ►deposits. The term denotes efforts by a bank to overcome liquidity shortages by increasing the total of its deposits, rather than by reducing its loans, or ►assets. Such increases are actively sought through the issue of ►instruments such as ►certificates of deposit, rather than passively awaited in the form of new conventional deposits by bank customers.

LIBID London interbank bid rate. ►London interbank offered rate.

LIBOR ►London interbank offered rate.

licensed deposit taker (LDT) A financial institution, other than a bank, authorized under the ►Banking Act 1979, and similar US legislation, to take ►deposits from the general public.

life assurance A branch of insurance in which compensation is made available to designated survivors of a deceased person, or to a person on their own survival of a fixed term of years, in return for payments, or premiums. Life assurance is based on the mathematics of probability, which determine the level of premium to be paid, and on those of compound interest, which determine the growth over time, through investment, of the fund constituted by the intake of premiums (►insurance; mortality). The two together ensure a fund adequate to provide the compensation required. Basic life assurance therefore covers the whole life of the insured person and is so named. However, life assurance may be taken out for less than the whole life and is then named *term assurance*. In this case the insured sum is paid only in the event of the insured person dying within the term.

An integral part of life assurance financing is the fund of collected premiums, invested in its turn for capital growth and income. Over the course of time insurance companies become more expert investors, and in recent decades stock market values grew strongly. The fund was thus found increasingly to'be surplus to payment needs. A further important refinement then emerged in the shape of *endowment assurance*. This is a development of term insurance in which the lump sum is payable either on death during the term, or certainly at the end of the term. A further variation of this has been endowment assurance with profits, in which the lump sum payable is raised in line with the growth in profits through the allocation to the policy of further sums, known as *bonuses*; these bonuses are declared regularly, normally annually, under the name *reversionary bonuses*. A further bonus, formally discretionary but normally declared, is determined at the end of the policy, or at the prior death of the holder. All bonuses are held as credits until death or termination of the policy. Given the certainty of an eventual lump-sum payment, endowment policies quickly lent themselves to the purchase of assets against this expectation. Thus endowment policies came to be used as a means of paying off mortgages for home buying; a later development was the concept of ►unit-linked life assurance.

Premiums are normally paid annually or at lesser intervals and are known as *regular premiums*. In some cases, particularly with unit-linked life assurance, one large premium only may be paid at the outset of the insured period; this is termed a *single premium*. In the latter case the life policy is more usually termed a ►bond.

Life Assurance and Unit Trust Regulatory Organization (LAUTRO) ►Financial Services Act.

life assurance premium relief (LAPR) A tax relief given on premiums paid for 'qualifying' life assurance policies issued in the UK up to March 1984. Policies 'qualify' by reason of conformance with certain requirements regarding size, regularity and duration of premium payments, size of final pay-out, and others. The relief was withdrawn in the 1984 Budget for all policies issued thereafter. ►life assurance; unit-linked life assurance.

Life Insurance Association (LIA) (UK) An association of life insurance intermediaries founded in 1972 and comprising some 23,000 members. Its objects are to improve professional standards, to promote knowledge and understanding of the life insurance industry and to foster good relations with government and other bodies.

lifeboat operation ►secondary bank.

LIFFE ►London International Financial Futures Exchange.

LIMEAN London interbank mean rate. The mean (►average) between ►London interbank offered rate (LIBOR) and *London interbank bid rate* (LIBID).

limit The permitted range within which prices may move, within a specified period, usually a day, in ►commodity markets.

limit order ►order.

limited company ►incorporation.

limited liability The restriction of an owner's loss in a business to the amount of ►capital that they have invested in it. Should a ►company be put into ►liquidation, the owner as ►equity shareholder can lose, at most, only the value of their shares, although director shareholders may be subject to other ►liabilities such as personal guarantees for bank borrowing.

line 1. ►line of credit. 2. A large block of shares. 3. Acceptance of an ►insurance risk by an ►underwriter, whether as an assumption of the whole of the risk or of a part.

line of credit 1. An agreed amount of loan arranged between a bank and its customer, normally to be ►drawn down in stages. ►overdraft. 2. A loan from the ►International Monetary Fund to a member country, the total amount of which is fixed, but normally available in stages.

liquid assets ➤Assets which consist of cash or other assets such as ➤Treasury bills which can be quickly turned into cash.

liquidate The act of cancelling, or closing out, a ➤futures contract where the owner of the contract is ➤long; normally done by physical sale of the underlying asset or by purchase of an offsetting contract. The term is also used, although more rarely, for ➤short positions, where the term ➤cover is more usual. ➤➤liquidation.

liquidation The termination, dissolution or winding up of a limited company (➤incorporation). Liquidation may be initiated by the shareholders or directors (voluntary liquidation) or by its creditors. If the company is solvent (➤bankruptcy) the ordinary shareholders will receive any surplus after the company's liabilities have been met.

liquidity 1. In general, availability of funds to meet claims. An economic agent is considered to have high liquidity, or to be highly liquid, if all its financial holdings, or ➤assets, are in cash; and to have low liquidity if its holdings are all in forms, such as property, commodities and long-term securities, that are difficult to convert into exact amounts of ready cash. 2. In ➤banking, liquidity refers to a commercial bank's ability to meet withdrawals of deposits, and relates to the bank's holdings of cash and short-term assets. 3. In ➤balance of payments contexts, liquidity relates to a country's ability to cover a shortfall on its overall external accounts, and refers essentially to that country's ➤reserves. International liquidity is the total of all national reserves. 4. In ➤monetary control terminology, liquidity denotes the total amount of money and very short-term financial assets in the economy. 5. In ➤securities markets, liquidity refers to the quantity of tradable ➤instruments available. The greater the number of ➤stocks at issue, the more ➤market makers there are; and the more widely held the stock, the greater the liquidity of the market in any given stock is likely to be. In a liquid market a trader can buy and sell stock without moving the price. Stocks on the ➤London Stock Exchange are classified into *liquid* and *less liquid* categories. ➤➤normal market size.

liquidity ratio 1. The proportion of the total ➤assets of a bank that are held in the form of cash (➤cash ratio) and ➤liquid assets. There is no longer a mandatory liquidity or reserve asset ratio for UK banks, although all larger banks are required to deposit 0.5% of ➤eligible liabilities with the ➤Bank of England. ➤➤capital adequacy; Federal Reserve System. 2. The ratio of liquid assets to the current ➤liabilities of a business. This is also called the cash ratio.

liquidity risk The risk in securities trading that the price of a ➤security may fluctuate excessively owing to the lack of a sufficient volume of trading in the market.

liquidity trap A monetary situation enunciated by J. M. Keynes in which ➤interest rates fall so low that only a rise can be anticipated. Since, however, any rise would only depress the price of ►bonds, the compulsion to remain in ►cash persists. At this point no increase in the ►money supply can increase people's preference for cash (liquidity preference) or therefore have any effect on incomes.

LIRMA ►London International Insurance and Reinsurance Market Association.

Lisbon Stock Exchange The principal ►stock exchange in Portugal. There is another one in Oporto. The exchanges are regulated (►regulation) by the Bank of Portugal, the ►central bank. In Portuguese the exchange is the *Bolsa de Valores de Lisboa*.

listed company A company whose ►shares are listed on an official ►stock exchange. Thus, a *quoted* company.

listed security A ►security that has been officially accepted for trading and ►quotation on a recognized ►stock exchange. The term 'listing' comes from the published list issued by the stock exchange authorities and known in the UK as the *Stock Exchange Daily Official List* (►official list).

listing ►listed security.

listing agreement ►general undertaking.

Little Board ►American Stock Exchange.

Liverpool Cotton Association (UK) A ►commodity market in cotton, set up in 1841, for many years a world centre for cotton ►physical and ►futures contracts. However, government intervention in the physical market in later years greatly impeded futures transactions. None the less 20m bales are traded annually, and some 50% of all contracts made in the rest of the world are estimated to be drawn up under Liverpool rules.

Lloyd's adviser An adviser required to be retained by a corporate member of ►Lloyd's to furnish analyses to syndicates and to negotiate the member's participation in syndicates.

Lloyd's broker ►Lloyd's.

Lloyd's Names' Associations Working Party A co-ordinating body created to promote common policies among the ►Lloyd's ►action groups.

Lloyd's An insurance institution based in London, the capital of which is provided by a large number of individual members each assuming unlimited personal liability for claims. The institution offers ►general insurance and ►reinsurance and some limited ►life assurance. Members ►underwrite an amount of ►policies in proportion to the deposit they make with the institution. Members are grouped in ►syndicates in which insurance policies are underwritten on behalf of the members by a professional underwriter. Business is accepted primarily from Lloyd's ►brokers. In 1987 there were 32,000 members, grouped into 370 syndicates, with a total ►premium income of over £3bn. As a result of severe losses incurred in 1989–91, active membership fell below 20,000, with a consequent shrinkage of available capacity from £11.5bn to £8.75bn. A programme of measures to isolate prior losses from current business, to reduce trading costs, to settle members' claims against underwriters and agents, to reduce hardship incurred by specially affected members, to attract corporate capital with limited liability, and to reorganize individual members' underwriting on a pooled basis (*Members' Agents Pooling Arrangement*) was undertaken. These measures were known collectively under the term *Reconstruction and Renewal (R & R)*. The isolation of prior losses was achieved by the creation of a major reinsurance entity known as *Equitas*. By reason partly of these measures, and partly of the stringencies imposed by losses, the number of syndicates fell to 228. However, total resources of Lloyd's, before current and future liabilities, rose from £16bn in 1988 to £24bn at the end of 1992.

Lloyd's was founded in the 18th century, taking its name from Edward Lloyd, the owner of the coffee house in which business was first conducted. It is now wholly international, deriving most of its business from abroad. ►►action group; active underwriter; allocated capacity; Association of Lloyd's Members; central fund; CentreWrite; errors and omissions; external member; funds at Lloyd's; Lloyd's adviser; Lloyd's Names' Associations Working Party; managing agent; members' agent; Newco; Old Years; overall premium limit; Premium Trust Fund; reinsurance to close; ring fence; stop loss insurance; syndicate; year of account.

LME ►London Metal Exchange.

load fund A ►mutual fund, the units in which are sold by commission brokers.

loading 1. Of insurance, that part of the premium that provides for administrative expenses, contingencies and profit. 2. Of banking, an additional charge made to the customer's account to recover the cost of additional services or account-handling difficulties. 3. Of unit trusts, the charge incorporated in prices and premiums to defray administrative expenses. 4. Of loans, the charging of interest. ►front-end loading.

loan The lending of a sum of money. Loans may be secured or unsecured (►securities), ►interest bearing or interest free, long term or short term, redeemable or irredeemable (►redeemable security). Loans may be made by individuals, governments, companies, banks, ►insurance and ►hire-purchase companies, ►building societies and other ►financial intermediaries, or by ►pawnbrokers, or by the issue of ►securities. ►►finance; term loans.

loan capital Fixed-interest borrowed funds, e.g. ►debentures.

loan certificate (Nor.) ►Commercial paper.

loan guarantee ►credit guarantee.

loan participation certificate (US) A device introduced by US banks on the occasion of high market interest rates in 1969, consisting of a loan to which a depositor had partial proprietary rights, thus enabling the banks to pay interest on their liabilities above the maximum level set by the supervisory authorities.

loan selling A term used to describe the issue of ►debt instruments, particularly ►Euromarket securities such as ►floating rate notes and ►Euronotes in ►note issuance facilities. Also sale of outstanding loans, particularly in Third World countries with external payments difficulties, by the lending bank to another bank or financial institution. The transaction is normally at a ►discount.

loan stock ►stock.

local (US) A dealer in ►financial futures or in ►traded options who is independent and acts on their own account.

local area network (LAN) A connected set of ►microcomputers, which allows individual users to access computer programs, data, storage space (e.g. ►hard disks) and peripheral equipment such as printers and ►modems, usually found on a central unit called the file server. The LAN includes the connecting wiring and the necessary computer software.

local authority bill A ►bill of exchange drawn on a local authority.

local authority stock A ►bond issued by a UK local authority.

local taxation ►Taxation levied by (or for) local rather than central government. In the UK local government rates were proportional to the estimated rentable value of business and domestic premises. From 1990 (in England) rates on domestic property were replaced with the *community charge*, a per capita tax for each occupant aged 18 or over. The community charge was extremely unpopular and was replaced in 1993/4 by the *council* tax. This tax is based on the values of property in 1990, defined by a series of bands. There is a rebate for people living alone and various other reliefs. Business properties continue to be based upon local valuations as before but are set by government on a uniform basis throughout the country, hence their name the *uniform business rate* (UBR). In the USA the states levy ►sales tax. In France the principal local tax on business is the *taxe professionelle*, which is based on the rentable values of buildings and equipment but also includes a ►payroll tax. In Germany regional government (*Länder*) levies a tax on business that has three elements: a ►profits tax (*Gewerbeertragesteur*), a tax on ►assets (*Gewerbekapitalsteuer*) and a tax on the capital value of buildings and land (*Grundsteuer*). ►►poll tax.

loco A ►commodity market term referring to the location of dealing in a commodity, e.g. tin may be traded *loco* London.

Loi Monory (Fr.) A law introduced by H. René Monory in 1978 to stimulate

➤stock exchange investment in the ➤securities of domestic companies. Individuals may deduct their share purchases up to a specified limit from their taxable income.

Lombard rate (Ger.) **1**. A generic term for lending against ➤security, normally against a ➤financial instrument. **2**. The interest rate at which the ➤Bundesbank lends in the normal course of events to the German commercial bank system. Such lending is always against ➤security. Lombard rate is normally set about a half-point above ➤discount rate.

Lombardsatz, Lombardzinssatz, Lombardzinsfuss (Ger.) ➤Lombard rate.

Lomé Convention ➤European Development Fund.

London and New Zealand Futures Association (UK) A ➤commodity market, set up in Bradford in 1953, dealing in ➤futures contracts for New Zealand crossbred wool. A member of the ➤International Commodities Clearing House.

London Bankers' Clearing House ➤clearing house.

London Bullion Market Association (LBMA) An association established in 1987 of participants in the London gold and silver ➤bullion market. Membership comprises some 62 firms, of which 14 are recognized market makers; 13 countries have interests in LBMA member firms. Members deal on a ➤spot, ➤forward or ➤options basis. The LMBA liaises closely with the market's supervisor, the ➤Bank of England, and sets standards for bullion delivery. Five members of the LBMA are responsible for the twice-daily 'fixing' (i.e. setting) of the price of ➤gold.

London Club An association of international commercial banks with the purpose of negotiating in common the terms and conditions of ➤sovereign loans.

London Cocoa Terminal Market Association Ltd A ➤commodity market, dealing principally in ➤futures contracts, opened in 1928 and stemming from the Cocoa Association of London, formed two years earlier. Futures trading lapsed during the price controls of the Second World War but resumed in 1951. The market, along with that in New York, was the largest in the world. Much ➤arbitrage trading was conducted between the two markets. The London market was a member of the ➤International Commodities Clearing House. The association was in 1987 merged with the ➤Futures and Options Exchange (FOX), the latter itself later merging with the ➤London International Financial Futures Exchanges (LIFFE).

London Commodity Exchange ➤Futures and Options Exchange.

London daily prices (LDP) Prices assessed each day for white sugar at the ➤United Sugar Terminal Market in London, then transmitted and used widely across the world for ➤physical trade in the commodity. There is no trading as such on the London market; the price is arrived at by the market's price committee in the light of reported business and dealings in the ➤futures market.

London FOX ►Futures and Options Exchange.

London Gold Futures Market Ltd A market in ►futures contracts in ►gold, set up in 1982 by the members of the ►London Gold Market in consultation with the ►London Metal Exchange and the ►International Commodities Clearing House. With a dollar unit of ►currency, the market is firmly established alongside other gold futures markets in the USA, Australia, Hong Kong and Tokyo.

London Gold Market Ltd A long-standing market comprising five dealers – Rothschild, Midland Montagu, Mocatta & Goldsmid (part of the Standard Chartered Group), Mase Westpac (owned by Republic National Bank of New York) and Sharps Pixley (owned by Deutsche Bank). The group meets twice daily at Rothschild's to fix the London price of gold. The price has long been a highly influential guide to the world market, although in recent years Zurich has become a strong rival. The market has in latter years formed itself into a company, in which each member has an equal share, although chairmanship at the fixing sessions resides permanently with Rothschild.

London Grain Futures Market Set up in 1925, the market was a ►commodity market for European Union varieties of wheat and barley, and deals in ►futures contracts. The market generated ruling prices for most trades throughout the European Union. The market was in 1997 merged with the ►Futures and Options Exchange (FOX), the latter itself later merging with the ►London International Financial Futures Exchange (LIFFE).

London interbank bid rate (LIBID) ►London interbank offered rate (LIBOR).

London interbank offered rate (LIBOR) (UK) The rate of ►interest offered on ►loans to first-class banks in the London ►inter-bank market for a specified period (usually three or six months). Owing to the heavy volume of interbank dealing, the three-month and six-month rates have come to be widely used as a basis of reference for the setting of many other rates. It is closely related to ►base rate but is closer to *prime rate* in US terms. The rate may apply to sterling or ►Eurodollars. The corresponding rate for ►deposits is the *interbank market bid rate* (IBMBR), the *interbank bid rate* (IBBR) or the *London interbank bid rate* (LIBID). Some other financial centres have interbank bid and offer rates, e.g. the *Paris interbank offered rate* (PIBOR) and the *Tokyo interbank offered rate* (TIBOR).

London International Financial Futures Exchange (LIFFE) An exchange established in London in September 1982 for trading in ►financial futures and ►options. The decision to set up a London market followed the success of the financial futures market in Chicago (►Chicago Board of Trade) and of that started in Sydney in 1979. The market is centred on a clearing house through which all transactions pass and that acts as a financially independent guarantor and regulator of the exchange. The exchange is also under the supervision of the ►Bank of England, which may, if needed, intervene. The market began by trading in four ►currency futures contracts (sterling, D-marks, yen and Swiss francs against the dollar) and three interest rate ►futures (►rate of interest). Given the large size of the closely similar ►forward market, the currency futures became less popular than the interest rate futures. By 1985 LIFFE was trading in three more futures contracts and two ►option contracts, the subjects of these including short-term sterling, long-term ►gilts, the FT/SE Index (►Financial Times share indexes) and US ►Treasury bonds. Options on three-month sterling interest rate futures were introduced in November 1987; trade in Japanese government bond futures began in July 1987. In 1996 the ►Futures and Options Market (FOX) was merged with LIFFE as a separate department, LIFFE Commodity Products, but with unchanged operations.

London International Insurance and Reinsurance Market Association (LIRMA) An international body comprising ►insurance and ►reinsurance companies in the UK and other member countries of the ►European Union (EU), assisting members' market needs in the international wholesale insurance market, and representing members' interests to governments. The association was formed in 1991 by a merger of the Reinsurance Officers Association and the Policy Signing and Accounting Centre. The association has a 50% interest, with the ►Institute of London Underwriters (ILU), and in the London Processing Centre for the checking, signing and sealing of members' policy documents. LIRMA has a membership of some 200 companies.

London Jute Association Set up in 1875, the association is not a marketing body but administers the contracts under which jute is sold throughout the world. There are few, if any, ►futures transactions.

London Meat Futures Exchange Ltd Set up in 1984, this is a ►commodity market for pigmeat, dealing in ►futures contracts. A member of the ►International Commodities Clearing House.

London Metal Exchange (LME) With origins dating back to the 18th century, and incorporated in 1881, the exchange is the London ►commodity market for trade in metals and the world ►futures, ►options and cash market for trades in aluminium, aluminium alloy, copper, lead, nickel, tin and zinc. Some nine-tenths of the total trade is in the form of futures and options. The market is daily for cash and contracts up to three months; and weekly, and then monthly, for contracts up to 15 and 27 months. Dealing in aluminium and nickel began in 1978 and 1979 respectively; dealing in aluminium alloy began in 1993; dealing in the other metals is of long standing. Membership is wholly international. Prices are set by 'ring members', i.e. those authorized to deal on the 'ring' or trading floor; the number has varied between 30 and 15.

London Potato Futures Market A ►commodity market, trading in ►futures contracts, set up in 1980. Futures dealings are possible given the exemption of potatoes from ►European Union pricing rules, although the UK Potato Marketing Board attempts to control production. Dealing is in all varieties of potatoes, with some ►arbitrage in the Bintje variety possible with the Dutch market, the only other potato futures market in Europe. The market was a member of the ►International Commodities Clearing House. The market was in 1987 merged with the ►Futures and Options Exchange (FOX), the latter itself later merging with the ►London International Financial Futures Exchange (LIFFE).

London Processing Centre ►London International Insurance and Reinsurance Market Association (LIRMA).

London Rubber Terminal Market Association A ►commodity market established in 1974 for dealing in ►futures contracts. The Rubber Terminal Market superseded the Rubber Settlement House, which had conducted futures trade for the previous 50 years. The market was a member of the ►International Commodities Clearing House. The association was in 1987 merged with the ►Futures and Options Exchange (FOX), the latter itself later merging with the ►London International Financial Futures Exchange (LIFFE).

London Soya Bean Meal Futures Market A ►commodity market, established in 1975, for trade in ►futures contracts in soya bean meal. The market provides ►hedging facilities, principally for trade between the UK and the rest of Europe; there is some ►arbitrage between the London and the Chicago markets. The market is a member of the ►International Commodities Clearing House.

London Stock Exchange (LSE) (UK) The London market in which ►securities are bought and sold. Its correct name is the International Stock Exchange of the United Kingdom (ISE). Members are formed into a declining number of firms that, following the ►Big Bang, now include major ►merchant banks, ►clearing banks and other financial intermediaries, some of which are foreign owned. All business is now conducted by telephone through an ►automated screen trading system, and the ►trading floor (including regional trading floors) is no longer used. The ►Stock Exchange Automated Quotation System (SEAQ) allows ►market makers and others to see competing quotations on their screens, and ►stockbrokers to select the best ►bid price or ►offer price for their clients. Prior to October 1986 the rules of the exchange did not permit ►jobbers to deal directly with the public, but only through stockbrokers; but now firms operate in ►dual capacity. An ►order driven electronic *Stock Exchange Trading System* (*SETS*), based on the new trading and information platform called *SEQUENCE*, was introduced in 1997, initially for the FTSE 100 Index companies (►Financial Times share indices). SETS handles transactions of more than 1,000 shares (500 were worth more than £5 each); other share ►bargains continue on SEAQ. ►►alpha securities; stocks, alternative investment market; CREST; Financial Services Act, normal market size; offer for sale; Securities Association; stock exchange.

London Sugar Futures Market A ➤commodity market, dealing in ➤futures contracts for raw sugar and white sugar, the descendant of the first London sugar futures market, formed in 1888. Closed during both world wars, the market reformed after each, the latest occasion being in 1957 when postwar sugar controls were relaxed. The market is not a ➤physical market but a daily price-fixing one. The London daily price, based on business in physical sugar and the tone of the futures market, is used worldwide as the basis of sales contracts. There is ➤arbitrage with the futures market in New York, which is roughly equivalent in size. The market was a member of the ➤International Commodities Clearing House. The market was in 1987 merged with the ➤Futures and Options Exchange (FOX), the latter itself later merging with the ➤London International Financial Futures Exchange (LIFFE).

London Traded Options Market (LTOM) An options market merged in 1991 with the ➤London International Financial Futures Exchange (LIFFE).

London Underwriting Centre A centre established in 1993 for non-marine ➤underwriters of 22 major ➤general insurance and ➤reinsurance companies offering the convenience of one-stop business for brokers. The centre regards itself as complementary to ➤Lloyd's and claims a capacity of £6bn, as against Lloyd's £8bn.

London Vegetable Oil Terminal Market A ➤commodity market, opened in 1967, dealing first in soya bean oil, coconut oil and sunflower seed oil, and from 1973 trading only in soya bean oil; concerned primarily with ➤futures contracts. The market is a member of the ➤International Commodities Clearing House.

long 1. Of ➤commodity and ➤securities markets, having assets normally under a ➤futures or ➤forward contract, available for sale on the prescribed date, e.g. having bought a futures contract. 2. Of securities and currencies, having a holding larger than normal quantities. ➤➤position. 3. An abbreviation for ➤long term.

long-dated securities ➤dated securities.

long-form report (UK) A detailed confidential report for the ➤sponsor (➤issuing house) of a company being prepared for flotation (➤float) by the reporting account-ants. The long-form report is intended to satisfy the sponsors so that they can lend their name to the issue and identify matters that need to be rectified before going public. The report will provide the basis for the *short-form report* included in the ➤prospectus.

long hedge A ➤hedge effected by the purchase of a ➤futures contract.

long tail business Of insurance, certain forms of insurance, particularly in

➤liability business, claims under which may arise long after the policy is issued. Examples are claims in respect of ill-health from exposure to asbestos or to certain drugs.

long term 1. Of a ➤security, having a ➤maturity of long duration, usually of more than 15 years. 2. Of a bank loan, repayable between five and 10 years. 3. Of a ➤money market instrument, having a maturity between three months and one year. 4. Of insurance, life insurance ➤annuity, ➤permanent health insurance, pension fund management (➤pensions) and capital redemption business.

long term care (LTC) Insurance against the costs incurred for nursing-home accommodation or home help in old age. Premiums vary according to the level of financing desired and are payable either annually or as a single ➤premium.

loss adjuster An independent expert called in where necessary by ➤insurers to assess an ➤insured's claim and to negotiate a settlement with the latter. Normally used for large claims.

Loss Prevention Council (LPC) (UK) A body set up in 1986, in succession to the Fire Officers Committee, responsible for fire prevention statistics; for standard insurance policy wording; for standards of construction; for the operation of fire extinguishing appliances; for fire fighting methods in general; and for approval of equipment. The LPC liaises closely with the ➤Association of British Insurers and ➤Lloyd's.

losses occurring policy An insurance policy specifying the ➤insurer's obligation to pay claims made in respect of losses incurred during the period of validity of the policy, regardless of the date of the claim or of the act causing the loss.

lot A minimum quantity unit traded in a ➤commodity market or a ➤securities market.

loyalty bonus ➤privatization.

LPC ➤Loss Prevention Council.

LSE ➤London Stock Exchange.

LTC ➤long term care.

LTOM ➤London Traded Options Market.

LUC ➤London Underwriting Centre.

lump sum 1. The amount calculated by ➤discounted cash flow for the immediate purchase of an ➤annuity. 2. The amount generated throughout the term of a ➤life assurance policy used for the purchase of a ➤pension. ➤➤equalization of pensions.

lunga scadenza (It.) ➤Long term.

Luxembourg Stock Exchange (LSE) The LSE is managed and self-regulated (►regulation) by the Société Anonyme de la Bourse. The volume of trading on the ►stock exchange is small, but Luxembourg is an important centre for the ►settlement of trading in ►Eurobonds (►Centrale de Livraison de Valeurs Mobilières).

M

Maastricht Treaty A treaty signed in February 1992 by the member states of the then European Community (EC) intended to inaugurate 'a new stage in the process of European integration'. The treaty declared the member states henceforth to be members of a ►European Union (EU), of which all inhabitants were citizens. Employing, like the Single European Act (SEA), the method of amending and expanding the original three treaties of the Community, the Maastricht Treaty provided for: (i) the establishment of full Economic and Monetary Union; (ii) the implementation of a common foreign and security policy; (iii) the development of close cooperation on justice and on home affairs; (iv) the strengthening of the common commercial, transport, capital and payments, environmental and other existing policies of the Union; (v) the endorsement of the principle of subsidiarity. Lastly (vi) there was attached to the treaty a protocol on social policy.

(i) The existing arrangements for the ►European Monetary System (EMS) were taken to be stage one of progress towards full Economic and Monetary Union. During stage two, beginning on 1 January 1994, general economic and financial convergence was to take place; a European Monetary Institute (EMI) was to be established with the task of taking over the functions of the European Monetary Co-operation Fund and of preparing for the third stage in consultation with the member states' central banks, *inter alia* in specifying the arrangements for the European System of Central Banks (ESCB). In stage three, to start not later than 1 January 1999, the move to a single currency, the ►euro, was to be made, with provisional derogations for member states not meeting the requisite ►convergence criteria; the ESCB and the European Central Bank (ECB) were to enter into their functions, and the EMI was to be liquidated.

(ii) There was to be close consultation between member states, with the presidency representing the European Union in matters where a common policy has been agreed in the Council, after liaison with the European Parliament. The Western European Union was to advise on and implement the European Union's actions and decisions in the field of security and defence.

(iii) The Union was to come to joint positions and, where appropriate, take joint action on: asylum, immigration, anti-drug addiction, anti-international fraud, and customs, police and judicial cooperation policies.

(iv) A number of tidying and reinforcing adjustments were made.

(v) In response to widening fears of overcentralization of Union action, the principle of 'subsidiarity', i.e. that the Union institutions should undertake actions only where these can be better performed than by the member states acting individually, was explicitly recognized.

(vi) The relevant documents consist of an agreement 'On Social Policy concluded between the Member States of the European Community with the Exception of the United Kingdom and Northern Ireland', which is annexed to a Protocol on Social Policy that explicitly recognizes the abstention from the agreement of the UK. (The documents are popularly miscalled 'the social chapter', in fact an existing section of the original EC Treaty.) The agreement records the intention of the signatory states to pursue so far unfulfilled aspirations of the Social Charter (►European Union), to which the UK was not a signatory.

Ratification of the Maastricht Treaty proved difficult, owing, it was surmised, to a general feeling that its provisions had gone too far, outpacing the member states' wishes for integration. A referendum in Denmark in June 1992 vetoed ratification. In September 1992 a referendum in France approved ratification by the smallest of margins a 'oui, mais'. The UK Parliament began a long-drawn-out wrangle over the 'social chapter'. The treaty was referred to the German constitutional court. Eventually a new referendum permitted Danish ratification in May 1993, UK ratification following two days later. That of Germany ensued in October 1993.

However, by then other events had weighed against attainment of the treaty's aim of strengthening and deepening the European Union. Severe currency turbulence led on 'Black Wednesday', 16 September 1992, to the withdrawal of the UK and Italy from the Exchange Rate Mechanism (ERM); and a repetition of the disorder in August of the following year compelled the extension of the ERM divergency margins to 15% on either side of the central parity, signalling the virtual lapsing of the whole system, amid grave doubts about the move to Economic and Monetary Union. Apart from this, continued dissatisfaction with the working of the common agricultural policy, coupled with external factors such as German unification and events in Eastern Europe and the former Soviet Union, combined to distract attention from issues of further Union integration. ►Amsterdam Treaty; Intergovernmental Conference.

Madrid Stock Exchange Since 1995 the four ►stock exchanges in Spain have been linked by a new electronic ►order driven trading system, *Sistem de Interconexión de las Bolsas Españolas* (SIBE), replacing its predecessor CATS (►Toronto Stock Exchange). The regulatory body is the *Comisión Nacional del Mercado de Valores* (the National Capital Market Commission). Foreign ownership of stockbroking firms has been deregulated. The principal index is the IBEX-35. There are exchanges in Barcelona, Bilbao and Valencia as well as in Madrid.

mailbox number ►electronic mail.

main market The market dealing in ►stocks and ►shares on the ►official list of the ►London Stock Exchange and not including second-tier or ►unlisted securities markets.

mainframe computer The largest size of computer.

mainstream corporation tax ➤corporation tax.

maintenance period (US) The period in which the banks must meet the reserve requirement set down by the ➤Federal Reserve, i.e. in which the average level of a bank's deposits in its reserve account at the Federal Reserve bank must be at least equal to the amount required. The maintenance period is normally of two weeks, termed statement weeks, running from a Thursday to the second Wednesday following.

major market index (MMI) (US) A ➤futures contract established by the ➤Chicago Board of Trade in 1983 and based on movements in the Dow-Jones Industrial Average Index (➤Dow-Jones indexes) of the stock exchange prices of 20 of the most heavily capitalized companies in the USA. The contract is licensed by the ➤American Stock Exchange, which trades ➤options in the index. In 1993 the contract was transferred to the ➤Chicago Mercantile Exchange.

Makler (Ger.) ➤Broker.

Maklergebühr (Ger.) ➤Broker's fee.

managed currency A ➤currency whose ➤parity is maintained at a declared level by the ➤central bank of the country concerned.

managed futures fund (US) A ➤mutual fund dealing in ➤derivatives. These funds grew from a total size of $4bn in 1986 to some $25bn in 1992.

managed unit trust (UK) A unit trust invested solely in other unit trusts belonging to the same group; first introduced in the UK in 1985. The purpose is to provide a lower-risk investment vehicle than a normal unit trust, a choice not easily made by the investor in the face of the more than 1,000 unit trusts in existence. The Department of Trade has laid down that managed unit trusts must be invested in at least five out of a possible choice of at least eight individual trusts, and be invested as to not more than 50% in any one. Doubts over ➤conflict of interest have remained, although biased purchases and sales would be speedily reflected in performance. Also known as *master trust* and *fund of funds*.

management buy-in ➤management buy-out.

management buy-out (MBO) The acquisition of all or part of the ➤share capital of a company by its directors and senior executives. Competitive pressures upon large companies in the 1980s have led to the disposal of many weak or peripheral subsidiaries in this way. The management are usually assisted by ➤loans from a venture capital (➤risk capital) or other financial organization, and both expect to seek public ➤flotation in due course. In a *management buy-in* an outside team of managers acquires a company in a similar way. A *buy-in management buy-out* (BIMBO) combines interests of both existing and new outside management.

managing agent The agent responsible for managing one or more ➤Lloyd's syndicates, and for employing the ➤active underwriter.

mandate A written document authorizing a named person to write ➤cheques on a bank account or to receive dividends, as in *bank mandate, dividend mandate*.

Manila Stock Exchange (MSE) Established in 1927, with a trading floor also in Makati. The ➤stock exchange and the regulatory body, the Securities Exchange Commission, are based on the US model, as is the ➤over-the-counter market.

MAPA Members' Agents Pooling Arrangement. ➤Lloyd's.

marché (Fr.) ➤Market.

marché à options (Fr.) Options market. ➤option.

marché à primes (Fr.) Market for a form of ➤call option, giving the holder the right to buy certain ➤securities on any one of three consecutive monthly dates ahead. Holders may abandon their option before ➤settlement on payment of a penalty (the *prime*).

Marché à Reglement Mensuel ➤Paris Bourse.

marché à terme (Fr.) The *forward* or monthly account market.

Marché à Terme des Instruments Financiers (MATIF) (Fr.) The French financial ➤futures market, established in 1986.

marché au comptant (Fr.) The ➤cash, ➤spot or ➤physical market.

marché conditionnel (Fr.) A generic term for the ➤options market, the ➤*marché à primes*, the ➤*stellage* market and the double option market (➤*opération du double*).

marché de l'argent (Fr.) ➤Money market.

Marché des Options Négotiables de Paris (Fr.) The French traded options (➤option) market, established in 1987.

marché des valeurs (Fr.) ➤securities market.

marché hors-cote (Fr.) The third-tier unofficial ➤unlisted securities market, not regulated by the ➤Commission des Opérations de Bourse.

Marché Libre OTC ➤Paris Bourse.

marché monétaire (Fr.) ➤Money market.

margin 1. Generally in finance, the *gross margin* is the difference between the price at which something is bought and the price at which it is sold; thus the contribution towards ➤overheads and other costs. **2.** In banking, the difference between the interest ➤rate paid to depositors or for funds on the ➤money market and the rate charged to borrowers. **3.** A deposit as partial surety that a ➤contract will be fulfilled, as in ➤commodity markets and ➤financial futures markets. Expressed as a percentage of the price paid (or sold), the *margin requirement* may necessitate further payments by the client if prices move against them. **4.** (US) The proportion of the price of a ➤security paid when giving an ➤order to a ➤broker, the rest being on ➤credit. **5.** The permitted divergence between national ➤currencies in the ➤European Monetary System.

margin call A requirement for an increase in the original deposit, or margin, placed on a ➤futures or ➤option contract, when the buyer has increased the size of the contract, or when market prices have become heavily adverse.

margin of solvency The required excess of an ➤insurance company's ➤assets over ➤liabilities, the amount and calculation of which is subject to exact standards set, for ➤European Union (EU) member countries, by EU directives.

margin requirement ➤margin.

margin trading A term describing the process by which ➤commodity speculators trade in ➤futures by subscribing only the ➤margin, i.e. the deposit, on a contract valued many times higher than the margin; thus permitting, if successful, a profit far exceeding the original outlay.

marginal cost ➤capital, cost of.

marker barrel The unit of petroleum sales of Saudi Arabia, used as a reference in assessing changes in the general oil price. The specification is: Saudi Arabian Light, API 40, Ras Tanura.

market Business or trade in any ➤commodity.

market capitalization The total value at market prices of the ➤securities at issue for a company or a stock market or sector of the stock market. Calculated by multiplying the number of shares issued by the market price per ➤share.

market clearing price The price at which all goods or services available in a market will find buyers.

market instrument Short-term ➤debt instrument.

market maker A ➤broker-dealer who is prepared to buy and sell specified ➤securities at all times and thus makes a market in them. Prior to the ➤Big Bang, this function was carried out by ➤jobbers, who were not allowed to deal with the public. Since the Big Bang all members of the ➤stock exchange may deal with the public as broker-dealers. Some specialize as market makers and others as ➤stockbrokers. Following the introduction of SETS (➤London Stock Exchange) market makers have been renamed *retail service providers*.

market order An instruction from a client to a ➤broker-dealer to buy or sell a

►security or ►commodity at the price prevailing at the time of execution of the transaction. ►order.

marketable ►negotiable.

marking to market Calculating the value of a ►securities portfolio by reference to current market prices, in order to establish the profit or loss made since a previous calculation.

markka The national ►currency unit of Finland.

Marktbewertung (Ger.) ►Market capitalization.

Marshall aid A programme of financial aid to Western European countries instituted by the USA after the Second World War; so called because the programme resulted from a proposal made by the US Secretary of State, General George C. Marshall, in June 1947. The form and distribution of aid were made according to the requirements set out by the recipient nations, grouped together in the ►Organization for European Economic Co-operation.

Maruyu (Jap.) A postal savings investment system, operated by the Postal Savings Bureau (PSB), under which deposits up to Y3m, defined as 'small savings', were free of tax; the system was withdrawn in April 1988. The PSB, founded in 1875, had by 1988 some 300m deposits, valued at Y286 trillion, mostly held in 10-year deposits at government-guaranteed interest rates. The system was abolished partly to create uniformity of treatment for savings, and partly to deal with the growth of illicit accounts, a trend illustrated by the fact that the number of accounts was 2.5 times the country's population.

masse monétaire (Fr.) ►Money supply.

master trust ►managed unit trust.

MAT Of insurance, an abbreviation for *marine, aviation and transport*, a recognized class of insurance business.

match (US) ►matched sale – purchase agreement.

matched bargains or bids A method of ►securities trading in which bids and offers (►bid price; offer price) are matched together. Used on the ►German stock exchanges, it is said to have greater ►transparency than the more common ►quote-driven systems. ►►order driven.

matched sale – purchase agreement (US) A sale of ►money-market instruments by the ►Federal Reserve for immediate effect, coupled with a simultaneous ►forward purchase of the same instruments, having as a result a distribution of the reserves of the banking system. Identical in effect to ►repurchase agreements, but used by the Federal Reserve to overcome the legal bar to its borrowing from the public, and thus to reverse repurchase agreements. First employed in 1966.

material facts A term used to define the information that an ➤insured must disclose under a contract of ➤insurance. ➤➤'prudent insurer'; *uberrimae fidei.*

mathematical reserves In ➤long term ➤insurance, a company's provision for future liabilities, less liabilities that have fallen due, and deposits repaid by reinsurers. Mathematical reserves are a concept used in the calculation of an insurer's ➤margin of solvency. Reserves are held by ➤long-term insurance businesses to cover all liabilities other than those already due for settlement. A frequent measure of the strength of the company is the excess of net assets over mathematical reserves.

MATIF (Fr.) ➤Marché à Terme des Instruments Financiers.

maturity The period between the creation of a financial ➤claim and the date on which it is to be paid. Often refers to the date of payment, e.g. the date on which a ➤bond becomes due for repayment.

maturity balance (US) The mix of ➤maturities of ➤securities (➤Treasury bills; Treasury bonds) and ➤Federal agency securities held by the ➤Federal Reserve for use in its ➤open market operations.

MBO ➤management buy-out.

MDAX ➤German stock exchanges.

mean ➤average.

median ➤percentile.

medical insurance ➤permanent health insurance.

medium term 1. Of a ➤security, having a ➤maturity of a medium duration, usually between five and 15 years. 2. Of a bank loan, for repayment between three and five years. 3. ➤finance.

medium-term financial assistance (MTFA) Loans of a ➤term of two to five years, available from ➤European Union countries to a member country in ➤balance of payments difficulties. The loans are made by donor countries up to a specified ceiling to which individual countries are committed, no one recipient country being entitled to receive more than 50% of the ceiling; financial and economic conditions may be placed on the recipient country in return for the loan.

medium-term note (MTN) ➤Euro-commercial paper, issued with a maturity of several years.

MEFF A term used in English-speaking markets to denote the Spanish ➤futures exchange, the Mercado Español de Futuros Financieros.

megabyte One million ➤bytes.

members' agent An agent responsible for advising ►external members of ►Lloyd's on the choice of syndicates and for administering the members' business affairs at Lloyd's.

memorandum of association The document that forms the basis of registration of a company, listing the subscribers to the ►capital and the number of ►shares, the name and address of the company and, where appropriate, its powers and objects. The memorandum also states that the ►liability of its members (►shareholders) is limited (►incorporation) (US = *articles of incorporation*). The *articles of association* set out the rules by which the company will be administered, e.g. the voting of directors and the calling of meetings (US = *corporate bylaws*).

Mercado de Valores de Buenos Aires ►Buenos Aires Stock Exchange.

Mercado Español de Futuros Financieros ►MEFF.

Mercato Italiano Futuri (MIF) The Italian ►futures market.

mercato ristretto (It.) A regulated market dealing in unlisted securities (►unlisted securities markets), based in Milan and five other centres. In its present form, regulated by CONSOB (►Commissione Nazionale per le Societá e la Borsa), the *mercato ristretto* dates from May 1978. ►►*terzo mercato*.

merchant banks Institutions that carry out a variety of financial services, including the acceptance of ►bills of exchange, the issue and ►placing of ►loans and ►securities, ►portfolio and ►unit trust management, ►foreign exchange dealing and some ►banking services. Several houses, often through subsidiaries, provide ►risk capital, deal in gold ►bullion, ►insurance and ►hire purchase, and are active in the ►Euromarket. Merchant banks advise companies on ►mergers and other financial matters, and many of them are well known, e.g. Rothschild, Barings, Hambro, Lazard and Schroder. There has been a recent trend, especially following the ►Big Bang, for merchant banks, including London firms on the ►stock exchange, to participate in financial ►conglomerates, so as to be able to offer a full range of financial services, including retail services. The term 'merchant banks' is now giving way to ►investment bank as their activities are absorbed into large global concerns. ►accepting house.

Mercosur A trade agreement, concluded in 1988, between Argentina, Brazil, Paraguay and Uruguay. The group also has a free trade association agreement with Chile and Bolivia.

merger The fusion of two or more separate companies into one. In current usage merger is a special case of combination, where both the merging companies wish to join together and do so on roughly equal terms, as distinct from a ►take-over, which occurs against the wishes of one company and is preceded by a contested bid. ►►leveraged buy-out.

merger accounting ➤consolidated accounts.

Mexican Stock Exchange The Bolsa Mexicana de Valores in Mexico City, established in 1894, has grown rapidly and now has the largest ➤market capitalization in Latin America. The stock price index is the *IPC Index (Indice de Precios y Cotizaciones)*.

mezzanine A term signifying an intermediate stage in a financing operation. It usually refers to ➤unsecured debt and ➤equity in ranking for payment in the event of ➤default (➤➤subordinated). It may carry an ➤option on some other claim to a stake in equity (an *equity kicker*). A form of *quasi-equity* combining features of both ➤debt and equity.

Mibtel index ➤Milan Stock Exchange.

microcomputer The smallest class of computer, also called *personal computer* or *PC*. PCs can be used for data processing on their own or as terminals connected to other PCs, ➤minicomputers or ➤mainframe computers through a ➤local area network or via a ➤modem and telephone lines.

Middle East ➤Tel Aviv Stock Exchange.

Midwest Stock Exchange Established in 1882 under the name Chicago Stock Exchange to deal in local railway, bank and energy company securities. In 1948, when the second largest stock exchange in the USA, it changed its name to the above. However, the market declined in relative size over succeeding years, in the face of strong competition from the ➤New York Stock Exchange, the ➤American Stock Exchange and the ➤over-the-counter market. In 1993 the exchange reverted to its original name.

MIF ➤Mercato Italiano Futuri.

Milan Stock Exchange The market has grown rapidly in international importance since 1985 as local ➤mutual funds emerged. Since 1996, all trading has been screen-based, and five-day rolling ➤settlement introduced. The most widely quoted share indices are the *Mibtel* and ➤Comit Indices. A new screen-based unlisted securities market is proposed (*Mercato Telematico Imprese* (MITEM). ➤➤*mercato ristretto*. The regulatory body is the ➤Commissione Nazionale per le Società e la Borsa (CONSOB).

milliard Originally the common term in English and French for *one thousand million*. Now superseded, at least in English, by the term *billion*.

Minex ➤Electronic Broking Service.

minicomputer A computer midway in size and data-processing capacity between a ➤microcomputer and a ➤mainframe computer. With recent increases in the power and storage capacity of personal computers the borderline between micros and minis has narrowed.

minimum contract size ➤lot.

minimum lending rate (MLR) The interest rate at which the Bank of England lent to relieve shortages in the ➤money market. The rate could be set at such a level as to foster a rise or a fall in the general level of money market interest rates, but was generally neutral to the trend, being in fact fixed by a formula relating to ➤Treasury bill tender rate in the period 1972–8. MLR replaced ➤bank rate in 1972 but was discontinued in 1981, the Bank of England reserving the right to restore it periodically in the future.

Minneapolis Grain Exchange A ➤commodity market for grain, established in 1881, dealing in ➤futures contracts for spring wheat and white wheat, and in the ➤cash market for barley, maize, drum wheat, flaxseed, oats, rye, soya beans, spring wheat and sunflower seeds. Together with the Kansas and Chicago exchanges, it sets the world price for grains.

minority interests ➤consolidated accounts.

MIRAS ➤mortgage interest tax relief at source.

Mishtanim Index The ➤share price index of the ➤Tel Aviv Stock Exchange.

mismatch ➤floating rate note.

MITI (Jap.) Ministry of International Trade and Industry.

mittelfristig (Ger.) ➤Medium term.

mixed policy A policy for the ➤insurance of a ship under which the vessel and its cargo are insured for a particular voyage and for a particular period of time.

MLR ➤minimum lending rate.

MMDA ➤money market deposit account.

MNC ➤multinational company.

MNE ➤multinational company.

mobilization (Fr.) The act of converting a ➤claim into a ➤negotiable asset, i.e. by discounting a ➤bill of exchange.

mode ➤average.

modem A device providing an interface between a computer and a telephone line or other line used for transmitting data.

momentum investing ➤investment approaches.

MONEP ➤Marché des Options Negotiables de Paris.

monetarism ➤monetary school.

monetarist An adherent to monetary theories, particularly those of Professor Milton ➤Friedman.

monetary base That part of the ➤money supply that, in the view of the ➤monetary school, is the most dynamic in its effects and is the ultimate source of money supply growth. Defined in the USA as total bank reserves plus notes and coin held by the public. In the UK, ➤till money, bankers' balances with the ➤Bank of England, and notes and coin in general circulation are regarded as the monetary base, in close conformity with the US definition. Definitions vary according to country, but all are broadly in line with the above.

monetary control The operation by a central bank of measures to regulate the size of the ➤money supply. In some countries, such as France and the UK, monetary control is a matter of government policy, and the central bank acts in accordance with this. In other countries, such as Germany and the USA, the central bank is entirely independent, though the government may make its views known.

Monetary Control Act (US) An Act of 1980, making all US banks members of the ➤Federal Reserve System.

monetary policy The policy of a government or central bank in monetary affairs, having regard to broad goals such as economic growth and restraint of inflation. ➤➤monetary control; money supply.

Monetary Policy Committee (UK) A ➤Bank of England committee established in June 1997 to determine UK interest rates, following the decision of the Chancellor of the Exchequer to transfer this function to the Bank from the ➤Treasury. The committee consists of nine members, with the Governor of the Bank of England, Mr Eddie George, as chairman. The other members are: two deputy governors, two senior officials of the bank and four independent financial experts.

monetary school The school of monetary theory based on the teachings of Professor Milton ➤Friedman of Chicago University, also referred to as *monetarism*. ➤➤money supply.

Monetary Union ➤Maastricht Treaty.

monetization The financing of a budget deficit through sale of short-term government ➤debt, namely ➤Treasury bills, to the banking system (UK) or to the ➤Federal Reserve (US), and similarly to banking purchasers in other countries. Purchase of Treasury bills by banks adds to their reserves and thus to their capacity to create money. Purchase of Treasury bills by the Federal Reserve from the banking system similarly adds to the latter's reserves.

money The means of facilitating the exchange of goods and services and the accumulation of financial wealth, commonly recognizable as banknotes, coins and bank deposits. The theory of money ascribes to it three functions: a medium of exchange; a unit of value; and a store of wealth. Money is thus a convenient proxy for all goods and services, enabling these to be exchanged more readily than if they were bartered each against the other; by its division into convenient units, the value of goods and services can be denoted by specific amounts of money; accumulated stores of money are reservoirs of purchasing power, or of wealth. The amount of money available to a community has commonly been held to have some influence on the relative value, or price, of goods and services. In the 1970s and later, increased emphasis was placed on this characteristic, leading to the emergence of the theories of the ►monetary school, or monetarism. These theories led to governments' greater resort to ►monetary policy and ►monetary control and to various theories of, and attempts to define, the nature of money (►money supply), as well as to define the effect of changes in the quantity and circulation of money on the level of national income and of price.

money as money does A theory of money measurement, assigning weighting to money forms based on frequency of use in transactions, to be employed when adding them together. Also known as the *MQ* approach.

money at call ►call money.

money broker A ►broker operating in the ►interbank market, acting as intermediary between banks wishing to borrow and banks wishing to lend. Money brokers also operate in the ►foreign exchange, ►Eurodollar and ►Eurobond markets.

money center banks (US) Large banks which act as clearing banks (►clearing house) and provide international services such as money transfers and ►foreign exchange for smaller banks in a given region.

money market The market in short-term (normally up to one year) financial ►claims, e.g. ►bills of exchange, ►Treasury bills, ►interbank money and ►discount house deposits. The market is wholesale, i.e. in large quantities traded not by individuals but by banks, discount houses, finance houses, the ►Bank of England, the ►Federal Reserve and others; and most transactions are by ►discount. In the UK the money market is frequently referred to as the *discount market*, mainly because many of the transactions are carried out by the discount houses.

money market deposit account (MMDA) (US) A form of retail bank account introduced in 1982, based on holdings in the money market, interest on which was free of official maxima. There were restrictions on withdrawals. Also known as a *supersaver account*.

money market mutual fund A type of ►mutual fund created in the USA in the early 1970s, designed to take advantage of the rise in interest rates by investing in ►short-term ►money market ►instruments. From 1974, when their ►assets were first recorded, money market mutual funds grew rapidly, rising from $2.2bn to over $200bn in 1982, thereafter stabilizing.

money purchase Of a pension, when constituted by an annuity derived from the investment, at retirement date, of a capital fund accumulated through contributions during working life. Contrasted with occupational pension schemes, where the pension is a guaranteed proportion of earnings, obtained through investment in the same way, but supplemented where necessary by additional contribution by the company or scheme manager. All ►personal pensions are money purchase schemes.

money stock The total amount of ►money existing in the economy. When multiplied by its ►velocity, termed the ►money supply, for which it is used, loosely, as a synonym. ►►monetary control; monetary school.

money supply The quantity of money in circulation in the economy. This conventionally consists of all ►private-sector-held notes and coin, excluding those held within banks, and all bank ►deposits, excluding those held by banks themselves. The money supply in the UK is normally categorized as *total money supply*, that is, including all deposits held in the UK in all currencies; and *sterling money supply*, i.e. only those deposits denominated in sterling. The money supply was initially further subdivided into: *M1* = notes and coin, plus ►sight deposits; and *M3* = M1 plus *time deposits*.

In the course of time, further definitions were added to the above main categories, as follows. *M2* is an intermediate aggregate, designed to distinguish *transactions balances* (deposits held for purposes of expenditure) from *investment balances* (deposits held as long-term savings). Only transactions balances were considered to form part of the money supply. These, redefined as *retail deposits*, included all bank deposits of less than £100,000 from which early withdrawals could be made, all early withdrawable shares and deposits in ►building societies and all deposits with ►National Savings Bank ordinary accounts. Thus: M2 = M1 plus retail deposits. *M0* is a narrower category, subsequently introduced, which consisted effectively of the ►monetary base, i.e. the central stock on which all money supply expansion is based, namely notes and coin, including that held by banks, plus operational balances held by banks with the Bank of England.

Before this, a definition still wider than that of M2 had been essayed. *PSL1* (private-sector liquidity) = M3 (time deposits up to two years) plus all ►money market and ►certificate of deposit holdings; and *PSL2* = PSL1 plus all shorter-term holdings of building society and National Savings instruments (excluding holdings of money-market instruments by building societies themselves). In further search for definition, two more aggregates were added: *M4* = M1 plus most bank deposits plus holdings of money-market instruments; and *M5* = M4 plus building society deposits.

UK definitions are similar to those of other countries. In the USA, M1 = notes and coin (US = *currency*), sight deposits (US = *demand deposits*), travellers' cheques of non-bank issuers, ►NOW accounts, and ATS (automatic transfer service) and CUSD (credit union share draft) accounts. US *monetary base* = bank reserves plus notes and coin held by the public.

moneyness The degree to which a financial ►asset may be deemed, in theory, to be a form of money.

Montreal Stock Exchange ►Toronto Stock Exchange.

Moody's Investors Service ►Standard and Poor's Ratings.

moratorium An agreed suspension of repayments of ►principal and/or ►interest spread over a longer period. A number of countries have negotiated moratoria or rescheduling (which is effectively refinancing) on international loans.

Morgan Stanley Capital International World Index (MSCI Index) A global index of equity prices based on 1,375 ►shares from 19 countries and covering roughly 60% of the ►market capitalization of world ►stock exchanges. The *Financial Times* (►Financial Times share indices) and other organizations also publish world indices. ►►share indices.

mortality Mortality rates are calculated, e.g. per 1,000, of death by age groups, by area groups or other classifications. Mortality tables as used by insurance companies show average expectation of life according to age group.

mortgage A legal agreement conveying conditional ownership of ►assets as security for a loan and becoming void when the ►debt is repaid. A common form of ►loan for home purchase in most countries, the home being the asset providing the ►security.

mortgage-backed security A ►security, normally a bond or note, the ►servicing of which is provided by the returns on mortgages (or housing loans). A portfolio of mortgages, insured against default and held by a trustee, constitutes the security or collateral to the bond or note issue.

mortgage debentures ►debentures.

mortgage interest tax relief at source (MIRAS) Interest payable on a ►mortgage being free of tax, ►mortgagors in the UK, under an arrangement introduced in the 1983 Budget, deducted an amount equivalent to the standard rate of tax from their payment of interest to the ►mortgagee, thus taking for themselves their tax relief; the Inland Revenue subsequently refunded the mortgagee. Tax relief at higher rates was claimed in the mortgagor's normal tax return. Tax relief was later restricted to the *standard rate*, then the *lower rate*, and from 1995/6 has been restricted to 15%. ➤➤income tax.

mortgage protection policy An ➤insurance policy providing for continued payment of ➤mortgage interest, generally for a limited period, in cases where the ➤policy-holder is unable to pay the interest as a result, usually, of illness, accident or unemployment.

mortgagee The lender of funds under a ➤mortgage.

mortgagor The borrower of funds under a ➤mortgage.

Moscow Central Stock Exchange A stock exchange set up in the early 1990s, one of the 109 exchanges registered throughout Russia in 1993.

Moscow Interbank Currency Exchange A currency exchange made the basis of a bond market, in which, in 1993, 24 primary dealers traded in government bonds.

moving average A sequence of ➤averages calculated for the time series that damps down the fluctuations in values for that series. In a 12-month moving average, for example, the values for the latest month are added to the 12-month total, the value for month one is subtracted, and the result is divided by 12. Used in ➤technical analysis.

MPC ➤Monetary Policy Committee.

MQ ➤money as money does.

MSCI Index ➤Morgan Stanley Capital International World Index.

MSP ➤matched sale–purchase agreement.

MTN ➤medium-term note.

MTO Multilateral Trade Organization. ➤General Agreement on Tariffs and Trade (GATT).

multi-component Euronote facility A ➤Euronote facility providing for the issue of Euronotes in a number of different currencies according to the issuer's choice.

multi-option facility The term given to a short-term borrowing package comprising a number of different ➤instruments. These may include bankers' ➤acceptances, ➤Euronotes and ➤commercial paper. Most facilities are based on an ➤underwritten ➤credit, of which part may be 'available', i.e. to be drawn on at will, and part may be 'unavailable', i.e. to be drawn on only at notice, a lower commitment fee being payable on this portion.

Multi-Year Rescheduling Agreement (MYRA) An arrangement for the postponement to various years of the due dates for repayment of loans from commercial banks to developing countries, first instituted in 1985. The arrangement was intended to substitute clear and dependable repayment programmes for the *ad hoc* maturity postponements frequently practised.

Multilateral Trade Organization (MTO) ➤General Agreement on Tariffs and Trade (GATT).

multinational company (MNC) A company having production and other facilities in a number of countries outside the nation of origin. Also, and more correctly, called multinational enterprise (MNE), or *transnational corporation*. According to the United Nations there are about 35,000 multinationals controlling some 170,000 affiliates, though the largest 100 account for about 40% of cross-border ➤assets.

multiplier An increase in national income or some other money aggregate divided by the increase in expenditure generating that increase in income. In the *investment multiplier*, an increase in capital expenditure on £100m on roads, for example, will result in increased wage, salaries of employees and profits of contractors. These sums will be partly spent and partly saved, thus generating further increases in income and so on. The extent to which each increment of income is spent or saved will determine the final increase in national income, though if resources are not available to meet increased demand prices may rise. ➤money supply.

Muttergesellschaft (Ger.) ➤Parent company.

mutual 1. A company without ➤issued capital stock, legally owned by those who have deposited funds with it, perhaps by paying premiums on an ➤endowment policy. Common among ➤savings banks and ➤insurance companies. Profits, after retention of reserves, are distributed to depositors. Contrast ➤proprietary company. **2.** In the USA, also an open-ended investment trust. ➤mutual fund.

mutual fund (US) A pooled system of group investment, equivalent to a ➤unit trust in the UK, first developed in the USA in the 1930s. Total ➤assets of mutual funds grew rapidly until the 1970s, then stagnated until the 1980s, when growth again accelerated (total funds rising from some $135bn in 1980 to well over $350bn by 1985). The funds are invested chiefly in ➤stocks (company shares) and bonds, both of companies and of the public authorities. A major category emerging in recent times has been the ➤money-market mutual fund. ➤open-ended fund.

mutual offset An arrangement under which markets in different time zones agree to link so as to market each other's products and provide a facility for, or towards, ➤24-hour trading.

mutual savings banks (US) Banks accepting interest-bearing ➤deposits and owned by their depositors. Also called ➤thrifts.

Mutualité Française (Fr.) A federation of nearly 6,000 French health insurance ➤mutual societies, providing top-up health cover above the level set by the state social security system, for 30m French public and private sector employees.

MVA ➤economic value added.

N

naamloze vennootschap (NV) (Neth.) A public limited company.

NAFTA ➤North American Free Trade Agreement.

naked Said of the holding of a ➤security that is not covered, or ➤hedged. An expression more frequently used in reference to ➤derivatives.

name 1. The parties to the commercial transaction underlying a ➤bill of exchange, as recorded on that document (in the ➤clausing). 2. An external underwriting member of ➤Lloyd's insurance market.

NAPF ➤National Association of Pension Funds.

NASD ➤National Association of Securities Dealers.

NASDAQ International ➤National Association of Securities Dealers Automated Quotation System.

NASDAQ OTC Price Index A series of ➤share indices measuring changes in the prices of shares quoted on the ➤National Association of Securities Dealers Automated Quotation System. There are seven indices, including a composite index based on 5 February 1971.

NASDIM ➤National Association of Securities Dealers and Investment Managers.

National Association of Pension Funds (NAPF) The representative organization of providers of occupational pension schemes (➤pensions).

National Association of Securities Dealers (NASD) (US) ➤National Association of Securities Dealers Automated Quotation System.

National Association of Securities Dealers and Investment Managers (NASDIM) (UK) A now defunct body, formed in 1979 as the Association of Licensed Dealers and until 1987 the leading representative body for some 800 licensed securities dealers, who are now members of one of the *self-regulating organizations* recognized under the ➤Financial Services Act.

National Association of Securities Dealers Automated Quotation System (NASDAQ) (US) A series of computer-based information services and an ➤order execution system for the US ➤over-the-counter market. The system was set up in 1971. NASDAQ provides quotations by over 500 active ➤market makers on the

➤securities of over 4,000 companies that are actively traded, an average of eight dealers for each security and a minimum of two.

There are some 180,000 NASDAQ terminals in use, of which 25,000 are outside the USA. NASDAQ was designated a UK *recognized investment exchange* in 1988 (➤Financial Services Act). Brokers and institutional traders, having selected the market maker who offers the best price on their screens, may execute their deals by telephone or teletype or, since 1984, may enter orders directly through the Small Order Execution System (SOES). The SOES allows dealers to fill orders for 500 shares or less and 1,000 shares for NASDAQ ➤National Market System issues. NASDAQ International has operated from London since early 1992 and allows investors to trade US stocks before the ➤New York Stock Exchange opens.

The National Association of Securities Dealers (NASD) is a self-regulatory organization (under delegated powers from the ➤Securities and Exchange Commission) that set up and now regulates NASDAQ and the OTC market.

national bank (US) A ➤commercial bank that receives its charter from (is registered with) the Comptroller of the Currency (who is a federal government official) and is required to be a member of the ➤Federal Reserve System (Fed). A *state bank* receives its charter from a state banking regulatory authority and may opt or not to join the Fed.

national debt The outstanding borrowings of the government, including overseas borrowing. Most of it consists of government and government-guaranteed ➤securities. ➤➤public-sector borrowing requirement.

National Insurance (UK) A social security scheme which provides unemployment and sickness benefits, flat-rate ➤pensions and other benefits in return for regular contributions paid by employees.

National Market System (NMS) (US) A system providing information on the quoted price of ➤stocks, the latest price paid, the high and low for the day and the current ➤volume. NMS brokers are required to report this information through the system within 90 seconds of the trade. Congress mandated the creation of a NMS in its amendments to the 1934 Securities Exchange Act in 1975, which created the ➤Securities and Exchange Commission. The purpose of the NMS was to increase competition by linking the US stock exchanges together in a way that would ensure that prices for any given stock would be the same at all of them. However, the ➤New York Stock Exchange (NYSE) allows its members to trade on the exchange only the stocks listed on the exchange, and only on the ➤National Association of Securities Dealers Automated Quotation System does the NMS operate fully. However, for certain stocks the Intermarket Trading System (ITS) has since 1980 linked a number of stocks quoted on the NYSE, on the ➤American Stock Exchange and one or more of the regional exchanges.

National Savings Bank (NSB) (UK) A ➤savings bank administered by the

Department for National Savings and operating through the post office network. Formerly known as the Post Office Savings Bank (POSB).

National Savings certificate (UK) A ➤bond issued by the UK government. There have been over 40 different issues of these certificates, on which interest, an index-linked increase (➤indexation) or a bonus is payable on ➤maturity or earlier. The certificates can be cashed at any time, and interest is tax free.

National Securities Clearing Corporation (US) A clearing house jointly owned by the ➤New York Stock Exchange, the ➤American Stock Exchange and the ➤National Association of Securities Dealers, set up in 1977. It works through the Securities Industry Automation Corporation (SIAC), which provides the automation, data-processing and communication facilities.

National Stock Exchange (NSE) (India) A ➤stock exchange set up by the Indian government in 1994 based in Bombay but with nationwide coverage. The NSE has clearing centres in Bombay, Delhi, Madras and Calcutta and more than 1,500 remote ➤broker terminals. The NSE has more than twice the turnover of its nearest rival, the ➤Bombay Stock Exchange.

NAV ➤net assets.

NCI ➤new Community instrument.

near money Financial assets that are highly liquid but do not have a direct role in transactions and therefore cannot be fully regarded as ➤money.

nearby month ➤front month.

negotiable 1. Subject to agreement between the parties involved in a transaction. **2.** A negotiable instrument, e.g. a crossed ➤cheque or ➤bearer share, is one in which the title to ownership is transferred freely from hand to hand. **3.** The propensity of a financial claim, e.g. a ➤bill of exchange, ➤certificate of deposit, ➤Treasury bill or ➤bond, to be traded in financial markets, e.g. in the ➤money market. The term is interchangeable in this sense with *transferable* and *marketable*.

negotiable order of withdrawal ➤NOW accounts.

Nennwert (Ger.) Nominal value. ➤par value.

net assets, net asset value (NAV) The value of a company according to the ➤balance sheet. It is calculated by taking fixed ➤assets plus current assets less ➤liabilities owed to all except the owners of the company, and therefore is the same as ➤shareholders' equity and is also called *net worth*. Where ➤long term liabilities, e.g. bank loans, are not deducted in arriving at net assets, then this term is synonymous with ➤capital employed. Assets are valued at *historic cost* (➤costs, historical; depreciation). The market value may be greater than the net asset value. NAV for an ➤investment trust is the market value of ➤shares owned by the trust plus cash, usually divided by the number of shares at issue to give NAV per share. The price of investment trust shares may be at a ➤discount or at a ➤premium to the underlying NAV. ➤➤balance sheet; investment trust; working capital.

net borrowed reserves (US) ➤Borrowed reserves less ➤excess reserves, i.e. the amount of banks' reserves borrowed from the ➤Federal Reserve less the amount of reserves they hold over and above the required minimum.

net current assets ➤working capital.

net premium Of insurance, a ➤premium less the amount paid for ➤reinsurance, and/or less the amount paid in ➤commission or ➤brokerage.

net present value ➤discounted cash flow.

net price On ➤stock exchanges, net prices are net of ➤commission.

net profit ➤profit.

net tangible assets (NTA) Fixed ➤assets plus current assets minus intangible assets, such as ➤goodwill, and minus current ➤liabilities.

net worth ➤net assets.

Neuausgabe (Ger.) ➤New issue.

Neuer Markt ➤German Stock Exchange.

new Community instrument (NCI) A loan financed by direct international borrowing of the European Commission, initiated in the 1970s. The Commission, which had until then organized borrowings through separate bodies established for the purpose, e.g. the ➤European Investment Bank (EIB), became aware that, given its own standing, it would command advantageous rates itself in the international capital market. The funds thus raised are re-lent to public and private bodies in the ➤European Union (formerly European Community) on the same terms and conditions as by the EIB, and the lending programme is managed by the EIB.

new issue The sale of ➤securities, e.g. ➤loan stock or ➤equity, to raise new or additional ➤capital, either by way of a ➤placing, an offer for *subscription* (➤offer for sale) or a ➤rights issue. The term may also refer to the ➤flotation of the existing securities of a company on a ➤stock exchange or an ➤unlisted securities market for the first time, though such an issue may also involve the raising of additional capital. ➤new issue market.

new issue market That part of the ➤capital market that provides new long-term capital, specifically the ➤stock exchange. Borrowers in the new issue market may be raising capital for new investment or may be converting private capital into public capital; this is known as *going public* (➤flotation). ➤➤new issue; rights issue.

new time (UK) Trading on the ►London Stock Exchange in the following ►account period during the last two days of the current one.

New York Cotton Exchange A ►commodity market for cotton, i.e. and other agricultural products, including potatoes and orange juice, founded in 1870, dealing principally in ►futures. The exchange is the world's most active market for futures trading in cotton. The market also trades in liquefied propane gas futures as well as in ►currency and stock index products. It also transacts ►options in cotton futures.

New York Mercantile Exchange (NYMEX) A ►commodity market, founded in 1872 as the Butter and Cheese Market of New York, reincorporated in 1887 under its present name; it now deals in ►futures in crude oil, heating oil, leaded regular gasoline, platinum and palladium. NYMEX introduced the first petroleum futures contract, that on heating oil, in 1978. A merger with the ►Commodity Exchange of New York was projected in 1993, presaging a merger of two of the world's largest markets in energy and precious metals.

New York Stock Exchange (NYSE) (US) The leading New York ►stock exchange and largest in the world in terms of ►market capitalization (►►American Stock Exchange). Some 2,000 companies and 5,000 ►securities are listed on the NYSE. It is the oldest exchange in the USA, dating from 1792, and is also referred to as the Big Board. There are about 500 broking firms, with some 1,366 members or seats. These members trade as ►specialists in particular ►stocks on the ►trading floor, as ►floor brokers on behalf of clients or as ►floor traders on their own account. The NYSE is a self-regulating body, though it has to ensure compliance with the requirements of the ►Securities and Exchange Commission. ►►Dow-Jones indexes.

New Zealand Futures and Options Exchange (NZFOE) Established in 1985, this exchange trades ►financial futures, ►currencies and wool using an automated trading system. The NZFOE is owned by the ►Sydney Futures Exchange.

New Zealand Stock Exchange (NZSE) This exchange has its origins in the 1870s. The trading floors were closed in 1991 in favour of a screen-based trading system. Fixed ►commissions were abolished in 1986. The market share index is the NZSE 40. The exchange is regulated by the Securities Commission and the Stock Exchange Association.

Newco An insurance company, proposed in 1993 by the authorities of ►Lloyd's, which would have the task of reinsuring the liabilities of ►Old Years.

newly industrialized countries (NICs) Not counted as developing or Third World countries, although they have not yet achieved the status of an advanced country. ►►dragons; emerging markets; tigers.

NFA (US) National Futures Association.

nibu (Jap.) The second section of the ►stock exchange, devoted to dealing in lower-rated securities.

niche player A term used to describe a financial institution, generally small, concentrating on a specialized sector, rather than the full range, of the market. Also known as a *boutique*.

NIF ►note issuance facility.

Nikkei/Dow-Jones Average ►Nikkei Stock Average.

Nikkei Stock Average A ►share index based on an unweighted (►weighted average) average of the prices of 225 ►equities quoted on the ►Tokyo Stock Exchange. Published since 1949, the index was originally called the Nikkei/ Dow-Jones Average. Nikkei is the popular name for Nihou Keizai Shimbun, which calculates the index. The Nikkei 300 is capital-weighted and somewhat less volatile. ►►ISE/Nikkei 50 Index.

NMS ►National Market System; normal market size.

No. 145 government bond Most recently issued Japanese government ►bond as at mid-1993, and therefore the 'benchmark' bond, defining going yields. (Japanese government bonds are numbered in sequence.)

nomad Nominated adviser. A stockbroking firm (►stockbroker) approved by the ►London Stock Exchange to advise and sponsor companies on the ►Alternative Investment Market. ►►issuing house.

nominal The characteristic of an aggregate or level expressed in current money terms, i.e. inclusive of the effect of inflation; e.g. nominal ►money supply, ►rates of interest. Always implies a relation to a previous size or level. ►►par value; real.

nominal interest rate The ►rate of interest on a ►fixed-interest security, expressed as a percentage of the ►par value as opposed to its market price. ►yield.

nominal value ►par value.

nominal yield ►yield.

Nominalwert (Ger.) ►Nominal price.

nominee A person or ►company holding ►securities on behalf of another in order to preserve anonymity or to simplify ►settlement. Many ►stockbrokers have set up *nominee companies* in which their clients have *nominee accounts* recording their beneficial interest in ►shares legally owned by the nominee companies. Such a system avoids the necessity for the broker to send ►share certificates through the post and could be the basis for the *paperless settlement systems* now being considered in several countries. ►►CREST; Transfer and Automated Registration of Uncertified Stock (TAURUS).

nominee account ►nominee.

nominee company ►nominee.

non-bank Any financial transactor outside the commercial banking system. ►commercial banks.

non-borrowed reserves (US) Those reserves of the US commercial banks that are not derived from borrowings from the ►Federal Reserve, i.e. reserves accumulated through ordinary banking business.

non-obligatory expenditure Expenditure of the ►European Union not specifically laid down in the founding treaties. In regard to these, the European Parliament, which has the right of final adoption or rejection of the Union budget, may propose amendments that may be sustained despite disagreement by the European Council. ►►obligatory expenditure.

non-proportional treaty Of insurance, an agreement for the reinsurance of a varying amount of claims. ►►excess of loss treaty; reinsurance treaty; stop-loss treaty.

non-recourse ►recourse.

non-recourse finance A loan whose servicing and repayment is dependent solely on the profitability of the underlying project, and not on other funds potentially in the possession of the borrower. ►►factoring.

non-underwritten A ►note, particularly a ►Euronote, that is not ►underwritten. Where issued by a non-bank, such Euronotes are classified as ►Euro-commercial paper, and such issues are known as *Euro-commercial paper programmes*. The term is interchangeable with ►uncommitted.

Nordquote A common quotation dissemination system for the largest companies listed on the four Scandinavian ►stock exchanges. Begun in 1994, the experiment was abandoned the following year.

normal market size (NMS) (UK) A system for classifying ►stocks quoted on the ►London Stock Exchange by ►liquidity. The new system replaced the old ►Stock Exchange Automated Quotation System categories (alpha, beta and gamma; ►alpha securities) on 14 January 1991. NMS for each stock is calculated by multiplying the value of the average daily customer ►turnover in the previous year by 2.5% to give an estimated average value of the normal institutional ►bargain; this is then divided by the price of the stock to give that normal bargain size in terms of the number of shares. This number of shares is allocated to 12 NMS *bands*; e.g. if the NMS interim number of shares is between 1,334 and 2,400, the NMS band is 2,000; if it is between 2,401 and 3,750, it is 3,000. All stocks that fall into an NMS band of 2,000 or more are called *liquid*, while others are called *less liquid* (equivalent to the old gamma stock grouping). The system is used to set the size of transactions for which ➤market makers quote prices and for the publication of market data.

North American Free Trade Agreement (NAFTA) An agreement for a tariff-free area arising out of the Free Trade Area (FTA) established between the USA and Canada in 1989, and extended to Mexico by signature of the three heads of government in 1992, with ratification by the three legislatures sought in 1993. Two accords allaying the fears of US trade unions, consumer groups and environmentalists were attached by President Clinton to the agreement in 1993. The agreement entered into force on 1 January 1994.

***nostro* account** ➤*vostro* account.

note 1. An ➤instrument recording a promise to pay a specific sum of money by a given date; a *promissory note*. ➤➤commercial paper. 2. An inscription on an unpaid bill of exchange by a notary comprising their initials, the date and other details, used by the notary to draw up a ➤protest. 3. A banknote.

note issuance facility (NIF) A form of medium-term ➤Eurocredit, under which the borrower issues a series of short-term ➤instruments against a banker's guarantee over the whole ➤term, given in the form of either an ➤underwriting or a ➤back-up credit arrangement. Where the borrower is a bank, the instrument is usually a short-term ➤certificate of deposit; where the borrower is a ➤non-bank, the instrument is normally a *promissory note* (➤note). ➤Maturities of the instruments are usually three or six months. NIFs are variously known as RUFs (revolving underwriting facilities), *note purchase facilities* and ➤Euronote facilities. The advantage of an NIF to the investor is the high ➤liquidity of the instrument, in that it has a short term and the investor need not partake in the next issue in the series. The willingness of banks themselves to buy the instruments, and the comparatively narrow ➤margins offered, have made NIFs attractive to borrowers, particularly in view of the flexible ➤drawdown available.

The instruments are sold either to a group of purchasing banks or to a *tender panel*, invited by the syndicate of banks managing the facility, or they are sold through a ➤placement, ensured by a sole placing agent. The ➤syndicate either underwrites the issue or makes back-up credit available. The first well-publicized NIF was an issue by the New Zealand government, for $750m, in 1981. By 1985 there were estimated to be new issues worth $33bn, giving a total of $60bn NIFs in place.

note purchase facility ➤note issuance facility.

notice day The day on which notice must be given in the ➤commodity market of the intention to supply a commodity due under contract for delivery in that month (rather than to ➤cover the contract or to ➤liquidate it by purchase of an offsetting contract).

novus actus interveniens A legal term requiring that human intervention, coming between the insured ➤risk and the loss itself, shall be deemed to be the proximate cause of the loss. ➤➤proximity rule.

NOW account (US) A personal interest-bearing savings account at a bank or ➤savings and loan association on which a *negotiable order of withdrawal* (NOW; in effect a ➤cheque) may be drawn, making it an interest-bearing chequing account (➤current account). NOW accounts were legally permitted throughout the USA from January 1980, although until recently the interest rate payable was capped at 5½%.

NPV Net present value. ➤discounted cash flow.

NSB ➤National Savings Bank.

NSE (India) ➤National Stock Exchange.

NT dollar New Taiwan dollar, the national ➤currency unit of Taiwan.

numbered account A bank account identified by a number and not the name of the holder to ensure secrecy.

NV ➤*naamloze vennootschap.*

NYMEX ➤New York Mercantile Exchange.

NZFOE ➤New Zealand Futures and Options Exchange.

NZSE ➤New Zealand Stock Exchange.

O

OAT ➤*obligation à trésorerie.*

obiter dictum An incidental observation of a judge, not necessarily binding in the case being heard, but of possible application in subsequent matters.

obligation 1. A ➤debt. 2. A ➤debt instrument, normally a ➤bond.

obligation (Fr.) A ➤bond.

Obligation (Ger.) A ➤bond.

obligation à trésorerie (OAT) (Fr.) A French ➤Treasury bill.

obligation au porteur (Fr.) A bearer ➤bond. ➤bearer security.

obligation convertible en action (Fr.) A ➤convertible bond.

obligation de caisse (Fr.) A bank bond issued at medium term, not traded on the ➤stock exchange.

obligation d'état (Fr.) A government ➤bond.

obligatory expenditure Expenditure of the ➤European Union directly deriving from the founding treaties. The European Parliament, which has the final decision on approval or rejection of the Union budget, may propose amendments to obligatory expenditure; but if these are not agreed by the European Council, then its only recourse is to reject the budget as a whole. Main examples of obligatory expenditure are those under the common agricultural policy. ➤➤non-obligatory expenditure.

OBX (Norwegian) *Oslo Børs.* The Oslo Stock Exchange.

occupational pension scheme ➤pensions.

OEIC ➤open-ended investment company.

Oesterreichische Kontrollbank The semi-official Austrian financial institution, supported by government funds, issuing bonds in particular in the international and ➤Eurobond markets.

Oesterreichische Termin und Optionsbörse The Austrian ➤futures and options exchange.

off-balance-sheet finance Where a business ➤asset is not purchased and subject to ►depreciation, but is acquired by ►leasing or ►hire purchase, it may not appear on the ►balance sheet. Rental payments will, of course, be taken into account in the ►profit and loss account, but the indebtedness of the company and ►capital employed will be understated. However, in the USA and UK companies may be required to capitalize leased assets. ►►market capitalization.

offer for sale (UK) Shares may be offered to the public at a fixed price in an advertised offer for sale (US = *public offering*). Those who purchase the shares are said to have subscribed, i.e. it is an offer for subscription. More rarely an offer for ►tenders will be called for. In a tender, potential investors are invited to specify the number of shares they are prepared to buy at a specified price at or above the issuer's stipulated minimum price. The ►issuing house will set a price, the ►striking price, at which the whole issue can be sold at the highest price. Those who have made a tender offer at or above the striking price will receive the number of shares they ask for (unless the issue is ►oversubscribed); those whose offer price is below the striking price will receive no shares. Issues over a certain size (£50m) have to be offered to the public in their entirety, under the rules of the ►London Stock Exchange, instead of by a ►placing or an ►intermediaries offer. ►►introduction.

offer price The price at which a ►dealer or ►market maker will sell ►commodities or ►shares (US = *asked price*). ►Unit trust managers also quote an offer price at which they will sell units to the general public. Cf. ►bid price.

office A company or ►mutual society engaged in insurance.

official list (UK) The daily list of ►securities admitted for trading on the ►London Stock Exchange. It does not include securities quoted on the ►unlisted securities markets.

official prices Of the ►London Metal Exchange, the prices reached in the first trading session of each day, which are then made public and used as a reference for most world trade in the metals for the following 24 hours. Also known as *settlement prices*.

offre publique d'achat (Fr.) A ►cash take-over bid.

offre publique d'échange (Fr.) A bid for a ►take-over based on an exchange of ►shares.

offshore banking ►tax haven.

offshore financial centres ►tax haven.

offshore funds ►tax haven.

ohne Dividende (Ger.) ►Ex-dividend.

ohne Kupon (Ger.) *Ex-coupon.* ►ex-dividend.

OKB ➤Osterreichische Kontrollbank.

Old Lady of Threadneedle Street Popular nickname for the ➤Bank of England.

Old Years Term used at ➤Lloyd's to refer to the 1985 business year and to all preceding years. The feature of these years was that they embraced the severe losses arising out of US legislation on asbestosis and environmental pollution, and other losses. US asbestosis and environmental legislation had occasioned US employers and producers massive costs in compensation payments, going back up to 40 years, and in remedial works. US courts had so interpreted the wording of insurance contracts, also up to 40 years old, that insurers were required to pay employers' and producers' costs.

OM The Swedish ➤options market.

OMLX ➤Options Market London Exchange.

on-line A part of a computer system, e.g. a printer, is on-line when it is connected to and ready for use by the computer.

one-month money Money placed, i.e. an ➤instrument 'bought' in the ➤money market, with a ➤maturity of one month.

one-year money Money placed, i.e. an ➤instrument 'bought' in the ➤money market, with a ➤maturity of one year.

OPEC ➤Organization of Petroleum Exporting Countries.

open cover A policy for the ➤insurance of ships' cargoes similar to a ➤floating policy except that the duration of the policy is unlimited.

open-end credit ➤revolving credit.

open-ended fund An investment company in which units may be purchased from or sold to the fund manager, i.e. a ➤unit trust or ➤mutual funds company. The fund is open in the sense that its size depends upon its success in selling units, in contrast to an ➤investment trust. Units are bought and sold at a price that reflects the market value of the securities they represent, plus a management charge equal to the difference between the ➤bid price and ➤offer price.

open-ended investment company (OEIC) An ➤open-ended fund listed on a ➤stock exchange at a single unit share price; like an ➤investment trust but it can issue or redeem (➤redemption) ➤shares to match demand in a similar way to a ➤unit trust. Common in continental European countries and the United States. OEICs have recently been permitted in the UK.

open market desk (US) A familiar term for the section of the New York Federal Reserve Bank that conducts open market operations on behalf of the Federal

Reserve Board, and specifically of the Federal Open Market Committee. More exactly referred to as the *domestic open market desk.* ►Federal Reserve.

open market operations Dealings in the ►money market by a central bank, with the object of influencing short-term interest rates in pursuit of ►monetary control policies. The term is used to distinguish such activities from other policy measures available to central banks, such as ►reserve asset requirements, bond sales and direct lending.

open-mouth operations (US) Expression used to describe the ►Federal Reserve's use of public statements to induce a change in ►money-market conditions. The term is a play on the official usage: ►open market operations.

open outcry, open outcry system The practice in a ►stock exchange or ►commodity market whereby trading is done by oral calling of bids and offers by market members to the point where prices are settled and deals are concluded.

open position A ►position that is not ►covered, or ►hedged. Of trade in ►commodities, a position, or holding of contract, that has not been ►liquidated.

open year The business of ►Lloyd's syndicates is conducted on a three-year cycle; i.e. the results of any one year's transactions are not finalized until the third year thereafter; e.g. the accounts of business done in 1993 are not closed until the end of 1995. This procedure provides for the fact that claims on policies issued in one year continue to arise for some time after the end of the year, and facilitates the choice of a fair premium for ►reinsurance to close. The first and second years in the three-year cycle are known as 'open years'. The term is also used on occasion to refer to a ►run-off account.

opening price The price at which a ►security is quoted when a ►stock exchange, or other market, opens for business in the morning (►bid price; offer price). ►Market makers will adjust their prices from the level they reached when trading stopped on the previous day (►closing prices) in line with their expectations of the strength of supply and demand.

operating factors (US) Circumstances, such as the ►Federal Reserve float, influencing the ►liquidity of the US banking system, which must be taken into account when conducting the ►Federal Reserve's ►open market operations.

operating profit (or loss) Profit (or loss) before tax and ►interest, usually on the principal trading activities of the business and excluding extraordinary items (►below the line).

operating system The set of programs or software that controls the basic functions of a computer. Additional software is normally necessary to use the computer to carry out specific tasks such as word processing.

operating target (US) The monetary aggregate (►non-borrowed reserves;

reserves; Federal funds rate) taken by the ➤open market desk as its guide in its open market operations.

opération du double (Fr.) ➤Bourse transaction under which *put* (*option de vente*) and *call* (*option d'achat*) ➤options are simultaneously held.

OPIC ➤Overseas Private Investment Corporation.

OPL ➤overall premium limit.

option 1. A contract giving its beneficiary the right to buy or sell a financial ➤instrument or a ➤commodity, including gold, at a specified price within a specified period. The option can be freely exercised or disregarded, there being no obligation to transact. Where the right is to buy, the contract is termed a *call option*; where the right is to sell, it is termed a *put option*. The holder of the option is able to take advantage of a favourable movement in prices, losing only the premium payable for the option should prices move adversely. The writer, or seller, of the option is correspondingly more exposed to risk. 2. In the ➤foreign exchange market, a binding contract to buy or sell a currency at a specific price, the date of the transaction being left to the choice of the holder of the contract.

Trade in option contracts (hence *traded options*) was long practised between banks but developed, particularly in currency options, after these began to be traded on the Philadelphia Stock Exchange in 1982. Trade in securities options, or *interest rate options*, began later. Currency options were introduced on the ➤London International Financial Futures Exchange (LIFFE) and the ➤London Stock Exchange in 1985. Options on three-month sterling ➤futures were introduced on LIFFE in November 1987; trade in Japanese government bond futures began in July 1987. Chief centres for trade in options are the ➤Chicago Board Options Exchange, the ➤American Stock Exchange, the ➤European Options Exchange in Amsterdam and markets in Australia, France, Sweden and Switzerland. ➤➤futures options; over-the-counter market.

option d'achat (Fr.) *Call* ➤option.

option de vente (Fr.) *Put* ➤option.

Options Clearing Corporation A ➤clearing house for ➤over-the-counter derivatives, based in New York.

Options Market London Exchange An options market (➤option) opened in 1989 in conjunction with the Swedish Options Market (OM), trading in Swedish and Norwegian equity derivatives; in May 1997 a wood-pulp ➤futures trade, *Pulpex*, was also initiated.

Optionsschein (Ger.) A right held by shareholders in a new issue to buy more shares at an agreed price, the right itself being tradable.

order An instruction from a client to a ➤broker-dealer to buy or sell a ➤security.

An order may be a market order to buy or sell at the best price the dealer can obtain at the time of execution. Alternatively, the client may impose a stop order to buy or sell only if the price rises or falls to a specified level. Stop-loss orders are intended to protect the client from loss or to limit the client's loss in a falling market (US = *limit order*).

order driven A ►stock exchange system in which prices react to orders, as in the *auction system* in the ►New York Stock Exchange, where ►brokers and dealers bid for stock (*open outcry* or *auction*) around a *specialist* who maintains a market in chosen stocks by buying and selling for their own account and for broker clients. As distinct from ►quote driven. An order driven system may be automated so as to match bargains (►matched bargains) electronically, as in the new SETS (►London Stock Exchange).

ordinary branch Of insurance, life insurance business other than ►industrial branch business.

ordinary share (UK) A share in the ►equity capital of a business; holders of ordinary shares being entitled to all distributed ►profits after the holders of ►debentures and ►preference shares have been paid (US = *common stock*).

Organization for Economic Co-operation and Development (OECD) The successor to the ►Organization for European Economic Co-operation (OEEC), the OECD was constituted in 1961 out of the original membership of the OEEC, comprising most Western European countries, together with Canada and the USA, to which Finland, Japan, New Zealand and Australia were subsequently added. Recently, the Czech Republic, Hungary, Mexico and Turkey have become members. The OECD thus represents the industrialized world as a whole. The purposes of the OECD are to promote growth and high employment consistent with financial stability in its member countries; to foster international trade; and to contribute to the economic progress of the developing countries and of non-member countries. The OECD is based in Paris and operates through a number of major committees attended by ministers of the member countries. An early achievement was the further promotion of the code of liberalization adopted by its predecessor, which contributed substantially to the removal of ►exchange controls. The Economic Policy Committee has latterly become an important venue for international consultation and agreement on policy response to the economic situation. The OECD publishes a wide range of reports, among them regular assessments of the worldwide economic situation and of the economies of individual members. The Development Assistance Committee centralized the OECD's activities in respect to the developing world and established, among other things, a standard of aid contributions to which all members should aspire (0.7% of *gross national product*; ►gross domestic product).

Organization for European Economic Co-operation (OEEC) An organization set up in 1948 in response to the offer of ➤Marshall aid from the USA. Open to all European countries, membership comprised 17 nations of Western Europe; the Eastern European countries, including the Soviet Union, refused to join. The task of the OEEC was to reach common agreement on the allocation of Marshall aid to individual countries. This was done through a range of technical committees for separate industries and economic sectors, in accordance with the European Recovery Programme established by the council of the OEEC. In concert with this, the US Congress voted funds as far as possible in the amount deemed necessary. Under the programme, which continued from 1948 to 1951, some £12.1bn was disbursed by the USA, equivalent to some $55bn in 1997 prices. As a result of these efforts, total OEEC industrial production expanded by 50% between 1947 and 1952/3, and the volume of exports to third countries doubled. Other measures included a co-ordinated reduction of quantitative restrictions on trade, in conformity with the convention of the ➤General Agreement on Tariffs and Trade (GATT); the introduction in 1950 of a code of liberalization, placing trade in goods, services and capital on a multilateral rather than a bilateral basis; and the establishment of the European Payments Union (EPU), extending payments for trade from a bilateral to a multilateral system. The EPU was succeeded in 1958 by the European Monetary Agreement (EMA), further extending ➤convertibility and establishing a European fund for *ad hoc* credit; automatic credits were ended. By 1960, with a further major rise in output and trade, it was decided that broader purposes were now appropriate, and the convention was signed for the transformation of the OEEC into the ➤Organization for European Co-operation and Development (OECD).

Organization of Petroleum Exporting Countries (OPEC) An intergovernmental organization of oil-producing countries, established in 1960 and comprising Algeria, Ecuador, Gabon, Indonesia, Iran, Iraq, Kuwait, Libya, Nigeria, Qatar, Saudi Arabia, the Union of Arab Emirates (UAE) and Venezuela. During the 1960s the member countries nationalized the management of the oilfields, until then operated by the major international oil companies. In the course of the 'Yom Kippur' Arab–Israeli conflict of October 1973, the OPEC countries reduced output and embargoed supplies to Western countries, with a consequent sharp rise in oil prices. The cutbacks in production continued after the conclusion of peace, and developed into a co-ordinated programme of production and export restrictions designed to raise prices permanently. In the event oil prices rose from some $3 a barrel in 1972 to some $15 a barrel in the mid- to late 1970s, and to some $33 a barrel in 1981. This caused a major wave of worldwide inflation and recession, and, given the Arab countries' propensity to concentrate their substantial new wealth in short-term bank deposits, a severe imbalance in international monetary resources.

However, by the mid-1980s the stringent measures of energy conservation, the switch to other fuels and the opening up of major new oilfields that had occurred in importing countries had effectively ended the OPEC domination of prices. By the mid-1990s oil prices per barrel had stabilized in the $15–$20 range.

origin principle ➤value added tax.

OSC Ontario Securities Commission. ➤Toronto Stock Exchange.

OTOB ➤Oesterreichische Termin und Optionsbörse.

out of the money A situation where the ➤exercise price of an ➤option is adverse to the market price, i.e. where the exercise price is higher than the market price in the case of a *call option* and the reverse of this in the case of a *put option*. ➤➤in the money; intrinsic value.

outright forward In a ➤forward currency contract, a single sale or purchase, as against a ➤forward-forward, or a ➤swap, sale or purchase.

outright purchase/sale (US) The purchase or sale by the ➤Federal Reserve of ➤money-market instruments (➤Treasury bills, government ➤bonds) for retention or for indefinite disbursement, thus creating a drain on or an influx into the reserves of the banking system.

over-the-counter (OTC) market 1. A group of licensed dealers who provide two-way trading facilities in company ➤securities outside the ➤stock exchange. The term originated in the USA in the 1870s when ➤stocks were first bought across bank counters. The term is often used to refer generally to ➤unlisted securities markets and specifically (US) to the elaborate electronic dealing system, with ➤market makers across the country, called the ➤National Association of Securities Dealers Automated Quotation System (NASDAQ). However, NASDAQ trades also in large-company stocks including those listed on other stock exchanges. **2**. More generally any securities trading activity carried on outside stock exchanges, e.g. OTC ➤options, which are options written by a single seller for a single buyer under a private and confidential arrangement, as distinct from *traded options*.

overall premium limit (OPL) The maximum amount of insurance a member of ➤Lloyd's can ➤underwrite, i.e. the maximum amount of premiums they can accept. The OPL is calculated as a multiple of the member's ➤funds at Lloyd's.

overdraft (UK) A ➤loan facility on a customer's ➤current account at a bank permitting the customer to overdraw up to a certain limit for an agreed period. ➤Interest is payable on the amount of the loan facility taken up, and it may therefore be a relatively inexpensive way of financing a fluctuating requirement. ➤➤line of credit.

overfunding ➤funding.

overheads Costs that do not vary with output in the short run, e.g. rent, administrative salaries.

overlay manager ➤currency overlay manager.

overnight money Money placed in the ➤money market for repayment the next day.

overnight repo ➤repurchase agreement.

overseas banks (UK) **1**. Banks operating in the UK but foreign-controlled. There are over 600 such banks in the UK. **2**. UK-owned banks that conduct their business mainly abroad.

Overseas Private Investment Corporation A US government agency set up to encourage US private investment in emerging countries.

overseas sector A term used in economic and ➤money supply contexts to denote foreign transactors, i.e. individuals, companies and governments resident abroad that are trading with, or involved in investment transactions with, national residents. ➤➤private sector; public sector.

oversubscribed, oversubscription A ➤new issue is said to be oversubscribed when investors are prepared to purchase more shares at the offered price (or the ➤striking price) than are available. In these cases the ➤issuing house either conducts a ballot or lucky draw in which the successful applications are selected at random, or it scales down applications for above a certain minimum quantity of ➤shares. ➤offer for sale.

overtrading A business is said to be overtrading when it has insufficient ➤working capital to meet its debts when they fall due.

own resources A term derived from the French *ressources propres* to denote the autonomous revenues of the ➤European Union, in contrast to direct contributions from member states. The European Union's own resources consist of the proceeds of the common external tariff, agricultural ➤levies and 1% of ➤value added tax collections, all of which pass to the Union as of right under a decision taken in 1970.

P

P & I clubs ➤protection and indemnity clubs.

P&L ➤profit and loss account.

pagare (Sp.) Promissory note. ➤note.

pagare de empresa (Sp.) ➤Commercial paper.

paid-up capital That part of the ➤issued capital of a company that has been paid in by the shareholders. Partly paid shares are those on which only a proportion of the issue price of the shares was paid on subscription. This may arise where shares are issued in partly paid form, the second part being payable a few months later to increase the attractiveness of the issue.

Panda A Chinese 1 oz gold coin with a fine (➤fineness) gold content of 1 ➤troy ounce. First issued in 1982.

pair (Fr.) ➤Par.

paper A vernacular term for any ➤security, most generally applied to those in the ➤money market. Used more specifically for ➤notes issued by companies for trading at a ➤discount, namely ➤commercial paper.

paperless settlement systems ➤Transfer and Automated Registration of Uncertified Stock (TAURUS).

par 1. A ➤security is issued at par, its *nominal* or *face* value, and may thereafter trade above or below par, or still at par. **2.** The official fixed ➤rate of exchange of a currency, as it was notified to the ➤International Monetary Fund (IMF) up to the time of the abolition of fixed exchange rates in 1978. The second amendment to the articles of agreement of the IMF, adopted in 1978, declared the withdrawal of par values, subject to their reintroduction, calculated, however, in terms of ➤special drawing rights (SDRs) or any other denominator except ➤gold or US dollars, on a 85% vote of the members.

par banking (US) The practice of paying the full nominal value by one bank of a cheque drawn on another made universal in the USA by the ➤Federal Reserve in the early 20th century.

par bond A bond trading at ➤par, the latter generally as defined by the price of new issues or by prevailing yields.

par casier (Fr.) One of the three types of quotation on the French ►stock exchange, the others being *à la criée* and *par opposition*. *Par casier* involves the deposit of orders for ►securities in specified repositories, or 'pigeon-holes' (the meaning of *casier*), in the market, which are then collected and used to determine a ►market clearing price. The method is normally used in the ►spot market.

par opposition (Fr.) One of the three forms of quotation on the French ►stock exchange, the others being ►*par casier* and *à la criée*. The method of *par opposition* is to strike a price arbitraging (►arbitrage) the ►forward and the ►spot market.

par priced A security issued or trading at its ►par, or *nominal* or *face* value.

par value The price at which a ►share, or other ►security, is issued, which may of course be greater or less than its market price. Alternatively *nominal* or *face* value, though these terms are more usually applied to ►currency; e.g. a silver coin may be worth more than its face value. ►►parity.

parallel markt (Neth.) The now defunct second-tier ►unlisted securities market of the ►Amsterdam Stock Exchange. There were two sub-tiers in the Dutch second-tier market: one for companies that have been officially admitted, and one for companies that have not met all the requirements. The term *parallel markets* is also widely used to refer to other second tiers or unlisted securities markets.

parallel money markets Markets in short-term securities other than ►Treasury bills, ►bills of exchange and ►bonds and including ►Eurocurrency, ►certificates of deposit, loans to local authorities and interbank loans. ►interbank market.

parent company A company that owns 50% or more of the ►ordinary shares of a ►subsidiary company.

pari passu With equal ranking.

Paris Bourse (Fr.) The principal ►stock exchange in France, from 1991 incorporating the ►regional stock exchanges in Bordeaux, Lille, Lyon, Marseille, Nancy and Nantes. A member of the stock exchange in France is called an *agent de change* and will be a member of the ►Chambre Syndicale des Agents de Change, which, with the official ►Commission des Opérations de Bourse, supervises the securities markets. The *bourse* has three main segments: the *Marché à Reglement Mensuel* and the *Marché au Comptant*, which comprise the first segment or *premier marché*; the *second marché* for small and medium enterprises, and the *nouveau marché* for hi-tech high-growth stocks (►EURO.NM). In addition there is an unregulated *Marché Libre OTC*, formerly the *Marché Hors Cote*.

The *bourse* operates a screen-based electronic system called *SUPERCAC*, which has superseded CAC, which was based on CATS (►Toronto Stock Exchange). The *CAC General Index* is based on 250 ►shares and the *CAC 40*, the most commonly quoted Paris index, is used as a basis for ►futures contracts. ►►Compagnie des Agents de Change; Marché à Terme des Instruments Financiers.

Paris interbank offered rate (PIBOR) The French equivalent of ➤London interbank offered rate (LIBOR).

parity A term interchangeable with ➤exchange rate, most often used by international institutions, a further alternative term being ➤par value. ➤➤International Monetary Fund.

parquet (Fr.) A generic term for the Paris ➤stock market, originally the name only of the official market as distinct from the ➤coulisse.

part (Fr.) **1.** In general, a ➤share of any possession. **2.** A company share. **3.** A ➤shareholding. **4.** A financial interest. **5.** A contribution.

participating preference shares (UK) ➤preference shares.

participation (Fr.) A ➤shareholding.

particular average ➤average.

partly paid shares ➤paid-up capital.

partnership An ➤unincorporated business based on a contractual relationship between two or more people who share risks and profits. Each partner is liable for the ➤debts and business actions of the others, to the full extent of their own resources (although they are taxed as an individual). ➤➤fiscal transparency.

pass (US) ➤coupon pass.

pass through (US) An arrangement whereby the interest and capital repayments on the mortgages underlying a ➤collateralized mortgage security, and received by the servicing agent, are forwarded to the security holder. This may be a straight pass through, where the transfers proceed as the underlying payments are received, or a *modified* pass through, where the transfers to the security holder are guaranteed, irrespective of the payments received by the security agent.

passif (Fr.) **1.** ➤Liability. **2.** The liability side of a ➤balance sheet.

Patronat (Fr.) The federation of company associations equivalent to the UK Confederation of British Industry.

pawnbroker (UK) A person who lends money against a pledged article that the lender is free to sell if the ➤loan is not repaid with ➤interest within a stated period.

Pay As You Earn (PAYE) ➤income tax.

pay-out ratio ➤dividend cover.

payback, payback period The period over which the cumulative net revenue from an ➤investment project equals the original investment. Its main defects are that it does not allow for the time value of money or for ➤cash flows over the whole life of the project. ➤➤discounted cash flow.

PAYE Pay As You Earn. ➤income tax.

paying agent An intermediary, usually a bank, responsible for transmitting payments of interest and capital, received from the ➤fiscal agent, to holders of ➤bonds, normally international in character (e.g. ➤Eurobonds), against presentation of ➤coupons and bond certificates.

payroll tax A tax (➤taxation) levied on employers' wage and salary bills.

PC Personal computer. ➤microcomputer.

PDVSA ➤*Petroleos de Venezuela SA*.

P/E ratio ➤price–earnings ratio.

peg To maintain a national ➤currency at a fixed exchange value in terms of another. ➤➤crawling peg.

PEG ➤price–earnings growth factor.

penny share (UK) A share ➤quoted on the ➤London Stock Exchange priced at less than £1, e.g. 18p. Penny shares seem cheap and are for this reason popular with some speculators, but what is really important is the ➤yield of a share and the prospects for the company. ➤heavy share.

pension (Fr.) A borrowing in the French money market, the ➤security against which is held by the lender.

Pension Benefit Guarantee Corporation ➤Employee Retirement Income Security Act.

pension mortgage Use of the tax-free lump sum payable on the maturing of a ➤personal pension scheme to pay off a ➤mortgage. There is a tax advantage in that contributions to a pension scheme attract tax relief, whereas premiums on a life assurance policy, the other method of financing a mortgage, do not. A disadvantage is that a smaller amount remains from the lump sum to buy an ➤annuity. ➤➤life assurance.

pensions Regular income after a certain age and usually after retirement from work, provided by a state scheme or private scheme. Most countries have state schemes as well as private schemes. In Britain the flat-rate retirement pension is paid to men over 65 and women over 60 who have paid appropriate National Insurance contributions, and there is also a State Earnings-Related Pension Scheme (SERPS). There are two broad types of private scheme: *occupational pension schemes*, provided by employers, either contributory or non-contributory; and *personal annuity schemes*, for the self-employed or others not members of an occupational scheme. Under these schemes individuals pay contributions into a fund managed by a ➤life assurance company, or other ➤institutional investor, which provides a cash lump sum at retirement age; if it is to qualify for tax relief, all the premiums must be used to purchase an ►annuity. Occupational pension schemes may also be *self-administered*, i.e. managed by the employer.

Pension schemes may be *funded* (a capital reserve system), with contributions paid into a fund that is invested in ►securities and other ►assets and from which pensions are ultimately paid. Such funds, which received special tax treatment, are important operators in securities markets (►institutional investor). Pension schemes may also be *unfunded*, as in the UK National Insurance scheme and most other state schemes, where pensions for retirees are paid out of the contributions of those in work.

►►Employee Retirement Income Security Act; equalization of pensions; individual retirement account; Keogh plan; personal pension.

Pensions Act 1995 (UK) An Act which came into force in April 1997 for the further regulation of UK occupational pension schemes. This established *inter alia*: a 'minimum funding requirement' intended to safeguard scheme members' rights in the event of the employer's insolvency; a new regulatory body, the Occupational Pensions Regulatory Body; an increase in the numbers of trustees drawn from scheme membership; and fuller information for scheme members. ►►Pensions.

People's Bank of China The Chinese ►central bank.

People's Insurance Company of China (PICC) A state-run insurance company in China. The PICC is the country's largest insurer.

per mille 'Per thousand': a term used to express very fine interest rates, thus '5 *per mille*' equals 0.5%.

per se By itself; in itself.

percentile The xth percentile is that value of a distribution of numbers below which are x per cent of the number of observations. The 50th percentile (which is called the *median*), for example, divides the distribution into two equal parts. The *quartiles* are at 25% and 75%. Similarly, *deciles* subdivide the distribution into tenths.

peril Of insurance, one of several possible occurrences, all of which constitute the ►risk against which insurance is provided.

peripherals ►local area network.

permanent health insurance (PHI) ►Insurance under which individuals rendered unable to work through illness or accident receive income during the period of incapacity. Any eligibility for benefit ceases when the policy-holder reaches retirement age. The insurance is so called because the insurer remains *permanently* in risk from the inception of the policy.

permanent interest-bearing shares (Pibs) (UK) A form of investment in a building society. The ►shares are perpetual, i.e. redeemable only on the winding-up of the society and then ranking after all other liabilities. Interest is paid after payment on all other liabilities. Where a building society converts itself into a limited company, i.e. a bank, Pibs are automatically converted into ►subordinated debt of that company.

perpetual annuity An annual sum of money paid over an indefinite period of time.

perpetual FRN (floating rate note) A ►floating rate note having no ►maturity, i.e. not to be repaid; used chiefly as an investment ►instrument.

personal annuity schemes ►pensions.

personal equity plan (PEP) (UK) A scheme introduced in the Finance Act 1986 to provide tax relief on the proceeds of personal investments in ►equities listed on the ►stock exchange. In any one year a maximum of £6,000 per annum plus £3,000 in a single company PEP per individual may be invested. There is no tax on ►capital gains, and ►dividends are free of ►income tax if reinvested. To qualify for these benefits, the shares must be held from the start of the plan until 31 December of the following year. The plan must be administered by a financial institution, and some ►investment trusts and ►unit trusts have PEP status (*qualifying trusts*). ►►individual savings account.

personal financial planning (PFP) Commercially provided advice on the financial affairs of individuals looked at as a whole, but with emphasis upon ►pensions, ►life assurance, ►taxation and ►investment. PFP concentrates on the creation and protection of ►capital, the maximization and balancing of capital growth and income in accordance with the wishes and tax circumstances of the client. PFP also aims to make provision for contingencies including house purchase, tax liabilities, the acquisition of shares in partnerships or other enterprises, school fees, sickness and disablement, retirement and death. PFP is not normally concerned with maximizing ►earned income, but it is concerned with the form in which that income is taken, in other words, with the mix of the remuneration package. PFP services are provided by ►financial intermediaries that also provide their own savings media, such as the ►commercial banks, and by specialist consultants, ►insurance brokers, accountants and solicitors, all of these advisers being subject to the provision of the ►Financial Services Act.

personal identification number (PIN) A number unique to an individual required to gain access via a ►key pad to computer-controlled equipment such as a security lock or an ►automatic teller machine.

Personal Investment Authority (PIA) (UK) A self-regulatory organization for the regulation of retail financial products. The PIA replaced FIMBRA and LAUTRO and some activities of IMRO and the SFA in 1994 and is itself to be absorbed into the FSA. ►Financial Services Act.

personal loan (UK) A ►bank loan made without ►collateral security to a private customer, usually for specific purposes. A ►term loan.

personal pension A ►pension deriving from a pension account in the name of a single individual, as compared with an occupational pension or company scheme. Personal pensions were made available to UK employees under the Social Security Act 1985; until then employees had access only to occupational pensions. Personal pensions are all ►money purchase schemes; taxation and contribution rules are the same as for self-employed pension schemes. Personal pensions can move with individuals when they change jobs, thus the term *portable pensions*. In the USA personal pensions were introduced in 1975 as ►individual retirement accounts (IRAs).

personal reserve Moneys arising from ►Lloyd's members' ►underwriting profits that they place with their ►funds at Lloyd's. ►Members' agents are empowered to insist on a minimum amount, but there is no upper limit.

Petrobas The state-owned oil company of Brazil.

Petroleos de Venezuela SA **(PDVSA)** (Venezuela) The state-owned oil company of Venezuela.

petroleum revenue tax (PRT) (UK) A tax on the profits of oil companies deductible from ►corporation tax. It was introduced to increase revenue from the profits earned on the development of oilfields in the North Sea.

Pfandbrief (Ger.) A loan instrument issued to refinance mortgages or public-sector projects, closely regulated under law. *Pfandbriefe* may be issued only by authorized banks, themselves fully liable for the issue. Underlying mortgages may not exceed 60% of the property value; public-sector projects must be secured by public-sector loans. *Pfandbriefe* must also be covered by separate funds with at least equivalent yields; holders have first claim on assets in case of default. *Pfandbriefe* are vetted by a state-appointed trustee.

PFI ►private finance initiative.

PHI ►permanent health insurance.

Philharmoniker An Austrian 1 oz gold coin of 999.9 ►fineness and with a fine gold content of 1 ►troy ounce, first issued in 1989.

physical A ►commodity, sold on a ►commodity market, available for immediate or very early delivery. So called because the commodity is physically at hand, as against commodities that are the subject of ►futures, ►forward and ►option contracts of sale. The term is used synonymously with 'actual', 'cash' and 'spot'.

physical price The price of a commodity immediately available for sale and delivery. Also known as cash or actual price. ►►forward; futures; option.

PIA ➤Personal Investment Authority.

PIBOR ➤Paris interbank offered rate.

Pibs permanent health insurance.

PICC ➤People's Insurance Company of China.

PIN ➤personal identification number.

pink sheets ➤Listings of ➤bid prices and ➤offer prices for ➤market makers in ➤over-the-counter markets. Published in the USA by the National Quotation Bureau, which also publishes *yellow sheets* for corporate bonds.

pit trader A ➤dealer in an area of or on a platform on the floor of a ➤stock exchange or ➤commodity market trading by ➤open outcry.

PIX (Finland) The Finnish Wood-pulp price index. ➤Finnish Options Exchange (FOEX).

placement ➤placing.

placement (Fr.) An ➤investment.

placing (UK) The sale of new shares to institutions or private individuals, as distinct from an ➤introduction or ➤offer for sale (US = *placement*). The placing of shares is common for ➤private companies, where it may be carried out by the company directly with investors (a private placing) or with the help of a ➤stockbroker. For ➤public companies wishing to place shares as a route towards a ➤listing, a ➤sponsor will be used; this is sometimes called a public placing (➤introduction). ➤Stock exchange authorities allow listed companies to use placing only for small issues, since not all investors have the opportunity to buy at the same price. For larger issues an offer for sale is required, but this is a more costly means of raising capital. ➤➤intermediaries offer.

plastic money ➤credit card.

Plaza Agreement (1985) An agreement reached at a meeting at the Plaza Hotel, New York, in September 1985 of the *Group of Five* – the USA, the UK, Japan, France and West Germany – to the effect that measures would be taken to establish greater international currency stability, and exchange rates more closely reflecting the economic situation of the countries involved.

Plc ➤incorporation.

plus value (Fr.) **1.** ➤Appreciation of capital. **2.** Surplus value, i.e. the Marxian concept of the true value of labour as contrasted with the value of wages paid.

PMI ➤private medical insurance.

poison pill A defensive action to discourage a hostile ►take-over bid, such as the sale of a major ►asset. ►corporate raider.

polarization (UK) The new regulatory framework in the investment industry (►Financial Services Act) does not allow banks, ►building societies and other ►financial intermediaries to sell their own financial products, such as ►unit trusts, and present themselves at the same time as advisers on such products. They must polarize: act either as independents, offering advice on, and sales of, all competing products; or as agents, selling only their own services. Some institutions have chosen one route, some the other. ►►independent financial adviser (IFA); independent intermediary.

policy A contract for ►insurance.

policy-holder The possessor of an insurance ►policy.

Policy Signing and Accounting Centre (PSAC) ►London International Insurance and Reinsurance Market Association.

political risk The risk, in securities trading, that a deal may be seriously threatened by a change in official policy such as in regard to ►taxation, ►tariffs, ►quotas, ►currency controls, foreign ownership, nationalization, interest rates, etc.

poll tax A tax levied equally on each adult member of a community; hence the unofficial name given to the community charge in the UK (►local taxation).

pooled pension funds An assemblage of ►pension funds collectively managed by the fund manager.

Ponzi scheme (US) An investment swindle in which the perpetrator pockets the investment and pays interest or profits to investors out of new money flowing into the scheme. The name comes from a 1920s scandal involving a Charles Ponzi.

pooling of interests ►consolidated accounts.

portable pension (UK) ►personal pension.

portfolio 1. A group of ►securities held as an investment. 2. A branch or class of insurance business.

portfolio insurance A ►stock exchange technique whereby offsetting transactions in the ►futures market are used to compensate for changes in the current market.

portfolio investment ►balance of payments.

portfolio theory Economic analysis of the means by which investors can minimize risk and maximize returns. Central to ►portfolio theory are the notions that risk can be reduced by diversifying holdings of ►assets, while returns are a function of expected risk. Statistical analysis of ►share prices is used to provide guidance on portfolio composition. ➤➤alpha coefficient; capital asset pricing model.

POSB Post Office Savings Bank. ➤National Savings Bank.

position 1. The extent of a person's financial commitment to a ➤stock, ➤commodity or ➤currency. If a ➤dealer, for example, sells 100 ➤shares they do not own, they have sold short or have a short position of 100 in the shares. If they own 100 shares, they have long position of 100 in the stock on their books. They will take a ➤bear position, i.e. a short position, if they expect the price of the stock to fall and can buy the stock to meet their sale more cheaply later on; and a ➤bull, or long, position if they expect the price to rise. **2.** The acquisition by the arranging bank of one-half of a ➤swap deal in order to complete the deal with the intention in due course of finding a counter-party.

Post-Market Trading (PMT) An ➤automated screen trading system operated by the ➤Chicago Mercantile Exchange in collaboration with ➤Reuters.

Postal Savings Bureau ➤Maruyu.

Potato Terminal Market (Neth.) A ➤futures market, set up in 1958, operating in Rotterdam and Amsterdam, dealing in the Bintje variety. The only ➤commodity market dealing in potato futures of note in Europe, apart from the ➤London Potato Futures Market.

pound cost averaging (UK) The investment of a fixed money sum on (say) a monthly basis in a ➤share (say in an ➤investment trust) will produce a lower average price per share than the purchase of a fixed number of shares each month. The reason is simply that if prices fluctuate over time, more shares will be bought when the price is low and fewer when it is high. (US = *dollar cost averaging* or *constant dollar plan*.)

PPP ➤purchasing power parity.

pre-emptive rights (UK) The right of shareholders of a ➤company to have first refusal to purchase any new ➤shares issued by the company. These rights have legal backing in the UK. ➤➤rights issue.

preference shares (UK) Holders of preference shares precede the holders of ➤ordinary shares, but follow ➤debenture holders, in the payment of ➤dividends and in the return of ➤capital if the issuing company is liquidated (➤liquidation). Preference shares (US = *preferred stock*) normally entitle the holder to a fixed rate of dividend, i.e. are *non-participating*, but *participating preference shares* also entitle the holder to a share of residual ➤profits. Preference shares carry limited voting rights and may be redeemable or not (➤redeemable securities). *Cumulative preference shares* carry forward the entitlement to preferential dividends, if unpaid, from one year to the next while *non-cumulative* preference shares do not. For *stepped preference shares* ➤investment trust.

preferred stock (US) ►preference shares.

Preis (Ger.) The price of an individual ►share; as against *Kurs*, the going market price for the class of shares.

pre-market Trading between members of a ►commodity market before the trading session on the floor begins.

premier cours (Fr.) ►Opening price.

premium 1. In ►insurance, the sum of money paid, either once (single premium) or continuously (regular premium), to buy an insurance policy. 2. In the ►forward and ►futures currency and ►commodity markets, the amount by which a later-date price exceeds an early-date price. 3. Of ►securities, the amount by which the ►secondary market price exceeds the ►issue price or ►par value. 4. Of ►options, the initial down payment, normally of 10%, required. 5. The amount by which the price of an ►investment trust share exceeds the ►net asset value.

premium income The total flow of insurance policy premiums into an insurance company.

premium pool An arrangement whereby several insurance companies derive business jointly through a single ►broker. ►►dollar pool.

Premium Trust Fund The fund into which all premiums received on insurance and reinsurance policies issued by ►Lloyd's must be paid, and from which claims and other underwriting liabilities are paid. The fund is administered under a trust deed approved by the ►Department of Trade and Industry.

present value ►discounted cash flow.

Prestel ►viewdata.

prêt (Fr.) A ►loan.

price – earnings growth factor (PEG) A ►financial ratio used to assist in ►share selection. The PEG factor is calculated by dividing the prospective ►price – earnings (P/E) ratio of a share by the estimated future growth rate in ►earnings per share. A share with earnings growth of 15% and a P/E of 25 would have a PEG factor of 1.67 (25 ÷ 15). Jim Slater, who devised this measure, says that on this measure alone shares may be attractive at a PEG of 1.00 or less, but he warns that other factors need to be taken into account, while the method is designed to measure ►growth stocks and not ►cyclical or ►recovery stocks. It will also be noted that the method relies upon earnings forecasts by ►investment analysts which may prove wrong.

price – earnings (P/E) ratio (PER) The quoted price of an ►ordinary share divided by the most recent year's ►earnings per share, also known as the *multiple*. In the UK the net distribution method is usually used in calculating the PER, in which earnings are defined as the net-of-tax dividends plus ►retained earnings (►►corporation tax). High P/E ratios reflect favourable investors' assessments of the future earning power of the company.

price index ►share indices.

primary 1. Of the stock market, that part of the market concerned with new ►issues; cf. ►secondary market. 2. Of the ►Federal Reserve System, a ►dealer in government ►securities through whom ►open market operations are conducted. 3. Of ►insurance, business conducted by an ►insurer with the general public, rather than ►reinsurance. 4. Of the ►commodities market, a product in its natural state, having undergone little or no refining or processing, e.g. raw wool, metal ores.

primary dealer 1. A ►securities dealer with whom the ►open market desk deals, in conducting its open market operations (US). 2. A securities dealer appointed by the Bank of England to deal as a ►market maker in ►gilts (UK).

primary market ►new issue market.

prime (Fr.) 1. An insurance premium. 2. An additional payment.

prime rate (US) ►base rate.

principal 1. A person acting on their own account, and buying and selling at their own risk, as distinct from someone acting as an ►agent for another, e.g. a ►broker. 2. The amount of a debt, i.e. the capital sum, excluding any ►premium or ►interest.

prise de contrôle (Fr.) A ►take-over.

private In economic and financial language, a term used to denote non-state or non-governmental matters. ►►public.

private company (UK) ►incorporation.

private equity Institutional investment in ►unlisted companies. ►►venture capital.

private finance initiative (PFI) A UK government-sponsored programme of public-sector construction projects in which financing costs are shared with private-sector enterprises.

private medical insurance (PMI) ►Insurance covering the costs of individuals' use of medical facilities in the private sector.

private placing ►placing.

private sector The part of the economy that does not belong to the government, central or local, or to trading corporations and other non-trading entities owned by the government. The private sector comprises chiefly privately owned financial institutions and companies, and individuals. A distinction is also made between the banking private sector, i.e. those financial institutions that are banks, and the non-banking private sector. The term is used widely in economic and ►money supply contexts. ►►overseas sector; public sector.

private trading system (US) A screen-based trading system used by ►institutional investors and ►broker-dealers not wishing to use the ►stock exchanges on grounds of cost, secrecy or other reasons.

private unrequited transfers A term used in ►balance of payments statistics to cover remittances by foreign workers to relatives and others in their countries of origin. Also includes charitable donations and other non-commercial transfers.

privatization The sale of government-owned ►equity in nationalized industry or other commercial enterprises to private investors. Privatization, which used to be called *denationalization*, may involve the retention of either a majority or a minority holding by government, though the UK government in several cases has retained a *golden share*, which is intended to give it power of veto in an unwelcome take-over bid, e.g. one from overseas. A large proportion of state-owned industry has been privatized in the UK since 1981, with the declared objective of promoting competition, efficiency and individual share ownership. Inducements, such as *loyalty bonuses* (e.g. a 10% free issue of shares to investors who retain their holdings beyond a certain date), not normally employed in the ►new issue market, have been used. Privatizations have included British Gas, British Telecom, Jaguar and the electricity and water companies. Many other countries, including France and ►newly industrialized countries in ►Eastern Europe, have embarked upon a privatization programme. Recent examples are Banque Nationale de Paris and Singapore Telecom. ►►privatization voucher.

privatization voucher A voucher exchangeable for a share in a privatized company, with a nominal value of Rbls10,000, distributed to Russian citizens as part of the privatization programme. By the end of 1992, 150m such vouchers had been issued. These were quickly utilized, given the privatization of 3% to 4% of Russian manufacturing companies each month in the period, with the emergence of some 35m shareholders.

prix d'émission (Fr.) The ►striking price in a sale of ►securities by ►offer for sale by ►tender.

prix d'offre (Fr.) The ►reserve price in a new issue of ►securities.

professional indemnity insurance ►Insurance providing compensation against damages incurred on grounds of negligence, available to those in professional occupations, such as doctors, lawyers and accountants.

profit *Net profit* before tax is the residual after deduction of all money costs, i.e. sales revenue minus wages, salaries, rent, fuel and raw materials, ►interest on

➤loans, and ➤depreciation. *Gross profit* is net profit before depreciation and interest. In manufacturing companies it is common to describe some elements in costs as the ➤cost of sales, and in distribution the term 'gross ➤margin' is used in calculating profit.

profit and loss account (P&L) (UK) A financial statement showing revenue, expenditure and the ➤profit or loss resulting from operations in a given period.

profit-sharing scheme (UK) Arrangements for giving employees a share in the ➤profits of the company they work for. These may take several forms. Employees may be granted *share options* under which they may purchase shares at a fixed price that may, after a time, be substantially less than the market price. The scheme may be restricted to certain classes of employee, as in *executive share options*. Alternatively employees may be allowed to purchase shares under a save-as-you-earn scheme. Other forms of profit sharing include ➤employees stock ownership plans, under which shares are distributed free, and schemes whereby a proportion of profits are set aside and distributed not to shareholders but to employees, either on a discretionary basis or as a percentage of earnings. Some profit-sharing schemes are eligible for relief from ➤capital gains tax and ➤income tax.

programme trading (UK) US = *program trading*. Computer-generated purchases or sales of ➤securities that occur when large premiums open up or disappear between the prices of securities and the prices of the same securities on the ➤futures market. A form of ➤arbitrage.

project finance The assembly of funds necessary for large-scale civil engineering and construction operations, including large housing projects. These are chiefly ➤loan funds, with possibly some admixture of ➤equity finance, of a ➤maturity matched as far as possible to the duration of construction; together with such government grants and credits as may be available; and backed, particularly in the case of foreign operations, by public or private ➤credit guarantees and political risk insurance. Where projects on foreign soil are concerned, optimum use of ➤foreign exchange is necessary. Significant finance is invariably obtained from international sources such as the International Development Association (IDA; ➤International Bank for Reconstruction and Development), the ➤Export–Import Bank, the development banks and the ➤Eurobond and ➤Eurodollar markets. Project finance is normally conducted by a consortium of banks, contractors and investment vehicles.

promissory note ➤note.

prompt date The delivery date set in a ➤commodity futures contract.

property income certificate (PINC) (UK) A ➤share in the ownership of a single building, giving holders the benefits of income and capital growth, but which can be traded. The trading of shares in individual buildings through PINCs is expected to be conducted on a new unitized property market or markets, but developments have been held up by problems in clarifying the tax status of this new investment vehicle.

proportional treaty Of insurance, an agreement for the ➤reinsurance of a fixed proportion of claims. ➤➤quota share reinsurance treaty; reinsurance treaty; surplus treaty.

proprietary company 1. An insurance company with issued capital stock; compare ➤mutual company. 2. In Australia, a ➤limited company.

prospectus A document containing company information in connection with a ➤new issue. With only a few exceptions, it is unlawful for a company to invite anyone to apply for shares unless the application form is accompanied by a prospectus containing certain information set out in the Companies Act 1985 (➤incorporation), or, in the case of a ➤London Stock Exchange company, in compliance with the regulations in the ➤Yellow Book.

protection and indemnity clubs ➤Mutual associations first founded in the early 19th century to provide protection to shipowners against risks not normally covered by conventional marine insurance. Members pay an annual levy or 'call' determined by the tonnage of the vessel concerned.

protest A document drawn up by a notary, certifying that a ➤bill of exchange has not been paid on the due date.

provisions Sums set aside in the accounts (and charged against profits) to provide for anticipated loss or expenditure, e.g. a bad debt. Provisions may not be made where the loss or expenditure is highly uncertain, as in a possible lawsuit, but noted as a *contingent liability*. Where losses do not materialize the provisions may be *written back*. Where, for example, a bad debt has proved impossible to recover it will be *written off*, i.e. removed from asset book values.

proviso clause (US) A clause inserted in 1966 in the written ➤directive given to the ➤open market desk after each meeting of the ➤Federal Open Market Committee, instructing the desk to maintain ➤free reserves at a given level, provided that growth of ➤bank credit proxy was not excessive.

proximity rule The rule in ➤insurance law that only the immediate, or proximate, cause of loss or damage is to be taken into account when deciding whether the insured ➤risk has occurred.

proxy ➤Shareholders unable to be present at a shareholder's meeting (➤annual general meeting) may authorize (give proxy to) another person (including the chairperson or other director) to vote on their behalf, either as they think fit or according to specific instructions.

PRT ➤petroleum revenue tax.

'prudent insurer' A term used to define the extent of the duty of disclosure of material facts incumbent on the ➤insured under a contract. The insured must disclose all those facts likely to be considered by a prudent insurer when deciding whether to insure a ➤risk.

prudential ratios ➤capital adequacy.

PSAC ➤Policy Signing and Accounting Centre; London International Insurance and Reinsurance Market Association.

PSB Postal Savings Bureau (Jap.). ➤Maruyu.

PSBR ➤public-sector borrowing requirement.

PSL Private-sector liquidity. ➤money supply.

PTS ➤private trading system.

public A term used in economic and financial language to denote state activities, in contrast to those of the general public, for which the term *private* is used. The two terms are to an evident degree anomalous; a term such as *state*, *official* or *governmental*, as against 'public', would have been more precise.

public dividend capital A form of UK long-term government finance for nationalized industries on which dividends are paid, rather than interest. The capital is not repayable. Since dividends are paid out of profits and these have rarely materialized in nationalized industries, little of this capital has been supplied.

public finance The provision of money for public expenditure by ➤taxation and borrowing. ➤➤budget.

public limited company (plc) ➤incorporation.

public offering ➤offer for sale.

public placing ➤placing.

public sector The part of the economy that consists of the central government, local government, the nationalized industries and other entities owned by central and local government. The term is used widely in economic and ➤money supply contexts. ➤➤overseas sector; private sector.

public-sector borrowing requirement (PSBR) (UK) A term used for the overall financial deficit of general government and the public corporations (state-owned enterprises), i.e. the amount needed to be borrowed, in a given financial year.

public subscription ➤offer for sale.

Public Works Loan Board (PWLB) (UK) A government institution set up to provide loan finance to local authorities, often at lower rates of interest than those obtainable in the capital market. For some time after the Second World War resort to the PWLB for local authorities' debt financing was compulsory: later this became optional.

Pulpex ➤Options Market London Exchange (OMLX).

pumping (US) The action of the ➤Federal Reserve in injecting a heavy addition to bank reserves, and thus provoking a fall in interest rates, before announcing a cut in the ➤discount rate. This enables the Federal Reserve to state that the lower discount rate was necessary in order to bring it into line with prevailing market rates. The stratagem, generally provoked by political considerations, has been described as a 'shortfall of candour'.

purchase Acquisitions of ownership of an ➤instrument or ➤bond through payment of its ➤face value with either a ➤discount or a ➤premium.

purchasing power parity (PPP) exchange rates ➤Exchange rates based on the relative prices of the same basket of goods in each country, instead of indicated by market or fixed rates. PPPs are used because exchange rates may be *over-* or *undervalued* in terms of relative domestic purchasing power. A currency may, for example, be overvalued in relation to its real purchasing power because of capital movements or ➤speculation.

pure risk Of insurance, a risk in which a loss will certainly arise if a given contingency, or ➤peril, occurs; and therefore a risk, in contrast to ➤speculative risks, which is insurable, since the occurrence can be calculated by the ➤law of large numbers.

put option ➤option.

PWLB ➤Public Works Loan Board.

pyramid investment scheme A scheme whereby each member subscribes a small sum, in return for which, provided only that the membership grows continuously, they will later receive a much larger payment. Such schemes must inevitably collapse, with large losses for the later subscribers. In 1993 the Caritas scheme in Romania, involving 3m people, about a sixth of the population, appeared to be on the point of breakdown.

pyramiding ➤holding company.

Q

qualifying trusts ➤personal equity plan.

quanto option An ➤option on an underlying foreign security in which immunity from ➤exchange rate risk is guaranteed.

quantum theory of money A theory devised by the Yale University Professor of Political Economy, Irving Fisher (1867–1947), to the effect that changes in the quantity of money available in an economy directly influence the general level of prices. The theory is expressed in the equation $MV = PT$, where M is the quantity of money, V is the velocity with which it circulates within the economy, P is the general level of prices, and T is the total number of transactions in the economy. The equation is a truism but is given significance by Fisher in his contention that V is constant and that T reflects the physical activity of the economy. Thus $M = kPT$. The theory was challenged by Keynes on the grounds that V could in fact vary with M, but it was revived by Milton ➤Friedman and made the point of departure for his ➤monetary school.

quartile ➤percentile.

quasi-equity ➤mezzanine.

quota An agreed fixed proportion of a financial obligation, thus: **1**. Of the ➤International Monetary Fund (IMF), that part of the organization's resources subscribed by each country and determined in relation to the country's participation in international trade. **2**. Of ➤reinsurance, that portion of the ➤cedant's risks that must be reinsured under a ➤quota share reinsurance treaty. **3**. Of ➤international commodity agreements, quantities of the commodity under consideration that contracting countries undertake to import, or quantities that exporting contracting countries undertake not to exceed.

quota share reinsurance treaty A ➤proportional treaty under which an insurer places an agreed proportion of any particular class of ➤risks with a ➤reinsurer, ceding to the reinsurer an equivalent proportion of the relevant premiums and receiving from them a refund, in the same proportion, of relevant claims paid.

quotation A price for ➤securities at which a ➤market maker will trade. ➤➤bid price; offer price.

quote driven A ➤stock market system (usually in relation to an electronic system) in which prices are initially determined by quotations of ➤dealers or ➤market makers. Ultimately prices are determined by supply and demand as in any other market, but the term is useful to distinguish between the systems in use on, e.g., the ►New York Stock Exchange, which are ►order driven, and those on the ►National Association of Securities Dealers Automated Quotation System and until, in part, recently the ►London Stock Exchange, which are quote driven. Electronic quote-driven systems are leading to the demise of the traditional ►trading floor.

quoted company A company (►incorporation) whose shares are listed on an official ►stock exchange. Compare ►unlisted company.

quotient cours bénéfice (Fr.) ►Price – earnings ratio.

Quotron A company now part of ►Reuters providing screen-based ►equity price quotations. Recently many competitors have emerged in the market for ►real-time stock market information, including those readable by hand-held mobile telecommunications equipment. ►►Telerate.

R

R & R Reconstruction and Renewal. ►Lloyd's.

rallonge ►short-term monetary support (STMS).

rally A sharp increase in the price of a ►stock, or in the general level of prices, following a decline.

ramp, ramping The purchase of securities for the sole purpose of increasing their price. A practice used in the ►Euronote market; also practised in the company share market in the course of a take-over bid – although it is illegal for a company to buy its own shares.

ratchet ►earn-out.

rate 1. An abbreviation of ►interest rate and applied mostly in the ►money market, e.g. interbank rate, bank bill rate, CD (►certificate of deposit) rate. 2. An abbreviation of ►rate of exchange, e.g. dollar rate, DM rate. 3. Of ►commercial paper in the USA, France, Australia and Canada, to assess the creditworthiness of the issuer; done by a ►rating agency. 4. To assess the creditworthiness of a ►security issuer, done by a rating agency.

rate anticipation swap A ►swap of securities made in the expectation of a change in interest rates.

rate of exchange The value of a ►currency in terms of another, i.e. the number of units of that currency required to obtain one unit of the other.

rate of interest The proportion of a sum of money that is paid over a specified period of time in payment for its ►loan. It may be a fixed rate of interest or a ►floating rate.

rate of return ►return on investment.

rate support grant A generalized grant from the UK central government to local governments, supplementing the latter's finances with the object of enabling them to attain comparable standards of service at comparable cost to local taxpayers.

rates ►local taxation.

rating ►Standard and Poor's Ratings.

rating agency A firm or organization set up to ►rate issuers of ►commercial paper, or ➤securities. In the UK, USA and other countries there are many rating agencies. In France the Agence d'Evaluation Financière (ADEF) was set up as a joint venture between the government agencies and institutional investors. In Australia rating is done by Australian Ratings. ➤➤credit rating.

RBA ➤Reserve Bank of Australia.

reaction function (US) The adjustment by the ➤Federal Reserve of its ➤monetary control to broad changes in the general economy.

real The characteristic of an aggregate or level that is expressed in money terms divested of the effect of inflation from a previous date, e.g. real ➤investment, ➤rates of interest, ➤money supply.

real The national ➤currency unit of Brazil.

real bills doctrine ➤elastic currency.

real-estate investment trusts (REITs) (US) Publicly ➤quoted trusts (➤investment trust) issuing ➤bonds secured by a package of commercial property. First launched in 1982, REITs had by 1993 moved from a ➤market capitalization of $3bn to one of $25bn. This growth was attributed to the popularity of the instrument with developers, given its low yield compared with that required by buyers of new-built property, a low yield level sustained by heavy demand from ➤mutual funds. REITs are a form of ➤securitization.

real time A computer and communications system in which the generation of data and the inputting and processing of that data occur virtually simultaneously, so that the output of the system, e.g. a ➤share price index, will reflect real changes (in prices) as they occur.

receivables Amounts due to a business, i.e. owed by ➤debtors.

receivership ➤bankruptcy.

reciprocal insurance ➤reinsurance.

recognized investment exchange ➤Financial Service Act.

recognized professional body (RPB) ➤Financial Services Act.

Reconstruction and Renewal (R & R) ➤Lloyd's.

recourse The right to claim indemnification from the seller of a financial instrument if the originator of that instrument does not honour the commitment given on it. A ➤bill of exchange stamped *non-recourse* or *without recourse* is not endorsed for payment. ➤factoring.

recovery stocks ➤Shares in companies which have suffered a re-rating downwards and which are now recommended in the hope or expectation that they will recover.

Red Book (UK) A familiar term for the ►Financial Statement and Budget Report issued on Budget day.

red chip A company, listed on the ►Hong Kong Stock Exchange, controlled by a business or government organization situated on the Chinese mainland.

red herring (US) A preliminary ►prospectus issued to test the market for a ►new issue; does not include a firm price. (UK = *pathfinder prospectus*.)

redeemable security ►Stocks or ►bonds that are repayable at their ►par value at a certain date, dates or specified eventuality. Most fixed-interest ►securities are redeemable, though ►consols bear no redemption date.

redemption The repayment of a ►loan or the ►par value of a ►security at ►maturity on the repurchase of a security such as a ►unit trust certificate.

redemption date The date at which a loan is repaid.

redemption yield ►yield.

rediscount The act of a ►central bank in ►discounting paper submitted to it by ►money market operators. So called because the paper has already been discounted in the market, and the central bank is acting in its capacity of ►lender of last resort; often referred to simply as discounting.

reducing-balance methods of depreciation ►depreciation.

réescompte (Fr.) ►Rediscount.

refinance 1. To take over or guarantee an existing loan; frequently by an official agency, such as the ►Export–Import Bank (US) or the ►Export Credit Guarantee Department (UK), *vis-à-vis* commercial banks providing export credit. **2**. To exchange one loan for another; done by ordinary borrowers either on the expiry of the original credit or to take advantage of an alternative loan on better terms. Compare ►funding.

regional bank (Jap.) One of the two categories of Japanese commercial banks. Restricted to local districts, they serve mainly local enterprises. Normally in possession of surplus funds, they are lenders to the ►call market. ►►city bank.

regional stock exchanges Many major countries have smaller ►stock exchanges in addition to the principal one, and they trade in the ►securities of local organiza-tions as well as in the securities listed on the main exchange. The UK used to have regional exchanges in several cities (►London Stock Exchange), while the USA has two major exchanges in New York, the ►New York Stock Exchange and the ►American Stock Exchange, and other regional exchanges that include Boston, Midwest (Chicago) and Pacific (Los Angeles). Although regional exchanges are more important in some countries, notably the ►German stock exchanges and the ►Swiss stock exchanges, in most countries the principal exchange accounts for the vast majority of trading in securities, and recently there has been a tendency for regional exchanges to be integrated under common management. ➤➤Paris Bourse; Tokyo Stock Exchange.

registered security ➤bearer security.

registrar A person or company appointed by a company to keep a record of the ownership of its ➤shares and to communicate with shareholders (US = *transfer agent*, where the registrar is not the company). The *share register* is a list of shareholders' names and addresses and the quantity of stock each one holds.

regular premium ➤life assurance; unit-linked life assurance.

regulation Generally, the supervision and control of the activities of private enterprise by government in the interests of efficiency, fairness, health and safety. All ➤stock exchanges are regulated (➤e.g. Financial Services Act; Securities and Exchange Commission), as are ➤banking and other aspects of finance (see e.g. ➤consumer credit; exchange control). Regulatory powers may be delegated by government to the financial services industry itself, or they may be exercised directly or through official regulatory agencies. Regulations may act as a barrier to entry and inhibit competition; following the lead of the USA and the UK, there has been a recent trend towards the *deregulation* of stock exchanges in particular, accompanied by some tightening of measures to protect individual investors (➤Big Bang).

Regulation Q (US) A ➤Federal Reserve regulation setting ceilings on rates of interest paid by banks on their deposits. In 1970 and 1973 the application of the regulation was lifted on ➤certificates of deposit (CDs) of maturities of 30 to 90 days, and over 90 days, respectively. Regulation Q was an important stimulus to the ➤Eurodollar market because it encouraged US banks to bid for funds at higher rates from their branches abroad.

reinstatement The restoration, following payment of a loss, of the original amount of cover pledged in a ➤reinsurance treaty; this may be subject to an increase in premium, or a maximum number of reinstatements may be specified in the treaty. Used chiefly in ➤excess of loss reinsurance in aviation, marine and property business, and also in catastrophe business.

reinsurance The practice of ➤insurers of passing on part of the ➤risks they assume to other parties in return for a proportional share of the ➤premium income. Although many large insurers themselves undertake reinsurance, the market is also served by large companies specializing in the activity. Reinsurance is essentially an international business. The largest reinsurer in the world is in Munich (Munich Re). Other large reinsurers are Cologne Re, Swiss Re (Zurich), General Re (USA) and the Gerling Group (Germany). ➤Lloyd's also conducts a substantial proportion of its business in reinsurance.

The reinsurance market grew significantly in the two decades from the 1960s; from a premium income of between $5bn and $6bn, handled by a small number of conservative-minded professional reinsurers, the market then grew to some $56 billion in the early 1980s, handled by many more professional reinsurers, by direct insurers entering into the business and also by ➤captive insurers. This strong growth was occasioned by an imbalance of ➤capacity as against demand. In the late 1980s, with a revival of profitable direct insurance, reinsurance growth eased. Reinsurance normally accounts for some 10% to 15% of direct business.

Reinsurance Offices Association (ROA) ➤London International Insurance and Reinsurance Market Association (LIRMA).

reinsurance to close (RITC) (UK) ➤Lloyd's syndicates have a legal life of one year only, and must reconstitute themselves in order to begin a new year (invariably the membership of the syndicates remains the same). Consequently, a syndicate must, before it closes at the end of the year, provide for the payment of any claims that may subsequently arise from the policies it has written during its life. It therefore reinsures against this with the new syndicate, paying a premium for this into the account of that syndicate. This is known as 'reinsurance to close'. The members of the old syndicate remain formally liable for any subsequent claims, but pass these claims on, under normal reinsurance practice, to the members of the new syndicate. As there may well be some change in membership between the two syndicates, great care is taken to ensure a level of RITC premium that is fair to both sides.

reinsurance treaty A contract between an ➤insurer and a reinsurer, whereby ➤risks held by the former are assumed by the latter in exchange for a proportional share in the premium income. Reinsurance treaties are binding over the whole range of the risks covered, as compared with ➤facultative reinsurance; and the insurers passing on the risks, i.e. ceding insurers, or cedants, are bound to declare their acceptance of all risks covered by such treaties, while reinsurers are bound to accept the cession of all such risks. Variations of reinsurance treaties are ➤proportional and ➤non-proportional treaties. The former include ➤quota share treaties.

REITs ➤real-estate investment trusts.

rendement (Fr.) **1.** ➤Yield. **2.** ➤Profit.

Rendite (Ger.) ➤Yield, ➤profit.

Renminbi The national currency of China. ➤*yuan*.

rente (Fr.) **1.** The flow of ➤interest on a ➤security. **2.** The interest-bearing security itself. **3.** A government ➤bond.

Rente (Ger.) **1.** The rate of ➤interest, return on a ➤security, or ➤capital. **2.** A pension. **3.** A ➤bond.

Rentenanleihe (Ger.) A government ►bond.

Rentenbank (Ger.) A credit bank.

renunciation In a ►rights issue a ►shareholder may decide not to subscribe to the new shares but to assign those rights to someone else by signing a renunciation form. The shareholder may decide to sell rights in this way where the rights issue is at a ►deep discount and where the right to subscribe has significant value.

reorganization ►bankruptcy.

repayment supplement (UK) Payment by the Inland Revenue of interest on overpaid tax, paid in respect of the number of years the tax sum was held by the Inland Revenue.

replacement risk ►counterparty risk.

replacement-cost depreciation ►depreciation.

repo repotate ►repurchase agreement.

report (Fr.) ►Contango.

reporting accountants A firm of accountants reporting to the ►sponsor of a ►new issue on the financial affairs of a ►company. ►►long form report.

reporting dealer (US) The official ►Federal Reserve designation for ►primary dealer.

reprise (Fr.) A recovery on the ►stock exchange.

repurchase agreement (repo) Short for *sale and repurchase agreement*. A transaction whereby funds are borrowed through the sale of ►short-term securities on the condition that the instruments are repurchased at a given date. Used principally between the ►central bank and the ►money market as a means of relieving short-term shortages of funds in the money market (perhaps overnight, hence, *overnight repo*) and thus as a means of ►monetary control by the central bank. Interest is paid on the instrument in the meantime. The operation was first developed in the USA and remains widely used as a borrowing method by large corporations and non-banking institutions. The instrument used is normally a US government security, usually ►Treasury bills. A *retail repo* involves a loan to a bank; it differs from a term ►deposit in that early withdrawals may be made without penalty. After the exemption of repurchase agreements from US reserve requirements in 1969, their use as a device for monetary control by the US Federal Reserve became widespread. Reverse repurchase agreements (*reverse repos*), whereby the sale of securities is by the Federal Reserve to the US money market, are also used. Repurchase agreements are also utilized in ►open market operations by other central banks, notably the ►Bank of England, the Banque de France and the ➤Bundesbank. An *overnight repo* is held between the closing and opening of the money market.

required reserves (US) ➤Reserves required to be held by US banks, prescribed in proportion to ➤deposits and other liabilities.

rescheduling An agreed alteration in the pattern of ➤interest payments or repayment of ➤principal. Rescheduling of debt between ➤developing countries and the ➤International Monetary Fund (IMF) and commercial banks is not uncommon, but it also occurs within advanced countries – e.g. in the UK Channel Tunnel project.

rescription (Fr.) A government short-term ➤instrument akin to a ➤Treasury bill.

reserve asset ratio The ratio of ➤reserve assets to ➤eligible liabilities required to be maintained by UK commercial banks under the arrangements for ➤monetary control introduced by the Bank of England in 1971, and known as *competition and credit control*. The system was superseded in 1981 by other arrangements under which the reserve asset ratio was abandoned.

reserve assets Holdings of a commercial bank, not used for loans or other transactions, and therefore available for use in the last resort to meet a shortage of funds. In most countries the level and constitution of reserve assets and their ratio to ➤deposits (➤reserve asset ratio) are prescribed by the regulatory authorities. ➤➤liquidity ratio.

Reserve Bank of Australia The central monetary authority of Australia.

Reserve banks ➤Federal Reserve System.

reserve price The lowest price at which someone is prepared to sell something. Thus a client may instruct a ➤broker to sell ➤securities or ➤commodities at or above a specified reserve price.

reserve requirement (US) The ratio of ➤reserves to ➤deposits, expressed as a fraction, prescribed by the US regulatory authorities. An alternative form of reference to ➤required reserves. ➤➤liquidity ratio.

reserves 1. Of countries, the ➤central bank's holdings of gold and foreign currencies and International Monetary Fund ➤drawing rights, for the purpose of providing for fluctuations in the country's ➤balance of payments; commonly referred to as the gold and foreign currency reserves. **2.** Of banks, cash and ➤short-term claims, e.g. claims on the central bank, ➤call money, ➤Treasury bills and ➤short-term gilts, held as backing for the bank's ➤deposit liabilities. Commonly referred to as ➤reserve assets. **3.** Amounts set aside from ➤profits in company accounts for an unspecified purpose. Reserves are part of ➤retained earnings, i.e. they are undistributed profits and belong to the ordinary shareholders of the company. In the USA the term *reserves* is often used in the UK sense of

➤provisions, which are sums set aside for specific anticipated purposes. **4.** Of ➤insurance, amounts set aside to meet underwriting liabilities; commonly referred to as *technical reserves*.

reserves maintenance period (US) A period during which banks must hold reserves at least equal on average to ➤required reserves; the period is normally of 14 days.

reserves market (US) A term applied to the transactions between the ➤Federal Reserve open market desk, banks, securities dealers and ➤Federal funds brokers in the ➤instruments making up the banking system's reserves. The main effect of such transactions is to regulate bank reserves in accordance with the Federal Reserve's ➤monetary policy.

reserves multiplier (US) An indicator used by the ➤Federal Reserve to assess the amount of bank deposits that will correspond to a given ➤reserve requirement.

reserve pressure (US) A situation brought about by the ➤open market operations of the ➤Federal Reserve in which the banking system requires to borrow at the ➤discount window.

Reskription (Ger.) A ➤public-sector short-term ➤bill, discounted (➤discounting) to the banking system, akin to a ➤Treasury bill. ➤➤*Schatzwechsel*.

ressources propres (Fr.) ➤Own resources.

retail banking ➤retail deposit; wholesale banking.

retail deposit 1. A ➤deposit placed by an individual customer, normally in relatively small amounts, with a bank, in contrast to a ➤wholesale deposit. **2.** In ➤money supply terminology, deposits held for expenditure purposes (*transactions balances*), as against those held for savings (*investment balances*). **3.** In ➤hire purchase, funds recruited by ➤finance houses from individual investors, rather than from the wholesale ➤money market. **4.** In ➤mortgage business, funds raised by mortgage banks (building societies) from individual depositors, rather than through wholesale borrowings from the money market or from other sources.

retail price index (RPI) An ➤index number measuring changes in the ➤weighted average of prices of a basket of goods and services (US = *consumer price index* (CPI)). Intended to measure changes in the cost of living. ➤➤indexation.

retail repo ➤repurchase agreement.

retained earnings Undistributed ➤profits that may simply be ➤reserves or may be used for investment in fixed ➤assets. When a company finances its capital expenditure from retained earnings rather than borrowings, it is said to be self-financing.

retention 1. The proportion of total risk in an ➤insurance agreement that the insurer retains on his own account, i.e. for which he does not arrange ►reinsurance. **2.** An amount of money which is held back for a specified period from payment under a contract for work, to provide against defects in the work carried out: repairs for any defects are paid for out of the money retained. **3.** ►Mortgage money held back by the ►mortgagee pending completion of repairs or improvements to the property.

retrocession The further insurance of ►risks assumed by a reinsurer. ►►reinsurance.

return on capital employed (ROCE) ►return on investment.

return on investment (ROI) A ►financial ratio showing ►profit as a percentage of total ►assets or ►capital employed (ROCE) or ►shareholders' funds. The numerator and denominator of the ratio need to be defined carefully, e.g. profit after interest and ►depreciation as a percentage of total assets at *historic cost* (►costs, historical).

Reuters A ►quoted company providing screen-based and teletype news, financial information and dealing services worldwide. In financial markets it is particularly strong in the provision of exchange rate quotations. Founded by P. J. Reuter in 1851, it was originally owed by the newspapers that used its services. The 3000 service provides historical data on 90,000 equities. ►Electronic Broking Service; Instinet; Quotron; Telerate.

Reuters 2000-2 ►Electronic Broking Service.

revaluation reserve Capital ►reserves created when the book value of existing ►assets is revalued to bring it into line with replacement costs, or when new shares are issued at a ►premium over ►par value.

reversal A fall or rise in the price of a ►stock against a previous trend.

reverse auction The process whereby an issuer of ►bonds, wishing to reduce the number at issue, invites holders to offer prices at which the issuer may repurchase them.

reverse monetization The theory, chiefly propounded by the Princeton University economist Alan S. Binder, that at times of high federal deficits the ►Federal Reserve will tend to restrict bank reserves.

reverse repo ►repurchase agreement.

reverse yield curve ►yield curve.

reversionary bonus ►life assurance.

revolving credit A ►loan facility that is renewed as it is repaid and may therefore be used repeatedly. Also referred to as *open-end credit* (US). ►Credit card loans are a form of revolving credit, since borrowers may make minimum repayments or repayment in full at the end of the account period, provided they remain within the credit limit. Retail *charge accounts*, where regular payments are made and credit is available up to a multiple of the regular payments, are another form of revolving credit.

revolving underwriting facility (RUF) ►note issuance facility (NIF).

RIE Recognized investment exchange. ►Financial Services Act.

Riga Stock Exchange The ►stock exchange in Latvia, which opened fully for trading in 1994.

rights issue An offer of new ►shares to existing shareholders. A company will offer the rights in a certain proportion to existing holdings, depending upon the amount of new ►equity capital it wishes to raise. Thus in a one-for-one rights issue, shareholders will be offered a number of new shares equal to the number they already hold. To ensure that the issue is taken up, the new shares are offered at well below the market price of the existing shares, i.e. at a ►discount, which will usually result in some fall in the price of existing shares. Rights issues are a relatively cheap way of raising ►capital for a quoted company, since the costs of preparing a brochure, ►underwriting, commission and press advertising involved in a new issue are avoided. ►new issue market.

Riksbanken (Swe.) The ►central bank of Sweden.

ring The trading floor of a ►commodity exchange. The term is also used for the trading session itself.

ring fence A measure to protect members of ►Lloyd's, underwriting in the 1994 business year and thereafter, from the effects of ►Old Years. A bylaw of 1993 forbids the acceptance of ►reinsurance to close of any policies issued in any year up to and including 1985. Liabilities of those years were intended in 1993 to be reinsured into ►Newco.

ringitt The national ►currency unit of Malaysia.

risk Of ►insurance, the contingent loss against which insurance is provided. In insurance contracts the term has the more precise connotation of an uncertainty for which the probability of occurrence is calculable. The term also applies, for insurance purposes, to the whole of the insurance cover provided, rather than to the individual contingencies or ►perils that may arise. ►►dynamic risk; static risk.

risk-adjusted assets ►Assets defined to include ►off-balance-sheet items. Under the ►Bank for International Settlements agreement on ►capital adequacy, the ►underwriting of securitized loans (►securitization) creates assets that do not, unlike traditional ►loans, appear on ►bank balance sheets. Risk-adjusted assets make an allowance for these items and under the agreement need to be covered in part by *prudential ratios* for capital reserves.

risk arbitrageur ➤corporate raider.

risk capital Long-term funds invested in enterprises particularly subject to risk, as in small or new ventures. Hence the alternative term ➤venture capital, a somewhat more precise term meaning ➤capital provided for a new or young business undertaking by people other than the proprietors. Venture capital is provided by ➤merchant banks but predominantly by specialized venture capital institutions, including ➤captives, and specialized venture capital ➤funds.

risk management The identification and acceptance or offsetting of the risks threatening the profitability or existence of an organization. ➤Insurance provides protection against death, fire or flood, ➤hedging against fluctuations in ➤exchange rates and accelerated ➤depreciation against the risk of obsolescence of fixed ➤assets. Also management by a company of events and activities so as to minimize the degree to which damage or loss may occur, so reducing dependence on insurance.

risk reversal A procedure for minimizing loss, whereby a ➤call option sale is combined with a simultaneous *put* option purchase.

risk-weighted assets ➤Assets held by a financial institution to which degrees of risk have been assigned, so that adequate ➤provisions can be set aside.

ROA ➤Reinsurance Offices Association; London International Insurance and Reinsurance Market Association.

ROCE ➤return on investment.

rocket scientist A mathematician and computer expert working usually in an ➤investment bank. Rocket scientists analyse ➤share prices and market movements and attempt to identify patterns to assist in forecasting. They also devise complex financial packages, including ➤securitization, ➤derivatives and ➤swaps.

rodo kinko (Jap.) A banking institution specializing in credit for small businesses.

ROI ➤return on investment.

roll-over In ➤derivatives, the transfer from one ➤delivery month to another, involving the sale/purchase of the ➤front month and of the later delivery month.

roll-over CD An arrangement whereby a ➤certificate of deposit (CD) ➤maturity is divided into shorter-term periods in respect to which individual CDs are issued, e.g. a three-year CD arrangement is effected through issues of a CD at six-monthly intervals. Purchasers commit themselves to buying the full services but are free to sell any of the individual CDs on the secondary market. Roll-over CDs were first issued in 1976 in the USA. The advantage to bankers is that of securing a longer-term deposit than they might obtain on a less flexible CD. The advantage to purchasers is the avoidance of the need to sell a long-term CD – always more difficult.

roll-over credit A loan by a bank or ►syndicate of banks, usually at ►medium term or longer, the funds for which are raised by the banks themselves through ►short-term borrowing, normally in the ►money market or ►interbank market. The interest then charged to the bank's client fluctuates in accordance with short-term money market rates, frequently ►London interbank offered rate (LIBOR), to which is added a ►spread.

roll-up funds (UK) Investment schemes involving rolled-up coupon funds, established in centres outside the jurisdiction of the UK Inland Revenue, i.e. abroad or, for example, in the Channel Islands, so enabling the reinvestment of the interest payments without liability to income tax. When eventually repatriated, the funds incur only ►capital gains tax. However, a ruling of the Inland Revenue in 1983 required the ►rolled-up coupons to be assessed as income.

rolled-up coupon An interest payment on a ►financial instrument or ►security, denoted by the ►coupon, which is not passed to the holder but is reinvested in the instrument, so adding to the latter's capital value and enabling, if repeated over time, a compounding of the interest. Most used where the interest can be classed as a capital investment by the holder and not a receipt of income (►capital gains), thus enabling the holder to avoid income tax. ►fund; roll-up funds; zero coupon bond.

rolling account ►settlement.

rolling settlement ►settlement.

rolling spot contract A ►currency derivatives contract introduced in 1993 by the ►Chicago Mercantile Exchange under which the contract is automatically rolled over each day (►roll-over) by the exchange, thus saving the trader the daily settlement costs incurred in normal ►spot market roll-overs.

roly-poly CD ►roll-over CD.

Room, the (UK) That part of ►Lloyd's premises in the City of London where ►working members carry on business. Also known as the *underwriting room*.

Roosa bonds (US) ►Bonds issued by the US Treasury during the Kennedy administration of the early 1960s, denominated in currencies other than the US dollar and held by central banks on a non-marketable basis. Roosa bonds enabled financing of the US federal deficit on a long-term basis in conditions of complete exchange security for the lender. In particular, the bonds were designed to induce the former West Germany, then unwilling to increase its dollar holdings, to continue to finance US Treasury needs. The bonds were named after Robert V. Roosa, their creator, then under-secretary at the US Treasury.

rosokuashi (Jap.) A ►chartist technique using box shapes on graphs to depict time periods.

round tripping Occurs when a non-financial company can borrow at lower than current and short-term market ►rates of interest and can therefore borrow and on-lend at a ►profit.

round-up stage (US) The stage at the monthly meeting of the ►Federal Open Market Committee at which comments are called from each of the 19 members.

RP ►Repurchase agreements.

RPB Recognized professional body. ►Financial Services Act.

RPIX The UK ►Retail Price Index, excluding mortgage interest payments.

RPIY The UK ►Retail Price Index, excluding mortgage interest payments and indirect taxes.

RTS Index (Russia) The ►share price index of the ►Moscow Central Stock Exchange. (RTS = *Russian Trading System*.)

Rubber Association of Singapore A major ►commodity market, dealing principally in natural rubber ►futures.

Rücknahmepreis (Ger.) ►Redemption price.

RUF Revolving underwriting facility. ►Euronote facility.

Rules 535(2) and 535(3) (UK) Formerly Rules 163(2) and 163(3), allowing ►brokers to deal in unlisted securities (►unlisted securities market) and mineral exploration ►shares respectively. ►►alternative investment market.

run A rush to get out of a ►currency or a ►share by selling it, or to withdraw money from a ►bank. Thus a 'run on the pound' means that holders of sterling are selling pounds for other currencies for fear that its value will fall. Such selling helps to bring about the feared event and withdrawal of deposits from a bank may force it to close its doors even though its ►assets may exceed its ►liabilities.

run-off account (UK) Where a ►syndicate finds, at the end of the three-year accounting cycle for a particular trading year, that it cannot reliably estimate the extent of claims that may still arise on the business of that year, and that it cannot therefore propose an acceptable premium for ►reinsurance to close, then the syndicate must remain open, and its members must retain their liability for such claims, until more certain prospects emerge. The business account for that year is then known as a run-off account.

run to settlement Said of a ►commodity sale contract allowed to run to the date where physical delivery of the commodity is due, i.e. a contract not ►liquidated or ►covered by purchase of an offsetting contract.

running yield ►yield.

rupiah The Indonesian national ►currency unit.

Russell 2000 The share price index of smaller companies quoted on the ►New York Stock Exchange.

Russia Country Fund A fund set up with the support of the Russian and US governments and of American private institutions, with the purpose of enabling US financial institutions, such as pension funds, to invest directly in private enterprises in Russia and other former Soviet states. The fund is ►closed-end and intends to raise $100m in ►project finance and ►venture capital for new business, expansions and ►privatization, with an emphasis on enterprises in the energy and environmental fields. The Russian government will contribute up to $25m. The ►Overseas Private Investment Corporation will provide a $50m ►loan guarantee to protect private institutions supplying the additional capital.

Russian Commodity and Raw Material Exchange A ►commodity exchange founded in Moscow by Konstantin Borovoi in 1990, planning also to introduce trade in equities.

S

'S' corporation ➤sub-chapter S corporations.

S&L ➤savings and loan associations.

SA ➤*société anonyme.*

SAEF ➤Stock Exchange Automatic Execution Facility.

saitori (Jap.) An intermediary in the ➤stock exchange, dealing only between members, similar to the ➤specialists on the New York Stock Exchange, except that the *saitori* are not allowed to take ➤positions for themselves.

sale Cession of ownership of an ➤instrument or ➤bond against payment of its ➤face value with either a ➤discount or a ➤premium.

sale and leaseback ➤leaseback.

sales and repurchase agreement ➤repurchase agreement.

sales tax A tax levied as a proportion of the retail price of a good or service. In contrast to ➤value added tax, a sales tax is levied only at the point of sale. Sales taxes are levied in the USA and many other countries.

samurai bond A ➤foreign bond issued in Japan by foreign issuers, denominated in yen.

samurai lease An international lease financed by the Japanese leasing industry under subsidy by the Japanese government. The transaction consisted of the purchase of foreign assets for leasing abroad. The practice was most common in the early 1980s and was used by the Japanese government to bring about a temporary increase in import payments.

Sanmekai (Jap.) The committee of ➤city banks that determines ➤short-term rates of interest.

São Paulo Stock Exchange Bolsas de Valores de São Paulo (BoVeSPa). One of the two largest ➤stock exchanges in Brazil, regulated by the Commissão de Valores Mobiliaros (CVM) or securities commission. Together with the exchange in Rio de Janeiro, BoVeSPa accounts for the bulk of trading in ➤securities, including ➤futures and ➤options, in Brazil, although there are also exchanges in seven other cities. The BoVeSPa Index is the most widely quoted ➤share index for Brazil.

sarakin (Jap.) Finance companies notorious for high interest rates charged to personal customers, frowned on by the government.

Sàrl (Fr.) ►société à responsabilité limitée.

Saturday-night special (US) A popular reference to 6 October 1979, on the evening of which the ►Federal Reserve announced its decision to abandon its policy of influencing the ►Federal funds rate, in favour of one of influencing the level of bank reserves.

savings Income not spent on consumption. Savings may be accumulated in a ►bank deposit account or ►current account or may be placed in a ►building society or ►savings bank or used to purchase ►securities, including ►savings bonds or ►National Savings certificates. Regular payments into ►pensions schemes or ►life assurance are referred to as contractual savings.

savings account ►deposit account.

savings and loan (S&L) associations (US) ►Savings banks that, like ►building societies, receive savings ►deposits (►retail deposit) and make mortgages. The deregulation of interest rates (►Depository Institutions Deregulation and Monetary Decontrol Act) created difficulties for S&Ls because they had commitments for long-term loans at fixed ►rates of interest, so that as deposit rates rose they were sometimes paying more to depositors than they were receiving from their borrowers. Also referred to as *savings and loan institutions* and ►thrifts, they exercise some banking functions, such as operating ►cheque accounts (US = *checking accounts*) and providing ►consumer credit and high-yield investment vehicles. S&Ls are largely ►mutual organizations, though many have incorporated (►incorporation) so as to broaden their access to ►capital markets. S&Ls are regulated either by the ►Federal Home Loan Bank Board or, in the case of state ►chartered S&Ls, by the state. ►►Garn–St Germain Act.

savings bank A bank that accepts ►interest bearing ►deposits of small amounts. The earliest savings banks were established in the private sector, but later they were set up or supported by governments, to encourage individual savings. In the UK the two main forms of savings bank are the ►National Savings Bank and, before ►privatization, the ►Trustee Savings Bank (TSB). The TSB, however, is now a full bank. The ►building societies share the basic objectives of the savings banks. ►►*caisses d'épargne*; savings and loan associations; *Sparkassen*.

savings bonds (US) ►Bonds issued by the US government at a ►discount to their *face value* (►par value) at which they are redeemed after ►maturity. Investors receive interest and a ►capital gain on maturity. The bonds, which are denominated by letters – E bonds, HH bonds, etc. – are free of state and local taxes and may be exchanged for other bonds so that liability to federal taxation may be deferred.

SBF (Fr.) ►Société des Bourses Françaises.

SBIC ➤small business investment company.

Schatz **bond** A term often used in English-speaking markets to mean *Schatzobligation*.

Schatzanweisung (Ger.) ➤*Schatzwechsel.*

Schatzbrief (Ger.) A ➤savings bond.

Schatzobligation (Ger.) A Treasury ➤bond.

Schatzschein (Ger.) ➤*Schatzwechsel.*

Schatzwechsel (Ger.) A ➤Treasury bill. Issued by ➤tap to the banking system for retention until ➤maturity. *Schatzwechsel* are normally for a ➤term of 90 days. Sometimes referred to as a *Reskription*.

Scheduled Territories (UK) A term used in UK ➤exchange control, abolished in 1979, to denote areas where sterling is the official ➤currency and where the exchange control regulations therefore did not apply. Also known as the *Sterling Area*. Embracing after the First World War the whole of the British Commonwealth, the Scheduled Territories by 1979 included no more than Great Britain, the Channel Islands and the Isle of Man.

Schlussdividende (Ger.) *Final dividend.* ➤dividend.

Schlusskurs (Ger.) ➤Closing price.

Schuldschein (Ger.) A ➤note in common use for the recruitment of ➤short-term funds, used by companies and by government, chief buyers being the insurance companies. Lower costs of issue offset interest rates slightly above the average.

Schuldscheindarlehen (Ger.) A loan based on a *Schuldschein*. The certificates for public-sector loans are traded in the ➤secondary market.

Schuldverschreibung (Ger.) A ➤bond or a ➤money-market instrument, the latter being particularly favoured by banks as a source of ➤short-term funds.

scrip issue ➤bonus issue.

SCMC ➤Société de Compensation des Marchés Conditionnels.

SDR ➤special drawing right.

SDR-linked deposit A private bank deposit denominated in ➤special drawing rights (SDRs). These are now recognized accounts for the payment of transactions.

SEA ➤Single European Act.

SEAQ ➤Stock Exchange Automated Quotation System.

seasonal borrowings (US) US banks' borrowings from the ➤Federal Reserve induced by seasonal fluctuations in credit demand. Seasonal borrowings constitute, together with ►adjustment credit, the ►borrowed reserves of US banks.

SEBI ►Bombay Stock Exchange.

second marché (Fr.) Second-tier ►unlisted securities market in Paris, with regional markets established in February 1983. The Belgian second-tier market is also called the *second marché*. ►►*tweede markt*.

second-tier market ►unlisted securities market.

secondary bank (UK) A bank (►banking) that has relatively few branches and therefore does not play a major role in the payments system as far as the general public is concerned. Included in the term are ►merchant banks, the British ►overseas banks and some ►finance houses. There was a secondary banking crisis in 1973 when the ►Bank of England mounted a lifeboat operation to rescue some of the banks.

secondary market A market in which ►securities or other ►assets are resold and repurchased, as distinct from a primary market in which assets are sold for the first time (►new issue market). The ►stock exchange is a secondary market, though it is also a primary market. The term is sometimes wrongly used to refer to *second tier* or ►unlisted securities markets.

secured Backed by a ►security (of a loan).

Securities and Exchange Act 1948 (Jap.) Legislation requiring the registration of ►broker-dealers governing ►securities trading in Japan, modelled on the US Securities Exchange Act 1934 (►Securities and Exchange Commission). Article 65 of the Act prohibits banks from owning more than 5% of any company or engaging in ►share broking (►broker) or acting as an ►issuing house. As in the USA (►Glass-Steagal Act), the evolution of international securities markets is resulting in pressures for change in Article 65. Japanese banks do engage in ►investment banking outside Japan through subsidiaries.

Securities and Exchange Commission (SEC) (US) Federal agency for the ►regulation of the markets in ►securities, set up in 1934 to administer the Securities Exchange Acts 1933 and 1934, which require most securities offered for sale to be registered. The SEC regulates the ►stock exchanges and ►brokers, including those on the ►over-the-counter market, investment advisers and others in industry. ►►Form 10-K.

Securities and Futures Authority ►Financial Services Act.

Securities and Investment Board ►Financial Services Act.

Securities Association, The (TSA) (UK) The former self-regulating organization for securities dealing. Formed in 1986 by the amalgamation of the ►London

Stock Exchange, now the International Stock Exchange, and the International Securities Regulatory Organization (ISRO), which then regulated dealers in ►Eurobonds and international equities in both registered and ►American depository receipt form. Neither ISRO nor the TSA now exist as such. The TSA merged with the Association of Futures Brokers and Dealers to form the Securities and Futures Authority in 1991. ►►Financial Services Act.

Securities Exchange of Thailand (SET) Set up in 1975 to succeed the Bangkok Stock Exchange, which in turn dated from 1962. Regulated by the Thai Ministry of Finance.

securities house ►Issuing house.

Securities Industry Automation Corporation ►National Securities Clearing Corporation.

Securities Investor Protection Corporation (SIPC) (US) A compensation scheme for investors in the event of the failure of ►market makers or ►dealers. All members of the ►National Association of Securities Dealers belong to this scheme.

securitization The substitution of ►securities for bank loans; i.e. a bank may, instead of lending to a customer, purchase or accept (►acceptance) a ►bill of exchange, a ►note or other ►security from them. Alternatively a would-be borrower, rather than apply to a bank, may issue a bill of exchange, note or other ►debt instrument to a non-bank purchaser or acceptor. Securitization was in part a revival of the capital markets, much impaired by the economic crisis of the 1970s and early 1980s, and in part a development of short-term security forms that give the lender ►negotiable instruments and enable banks to raise funds more easily. Securitization also relieves banks of reliance on the traditional interest rate differences on deposits and advances; and it enables them, in times of pressure on capital ratios, to avoid balance sheet additions. In so far as the security issues are managed or ►underwritten by the banks, a fee-earning opportunity is also opened to the banks. Since many of the securities have been short term, with ►floating rates of interest, investors have been more ready to buy them than fixed-rate bonds, whose return or capital value would have fallen with any rise in general market interest rates. ►►disintermediation.

securitized paper The ►instrument resulting from the conversion of a bank loan into a *marketable* (►negotiable) ►security. ►securitization.

security 1. A pledge of financial or physical property to be surrendered in the event of failure to repay a loan. **2**. Any medium of investment in the money market or ►capital market, e.g. a money-market ►instrument, a ►bond, a ►share. **3**. A term used to refer only to bonds, and shares, as distinct from ►money-market assets.

SEDOL number All UK quoted securities (not merely those on the ➤official list, but including the ➤alternative investment market) are given a *Stock Exchange Daily Official List* (SEDOL) number. This number also serves as the *International Securities Identification Number* (ISIN).

segregated pension fund A ➤pension fund managed as a distinct entity by the fund manager.

segundo mercado (Sp.) The markets in unlisted securities (➤unlisted securities market) in Barcelona (since 1982) and Madrid (since 1987). Also called *bolsa secundaria*.

SEHK ➤Hong Kong stock exchanges.

seignorage The difference between the value of metal used in minting coins and their face value.

seiji kabu (Jap.) Literally, a 'political security', i.e. a stock rumoured to be a preferred investment choice of politicians; thus held likely to appreciate. Such stocks are frequent subjects of ➤ramping.

self-assessment ➤income tax.

Self-Employment Individuals Retirement Act ➤Keogh plan.

self-financing ➤retained earnings.

self-regulating organizations ➤Financial Services Act.

self-select PEP A ➤personal equity plan for which the share ➤portfolio is selected by the individual investor rather than by a ➤financial intermediary; the latter must none the less administer the plan.

sell-side ➤investment analyst.

senior debt ➤subordinated.

SEPON Stock Exchange Pool Nominee. ➤Transfer Accounting; Lodgement for Investors; Stock Management for Jobbers (TALISMAN).

SEQUENCE ➤London Stock Exchange.

series Put or call options on the same underlying ➤instrument, having the same ➤striking price and the same ➤maturity.

SERPS State Earnings-Related Pension Scheme. ➤pensions.

services That part of the national economy not concerned with the production of tangible goods, i.e. activities such as insurance, transport, banking, securities and commodity dealing, electricity, gas and other utilities, and telecommunications. In most industrialized countries services account for half or more of all economic activity. The term is also applied in balance of payments terminology to denote the imports and exports of service industries.

servicing Payment of interest on a bank loan.

SES ➤Singapore Stock Exchange.

SESDAQ Stock Exchange of Singapore Dealing and Quotation System. ➤Singapore Stock Exchange.

SET ➤Securities Exchange of Thailand.

SETS ➤London Stock Exchange.

settle Of ➤currency and ➤security transactions, to pay the purchase price.

settlement 1. Payment of an obligation, e.g. payment in cash for ➤securities. Hence ➤account day on the ➤London Stock Exchange is also known as settlement day or the settlement date. Settlement procedures vary. In the UK stockholders' accounts fall due at the end of fixed periods (accounts). In the USA payment for securities is usually due on the fifth day after the transaction; this is known as a rolling account or rolling settlement system. This system is soon to be adopted in the UK. **2**. The transfer or intended transfer of property after a legal agreement or on the ➤execution of a will after death. ➤➤Transfer and Automated Registration of Uncertified Stock (TAURUS); CREST.

settlement date ➤settlement.

settlement day ➤settlement.

settlement prices ➤official prices.

settlement risk ➤counterparty risk.

seven-day money Money placed, i.e. an instrument bought, in the ➤money market with a ➤maturity of seven days.

Seventh Directive ➤consolidated accounts.

SFA ➤Securities and Futures Authority; Financial Services Act.

SFE ➤Sydney Futures Exchange.

Shanghai Securities Exchange ➤China.

share One of a number of equal portions in the nominal ➤capital of a company, entitling the owner to a proportion of distributed ➤profits and of residual value if the company goes into ➤liquidation; a form of ➤security. Shares may be fully or partly paid (➤paid-up capital), ➤voting shares or non-voting (sometimes called 'A' shares). ➤➤ordinary shares; preference shares; stock. Also a term used to denote deposits in a UK ➤building society; the usage is historical, referring to the depositor's participation in the funding of the society, and has no ►equity shareholding connotation.

share certificate A document issued by the ►registrar or their agent confirming legal title to the ownership of a stated number of ►equity shares. ►CREST.

share exchange scheme ►Unit trusts, ►investment trusts and other forms of managed ►portfolio investments are often willing to accept investments in the form of ►shares rather than cash. These schemes offer more attractive terms than the alternative of selling shares in the market and paying commission for those who wish to switch from direct ownership of shares into trusts. ►►switching discount.

share indices ►Index numbers indicating changes in the average prices of ►shares on the ►stock exchange. The indices are constructed by taking a selection of shares and (usually) weighting (►weighted average) the percentage changes in prices together as an indication of aggregate movements in share prices. Roughly speaking, a share index shows percentage changes in the market prices of a ►portfolio compared with its value in the base year of the index. ►►Dow-Jones indexes; Financial Times share indices; Hong Kong stock exchanges; Morgan Stanley Capital International World Index; NASDAQ OTC Price Index; Nikkei Stock Average; Standard and Poor's Ratings; Toronto Stock Exchange and other national ►stock exchange entries.

share options ►profit-sharing scheme.

share perks (UK) Benefits for ►shareholders over and above ►dividends, e.g. discounts on company products.

share premium Where ►shares are sold at a ►premium to their face value. The excess proceeds of sales of its own shares by a company at a premium are credited to a share premium account and shown as such in the ►balance sheet as part of the permanent capital of the business. The share premium account may not be used to pay ►dividends (though it may be used for a ►bonus issue).

share register ►registrar.

shareholder The owner of ►shares in a company.

shareholder value An ill-defined but popular term associated with the concentration by companies on their core activities and the disposal of unwanted subsidiaries. Changes of these kinds have frequently led to an upward re-rating of shares and hence to improved shareholder value.

shareholders' equity The total ►assets of a company minus its external ►liabilities (i.e. except those to ►equity shareholders). Put another way, the ►balance sheet will show shareholders' equity as ►paid-up capital, ►revaluation reserve and *undistributed profits* (►retained earnings). ►►net assets.

shelf registration (US) Under Rule 415, larger companies may since 1983 register advance details of ►securities with the ►Securities and Exchange Commission (SEC) without any date of issue, so that when they need to raise capital they make an issue 'off the shelf' without the delay involved in waiting for clearance of an application to the SEC.

Shenzhen Securities Exchange ►China.

shibosai (Jap.) The Japanese market for ►private placements.

shibosai **bond** (Jap.) A ►samurai bond, the subject of a *private placing* (►placing).

shintaka ginko (Jap.) ►Trust bank.

shinyo kinku (Jap.) A banking institution providing ►credit to small businesses; usually translated into English as a credit association. ►►credit union.

shinyo kumiai (Jap.) A credit association similar to a *shino kinku* but dealing with small businesses. ►►credit union.

shogun bond (Jap.) A ►bond denominated in a ►foreign currency, issued on the Japanese market by a non-resident.

shogun lease An international lease provided by the Japanese leasing industry, the contract being established in yen.

short 1. Of dealings in ►currencies, ►securities and ►commodities, a condition of net indebtedness, either by being liable to discharge a loan of one of these items, or by being committed to supply an amount at a future date, e.g. having sold a ►futures contract; or being committed or liable to supply at a future date at a price below the current rate, as in futures or ►options contracts. ►►position. 2. Of dealings in securities and ►money-market instruments, to shift a holding to a shorter-term (►term) form. 3. More generally to hold securities, currencies and money-market instruments in reduced quantity.

short covering To ►cover a ►short position.

short-dated securities ►dated securities.

short hedge A ►hedge effected by the sale of a ►futures contract.

short tail business ►Insurance business, such as motor insurance, where claims quickly follow losses.

short term 1. Of a ►security, having a short ►maturity, normally up to five years. 2. Of a bank loan, repayable within three years. 3. Of a ►money-market instrument, having a maturity of three months or less. 4. Of ►insurance, business other than life insurance. 5. ►finance.

short-term monetary support (STMS) A form of ►intervention mechanism under the ➤European Monetary System (EMS) under which the central bank of a country under ➤exchange rate pressure due to ➤balance of payments difficulties may borrow at three months from the central banks of other member countries; the ➤term may be extended, such an extension being known as a *rallonge*. This form of assistance is funded by member country subscriptions based on a ➤quota.

SIAC ➤Securities Industry Automated Corporation.

SIB Securities and Investment Board. ➤Financial Services Act.

SICAV ➤*société d'investissement à capital variable.*

sight deposit A bank ➤deposit, all or part of which may be withdrawn without notice (i.e. on sight). US = *demand deposit.* ➤➤current account.

SIMEX ➤Singapore International Monetary Exchange.

simple sum A theory of money measurement that regards all money forms as equal. Also known as the *all-or-nothing* theory.

sine die Indefinitely; of a postponement, or of the fixing of the date of a future event.

Singapore International Monetary Exchange (SIMEX) Deals in financial (especially ➤Eurodollar), energy and commodity ➤futures. SIMEX was established in 1984 and now has a mutual offset arrangement with the ➤Chicago Mercantile Exchange.

Singapore Stock Exchange (SES) In its present form dates from 1973 when the joint ➤stock exchange of Singapore and Malaysia were separated. There remain close links between the securities trading activities of the two countries. By 1990 the Malaysian government made its companies delist from the SES, but this was followed by the establishment of the Central Limit Order Book (CLOB) international computerized market in Singapore, which, although not officially recognized by the ➤Kuala Lumpur Stock Exchange, lists many Malaysian companies. There is a second tier. The Stock Exchange of Singapore Dealing and Automated Quotation System (SESDAQ) was launched in February 1987 and modelled on the ➤National Association of Securities Dealers Automated Quotation System (NASDAQ). The principal ➤share indices for ➤stock quoted on the SES are the *Straits Times Index* (STI) and the *Stock Exchange of Singapore Index* (SESI).

single capacity A term used to describe a situation where a ➤market maker on a ➤stock exchange deals only with other professionals and not with the investors. ➤➤dual capacity.

single company PEP A ►personal equity plan that is wholly invested in the ►shares of one ►quoted company.

Single European Act ►European Union (EU).

single premium ►life assurance.

sinking fund Provision for the repayment of ►debt, including the ►redemption of a ►security by the issuer, by accumulating a fund through regular payments that, with interest, will *amortize* the loan.

SIPC ►Securities Investor Protection Corporation.

Sistem de Interconexion de las Bolsas Españolas ►Madrid Stock Exchange.

skip day (US) Settlement of the purchase of a ►security, normally in the ►money market, two days after the transaction takes place.

slip The document setting out details of the ►insurance risk to be ►covered, used by ►brokers, particularly at ►Lloyd's. Signatures by ►insurers on the slip are evidence of acceptance of the risk.

Small Order Execution System ►National Association of Securities Dealers Automated Quotation System (NASDAQ).

small business investment company (SBIC) (US) A company set up with low-cost funds and taxation advantages from the US federal government to invest in small businesses, authorized under the Small Business Investment Act 1958. Similar institutions exist in Japan, while in France and other countries ►venture capital companies and ►investment trusts or their investors may be eligible for tax incentives. ►►Business Expansion Scheme; Venture Capital Trust Scheme.

small cap stocks (US) ►Shares in smaller ►quoted companies which have a low market capitalization compared with ►blue chips and mid-cap stocks. There are no generally agreed definitions, but small caps have capitalization of around $250m or less and big caps $2bn or so. The attraction of small cap stocks to some investors is that they are not fully researched and, though individually risky in aggregate, have tended to outperform big caps in the past.

small loan company ►finance house.

smaller companies market (SCM) (Ire.) The third-tier ►unlisted securities market (USM) in Ireland. Ireland also has a second-tier USM.

smart card A plastic card incorporating a microchip. Invented in France, where they are called *cartes à mémoire*, smart cards can be used as plastic money a credit facility being drawn down as it is used and recharged by the issuing bank or store; or they may be used at ➤automatic teller machines (cash dispensers). ➤➤credit card.

SMI ➤Swiss stock exchanges.

SMR ➤standard Malaysian rubber.

Snake ➤European Monetary System (EMS).

SNIF Note issuance facility. ➤Euronote facility.

sobashi (Jap.) A speculator, often engaged in ➤ramping.

Social Charter ➤European Union (EU).

Social Security Act 1986 (UK) ➤pensions.

sociedad anónima (Sp.) Public limited company. ➤incorporation.

società per azioni (SpA) (It.) Public limited company. ➤incorporation. A private company in Italy has 'Srl' after its name.

société anonyme (SA) (Fr.) Public limited company. ➤incorporation. Also in some non-French-speaking countries, e.g. Greece.

Société Anonyme de la Bourse ➤Luxembourg Stock Exchange.

société à responsabilité limitée (SàRL) (Fr.) Private limited company. ➤incorporation.

Société de Compensation des Marchés Conditionnels Operator of the French equity options market (➤Marché des Options Negotiables de Paris).

Societé des Bourses Françaises (Fr.) Association of French ➤stock exchanges.

société d'investissement à capital variable (SICAV) (Fr.) ➤Unit trust.

Société du Nouveau Marché A new ➤unlisted stock market set up in Paris in 1996, for hi-tech, high-growth ➤stocks and a member of the EURO.NM alliance.

SOES Small Order Execution System. ➤National Association of Securities Dealers Automated Quotation System (NASDAQ).

SOFFEX ➤Swiss Options and Financial Futures Exchange.

soft commodity A term applied to most ➤commodities other than metals, but chiefly referring to agricultural products such as tea, coffee, sugar and wheat, and to raised products such as wool, hides and skins.

soft currency ➤currency.

soft dollars (US) Payments made for services provided by a ➤stockbroker in the form of ➤commission to be earned on an agreed future level of trading. For example, a broker might carry out research on the understanding that a given level of trading would be based on the results. Cash payments or fees for research are referred to as *hard dollars*. Also practised in countries other than the USA in local currencies.

soft loan A loan made at below market rates of ➤interest.

sogo bank (Jap.) A bank specializing in house credit.

sogo shosha (Jap.) A term applying to the large corporations, e.g. Mitsubishi and Mitsui, engaged chiefly in distribution but also in finance and production.

sokai (Jap.) A shareholders' meeting.

sokaiya (Jap.) Literally, a shareholders'-meeting man; hence, a speculator. *Sokai-yas* have also been involved in corrupt practices in which they receive money from Japanese companies in return for a guarantee not to ask embarrassing questions at shareholders' meetings.

sold short ➤bear.

solde (Fr.) ➤Balance.

sole proprietorship An ➤unincorporated business owned by a single person and not benefiting from limited liability. ➤incorporation.

solvency The ability to pay one's debts in full on the due date. ➤➤solvency margin; solvency ratio.

solvency margin A required minimum surplus of an insurance company's ➤assets over its ➤liabilities, the composition of these two aggregates being strictly defined by the supervisory authorities, and varying according to the type of company and the class of business transacted.

solvency ratio Of banks, the relationship of own capital to total ➤liabilities.

solvent A condition in which total ➤assets exceed total ➤liabilities.

sources and uses of funds (UK) Statements of ➤flow of funds within a company during a period. Now a required element in the published financial accounts for all but the smallest companies, alongside the ➤balance sheet and the ➤profit and loss account. Also known as sources and applications (or disposition) of funds and in the USA as statement of *changes in financial position*. There are various forms of flow of funds statements, but typically they show all the ➤capital flows of a business between balance sheet dates. *Sources of funds* are ➤profits from trading operations, ➤depreciation provisions, sales of ➤assets and borrowing, including ➤equity and other capital issues. *Uses of funds* are purchases of fixed or financial assets, cash and distribution of income.

sovereign A national government in its role, for example, as a lender or borrower; hence ➤sovereign risk.

sovereign loan A bank loan to a government, usually of a developing country.

sovereign risk The hazard, in ➤securities trading involving another country, that ➤political risk may arise in that country. Also known as *country risk*.

SpA (It.) ➤*società per azioni*.

SPA ➤state pension age.

Sparkassen (Ger.) The oldest network of ➤savings banks, dating from the second half of the 18th century. The banks are guaranteed by local authorities.

Special Credit Controls Program (US) A series of emergency counter-inflation measures introduced in March 1980, applying limits to most forms of credit provided by most financial institutions. The programme was abandoned in May of the same year.

special deposits (UK) Deposits required to be placed by UK commercial banks with the ➤Bank of England. Special deposits have been used as an instrument of ➤monetary control and were first introduced in 1961. The intended effect is broadly to reduce the level of deposits held by the commercial banks and so to reduce their capacity for lending. Special deposits, when called for, are assessed as a proportion of the bank's ➤eligible liabilities. Interest is paid on special deposits by the Bank of England at a rate close to ➤Treasury bill rate.

special drawing right (SDR) A form of international ➤reserve created by the ➤International Monetary Fund (IMF) in 1970. The purpose was to assist international ➤liquidity by providing a complement to existing reserve vehicles such as gold, the US dollar and UK sterling, supply of the first of which was determined by production factors and of the others by ➤balance of payments outturns. SDRs are allocated by the IMF to its member countries in proportion to each country's ➤quota and are used, as is the rest of the quota, to acquire other national currencies when needed for balance of payments reasons. SDRs are therefore a universally recognized claim on national currencies and thus have the effect, although not yet all the characteristics, of a new currency.

SDRs were first given a value equal to 0.89 grammes of fine gold, or US$1, which was the then dollar/gold parity. With the subsequent devaluation of the dollar, the value was set to equal the sum of specified national currencies. In 1981 the SDR was simplified to a weighted average of the five leading currencies according to their share in world trade. SDRs are used as the ➤unit of account of the IMF and since 1980 have been the denomination for many ➤certificates of deposit and ➤bond issues.

special Lombard rate The rate of interest charged by the German ➤Bundesbank

251

to the banking system when normal lending against ➤Lombard rate has been suspended, and lending proceeds day by day at interest rates fixed each day by the Bundesbank. ➤discount window.

special reserve (UK) An amount that ➤Lloyd's members may, with relief from taxation, set aside from their ➤underwriting profits to meet future tax liabilities. The amount may not exceed a prescribed percentage of the relevant profits, may not be used for any purpose other than payment of tax, and becomes subject again to tax when used.

specialist (US) A member of the ➤New York Stock Exchange who makes a market in a number of ➤stocks by buying and selling on their own account and for ➤commission brokers (➤➤order driven). The role of specialists is similar to that of ➤jobbers under the system that operated on the ➤London Stock Exchange before the ➤Big Bang. A specialist operates from a *trading post*, a location on the ➤trading floor where particular securities are bought and sold.

specie Money in the form of coins.

speculation Dealing in a ➤commodity or financial ➤asset with a view to obtaining a profit on the prospective change in the market value of the item in question.

speculative risk Of insurance, a ➤risk arising out of entrepreneurial action, leading to gain or loss in a way not calculable by the ➤law of large numbers and therefore not insurable.

split-level trust ➤investment trust.

sponsor ➤issuing house.

spot Immediate or now.

spot month The first month for which ➤futures contracts are available.

spot price The present value of an ➤asset, as opposed to ➤futures, ➤forward or ➤option prices. It is applied to dealings in ➤currencies, ➤securities and ➤commodities, and synonymous for the latter with *cash*, *physical* or *actual* prices.

spread 1. The difference between the interest rate charged by a bank or banks on a loan and that paid by them for their funds. Most used in connection with syndicated international credits and Euromarket loans. The bank's funding rate is normally assumed to be a reference rate, such as ➤London interbank offered rate (LIBOR), *London interbank bid rate* (LIBID) or London interbank mean rate (➤LIMEAN). 2. The difference between the selling price asked by dealers in foreign exchange or securities and the price at which they have bought them. 3. Difference between the price at which an underwriter buys securities from an issuer and the price at which they sell them to the general public. 4. The gap between the highest-valued and lowest-valued currency in the ➤European Monetary

System (EMS), also termed the *margin*. **5**. The distribution of risks taken on by an insurer. **6**. The sale of a contract in the ►commodity, ►options or ►financial futures market and the purchase at the same time of a contract for a different item, or of a contract with different terms for the same item, the object being to achieve a profit on the movement in prices between the contracts. ►►straddle. **7**. The difference between the ►bid and ►offer price of units in a ►unit trust.

spreadsheet A (usually) rectangular grid or matrix, setting out large amounts of financial or other data. The data are written or printed in boxes or windows defined by the rows and columns of the sheet, e.g. years along the top and the components of ►cash flow down the left-hand side. Traditionally spreadsheet analysis was carried out on specially ruled paper. Now electronic spreadsheets can be composed on computer screens using proprietary software such as Lotus 1-2-3 that will sum rows and columns quickly after changes are entered in, and produce graphs, subtotals and other calculations at the press of a key.

Square Mile ►City.

Srl ►*società per azioni*.

SRO Self-regulating organization. ►Financial Services Act.

SSAP Statement of Standard Accounting Practice. ►accounting standards.

stability pact ►Amsterdam Treaty.

standard bar A gold bar weighing approximately 400 oz with a minimum ►fineness of 995; a silver bar of approximately 1,000 oz with a minimum fineness of 999.

stag A speculator who subscribes to ►new issues, in the expectation that they will rise to a ►premium over issue price, so that they (the speculator) will be able to sell their allotment of ►securities at a profit when dealings in them begin. Some people make multiple applications where there is a likelihood that the issue will be ►oversubscribed and a ballot or scaling down is expected, though multiple applications may be proscribed and illegal.

stamp duty (UK) A form of ►taxation that involves, or used to involve, the fixing of pre-paid stamps on legal or commercial documents. Stamp duties may be *ad valorem* or specific (►tax; *ad valorem*). Stamp duty is applied as a percentage of the value of share transactions in the UK.

Standard and Poor's 500 (S&P 500) (US) A ►share index measuring price changes in 500 ►securities quoted on the ►New York Stock Exchange (NYSE); 400 company ►stocks, 40 financial, 20 transportation and 40 public utility issues are included, each weighted in accordance with the number of stocks at issue.

Standard and Poor's Ratings (US) A classification of preferred stocks (►preference shares), ►bonds and ►common stocks according to risk. 'AAA' represents the highest-quality investment grade, in which the risk of default is minimal; 'BBB' are medium grade, and 'Bb' predominantly speculative; 'C' are the lowest quality of bond, paying no interest, and 'DDD' are in default or in arrears; 'D' are of questionable value. A similar service is provided by Moody's Investor Services, a subsidiary of Dun & Bradstreet.

standard deviation A measure of the ►dispersion of a group of numerical values from the mean or ►average. The standard deviation is calculated by taking the differences between each number in the group and the arithmetic average, squaring them to give the variance (i.e. multiplying each number by itself), summing them and taking the square root.

standard Malaysian rubber (SMR) A standard product in natural rubber, devised by the Malaysian government in the early 1960s in order to provide homogeneity in competition with synthetic rubber. SMR reduced factory processing time and allowed for quality control through adherence to specification rather than by visual inspection; it also facilitated packing and handling.

standby credit ►Credit guaranteed in a ►note issuance facility or ►Euronote facility. ►►back-up credit.

start-up A new independent business venture.

state bank ►national bank.

State Earnings-Related Pension Scheme (SERPS) ►pensions.

state of the art A doctrine to the effect that producers are not liable for harm caused by their product if, at the time the product was made, the product's potential for harm was unknown to science. This argument was advanced, for instance, to reject liability for the harm caused by asbestos in products manufactured at a time when the noxious characteristics of asbestos had not been discovered.

state pension age The age at which men and women become eligible for ►pensions provided by the state.

statement of changes in financial position ►sources and use of funds.

Statement of Standard Accounting Practice (SSAP) ►accounting standards.

statement week (US) The unit of time in which the ►Federal Reserve's directions for the average level of bank reserves must be observed. ►►maintenance period.

static risk Of insurance, a ►risk arising out of natural causes, e.g. fire, earthquake or human frailty such as theft.

stellage (Fr.) ➤Bourse transaction conveying the right, against a premium, to sell an underlying security at a given price on or before a stated date; it can also convey the right to buy.

step-lock option ➤ladder option.

stepped preference shares ➤investment trust.

sterilization (US) The contention of some theorists, notably R. I. McKinnon of Stanford University, that the US authorities, in not adjusting internal monetary conditions to changes in the dollar's ➤exchange rate, neutralize, or sterilize, the effect of growth in the world ➤money supply.

Sterling Area ➤Scheduled Territories.

sterling warrant into gilt-edged stock (SWING) Authorized by the ➤Bank of England in 1987, an ➤option to buy or sell a specific ➤gilt. The warrants are issued by the Bank of England, then sold by an appointed dealer.

STI Straits Times Index. ➤Singapore Stock Exchange.

stock 1. A particular type of ➤security, usually quoted in units of £100 value rather than in units or proportion of total ➤capital, as in ➤shares. Stock, or stocks, and shares have now become synonymous, and the original distinction between stocks and shares has become blurred. The term 'stock' in UK usage is now coming to mean exclusively a fixed-interest security, e.g. loan stock, but in the USA fixed-interest securities are referred to as ➤bonds, while other securities are called 'stocks' as in ➤common stocks. **2**. An accumulation of capital. **3**. An accumulation of a ➤commodity or of finished or semi-finished goods or materials. ➤inventories.

stock dividend ➤bonus issue.

stock exchange A market in which ➤securities are bought and sold. There are stock exchanges in most capital cities, as well as in the larger provincial cities in many countries. The ➤New York Stock Exchange, ➤London Stock Exchange and ➤Tokyo Stock Exchange are the largest in terms of ➤market capitalization and ➤turnover, although London lists the securities of more companies, particularly overseas companies, than either Tokyo or the NYSE.

Continental European exchanges are often referred to as *bourses* (Fr.). Stock exchanges facilitate ➤savings and ➤investment by making it possible for investors to dispose of securities quickly if they wish to do so (in the ➤secondary market) and for companies, governments and other organizations to raise new ➤capital in the primary market (➤new issue market). Ready marketability requires that: ➤new issues should be made and backed by reputable borrowers or institutions; information should be available on existing securities; competition should exist among ➤market makers; and there should be adequate ➤liquidity. There should be both a legal framework and market rules to prevent fraud and sharp practice (►regulation). There are various trading systems on stock exchanges (►order driven; quote driven), but many ►trading floors have given way to ►automated screen trading and telephone markets. These new technologies and deregulation have permitted the development of new systems for trading securities outside of stock exchanges (►IBIS; Instinet). ►►entries for stock exchanges, e.g. ►Singapore Stock Exchange, or country, e.g. ►China, or region, e.g. ►Eastern Europe. ►►unlisted securities market.

Stock Exchange Alternative Trading Service (SEATS) 1. A system for trading less liquid (►liquidity) ►securities introduced on the ►London Stock Exchange on 16 November 1992 to replace the ►Company Bulletin Board, where there is only either a single or no ►market maker. The screen displays the current ►quotations for the market maker (if any) and current public ►orders to provide a central point for business in these illiquid stocks. SEATS complements the ►Stock Exchange Automated Quotation System. **2.** An automated screen trading system on the ►Australian Stock Exchange.

Stock Exchange Automated Quotation System (SEAQ) (UK) A screen-based quotation system for ►securities that allows ►market makers on the ►London Stock Exchange to report their price quotes and trading volumes to users of the system. SEAQ was introduced in preparation for the ►Big Bang and has allowed all transactions on the exchange to be carried out by telephone rather than as formerly on the ►trading floor. It feeds into TOPIC (►Teletext Output of Price Information by Computer) and is linked into NASDAQ (►National Association of Securities Dealers Automated Quotation System). ►►alpha securities; normal market size; stocks.

Stock Exchange Automatic Execution Facility (SAEF) (UK) A computerized system for executing small purchase and sales ►orders for ►shares on the ►London Stock Exchange. SAEF automatically routes orders to the ►market maker offering the best price on the ►Stock Exchange Automated Quotation System, executes the order and produces ►contract notes, and enters the transaction into the TALIS-MAN (►Transfer Accounting, Lodgement for Investors, Stock Management for Jobbers) settlement system. TRADE and BEST are competing similar proprietary small order execution systems operated by the London ►market maker houses Barclays de Zoete Wedd and Kleinwort Grieveson Securities respectively. SAEF is similar to the small order execution system operated by the ►National Association of Securities Dealers Automated Quotation System.

Stock Exchange Daily Official List (UK) ►official list.

Stock Exchange pool nominees ►Transfer Accounting, Lodgement for Investors, Stock Management for Jobbers.

Stock Exchange Trading System ►London Stock Exchange.

stock index futures ►Futures contracts based on ►share indices.

stock market ►stock exchange.

stock split (US) A ►bonus issue of shares that reduces the unit quoted price but not the ►yield or market value of the investor's holding.

stockbroker A member of a ►stock exchange who buys and sells ►securities as an ►agent for clients in return for a ►commission (US = *commission broker*). ►►broker; floor broker; market maker.

Stockholm Stock Exchange (SSE) The Stockholm Fondbors, as it is called, is the ►stock exchange of Sweden. The exchange is regulated by the Bank Inspection Board (BIB) and the Riksbanker (►central bank). Since 1993 the exchange has been a ►limited liability company and in 1994 its shares were opened up to general ownership. ►►Nordquote.

stop-loss 1. The price at which a ►security is automatically sold to protect the investor against further loss. ►orders. **2.** Insurance against losses on the ►Lloyd's market. ►stop-loss insurance.

stop-loss insurance Insurance by ►names at ►Lloyd's of London against ►underwriting losses, an insurance normally contracted within the market itself.

stop-loss treaty A ►non-proportional treaty (►►reinsurance) under which the reinsurer refunds to the insurer the amount of claims paid that exceed a predetermined percentage of premiums received.

stop order ►order.

stop rate (US) The lowest accepted rate of interest on a ►repurchase agreement.

straddle Used interchangeably in the ►commodities, ►options and ►financial futures markets with the term ►spread. A straddle often signifies the simultaneous sale and purchase of ►call and *put* options or of different ►terms in the same financial futures or commodity market.

straight bond A ►bond at a fixed ►rate of interest without ►conversion (i.e. not replaceable with a new bond or ►equity).

straight-line method ►depreciation.

Straits Times Index (STI) ►Singapore Stock Exchange.

strangle The sale or purchase of put and call ►options with the same expiry date but different ►strike prices, done for speculative purposes.

strict liability A doctrine in law that a party causing harm or loss is liable, whether or not they acted negligently or with wrongful intent. The doctrine is opposed to that of ►state of the art. Strict liability has increasing adherence in

US and German jurisdiction, and legislation on comparable lines is contemplated by the European Commission (➤➤European Union). Limited defences are available under strict liability to defendants, thus distinguishing the concept from *absolute liability*, a rule permitting no exceptions, and one that strict liability has displaced.

striking price, strike price 1. Offer for sale. 2. The price paid by the holder of a ➤call option or to the holder of a *put* option when the option contract is executed. Normally, for commodities, the current market price at the time of sale of the option.

stripping The separate trading of the ➤capital and ➤interest of a ➤bond. ➤➤asset stripping; gilt strip.

Structural Adjustment Programme (SAP) ➤International Bank for Reconstruction and Development.

sub-chapter S corporations (US) Under sub-chapter S of the Internal Revenue Code, corporations with 35 or fewer non-corporate shareholders may elect to be subject to ➤income tax instead of ➤corporation tax. This allows a business to choose whichever tax regime is most favourable to it, e.g. where it would be advantageous to offset losses in the company against other personal income. When a ➤company is taxed in the normal way it may be referred to as a *C-corporation*.

subordinated Of a ➤liability, ranked below another liability in order of priority for payment. *Junior debt* is ranked after *senior debt* for repayment in the event of ➤default.

subsidiary Generally, a company controlled by another, parent company (➤consolidated accounts). Also referred to as an *affiliate*.

SUPERCAC ➤Paris Bourse.

supersaver account (US) ➤money-market deposit account.

supplementary special deposit (SSD) (UK) An additional deposit required to be placed by commercial banks with the Bank of England, over and above ➤special deposits. The system, known as 'the corset', was operated by the Bank of England in 1973–5, 1976–7 and 1978–80. It was abandoned permanently in June 1980. The object of the scheme was to reinforce the restraint of banks' deposit taking effected by special deposits. SSDs, which did not qualify for interest, were called in relation to the banks' ➤interest-bearing eligible liabilities (IBELs), a higher amount being required as the banks' IBELs exceeded a prescribed rate of growth. The scheme was largely frustrated by the ➤bill leak and by the abolition of exchange control in October 1979.

supply estimates ➤supply expenditure.

supply expenditure (UK) The part of UK central government expenditure that is financed by moneys voted by Parliament, i.e. expenditure not automatically arising from continuing statutory obligations. The parliamentary vote is given in response to detailed presentation of the expenditure needed, in the supply estimates. The moneys arising in this way are frequently referred to as 'the vote'.

surplus ACT ➤corporation tax.

surplus treaty Of ➤insurance, a ➤proportional treaty (➤➤reinsurance) under which the insurer cedes to the reinsurer that part of the ➤risk on which they (the insurer) do not wish to be liable themselves.

sushi bond (Jap.) A foreign-currency ➤bond that, when issued by a Japanese institution, is officially classified as a domestic bond. Such bonds are attractive to ➤trust banks and insurance companies whose foreign bond holdings are restricted.

swap **1**. A transaction whereby a ➤security of a certain value is sold to a buyer in exchange for the purchase, from the buyer, of a security having the same value; the purpose being to obtain an improvement, in the eyes of either of the parties, in the quality of the security, or to anticipate a change in yield, e.g. ➤intermarket spread swap, ➤rate anticipation swap. **2**. In ➤foreign exchange, the purchase/sale of a currency in the ➤spot market against the simultaneous purchase/sale of the same amount of the same currency in the ➤forward market. **3**. In international monetary relations, the opening by one ➤central bank of a ➤line of credit in its own currency against the opening of an equivalent line of credit in another currency by the relevant central bank. ➤➤currency interest rate swap; option.

swap line A ➤swap between the ➤central banks of different countries in that the borrowing central bank's complementary action is in the form of a ➤forward contract, rather than the simultaneous provision of its own currency. An extension of the principle of a ➤line of credit.

swap rate The difference between the ➤forward interest rate on, say, a ➤currency and the ➤spot rate expressed as a ➤discount or ➤premium on the latter.

swaption An ➤option to enter into a ➤swap contract.

sweep facility An automatic service available on some bank accounts or other ➤current accounts that shifts credit balances into a ➤deposit account where they will earn interest.

SWIFT Society for Worldwide Interbank Financial Telecommunications. A credit-transfer system between banks operated on a non-profit basis from Brussels. The system links some 1,500 banks in 68 countries.

SWING (UK) ➤sterling warrant into gilt-edged stock.

swing line (UK) An arrangement reconciling different ➤settlement dates in domestic and ►Euro-commercial paper markets. Borrowers switching, e.g., from domestic US ►commercial paper with one-day settlement to Euro-commercial paper with two- to three-day settlement first make two- or three-day drawings. With same-day settlement becoming more common in the Euro-commercial paper market, swing lines have more recently become less used.

Swiss Market Index ►Swiss stock exchanges.

Swiss Options and Financial Futures Exchange (SOFFEX) An ►options and ►futures market set up by the Basle, Geneva and Zurich stock exchanges, together with five Swiss banks, in May 1988, initial trading being in options on up to 15 first-line Swiss stocks.

Swiss stock exchanges The ►stock exchanges in Switzerland are now grouped under the *Schweizer Borse.* Zurich is the largest exchange, followed by Geneva and Basle. A second tier, the *deuxième marché,* was opened in 1988 and there is also an *avant-bourse* for pre-market trading in other shares. The *Swiss Market Index* (SMI) is the main exchange index.

switch ►swap.

switching Of a ►commodity, substituting a contract for delivery at a certain date for one for delivery of the same commodity at another date.

switching discount A ►discount or reduction in the ►offer price of a ►unit trust offered to investors in other unit trusts of the same group.

Sydney Futures Exchange (SFE) Trades ►financial futures, including contracts based on the *All Ordinaries Index,* and other futures and ►options, including ►commodity futures (wool and live cattle). The SFE also owns the ►New Zealand Futures and Options Exchange (NZFOE).

syndicate 1. A group of banks or other financial institutions formed to provide a ►credit or to ►underwrite or manage an issue of a ►security. **2.** The operating unit into which the ►Lloyd's insurance market is divided.

syndicated credit ►syndication.

syndicated lending ►syndication.

syndicated loan ►lead manager.

syndication To subject a ►credit or the issue of a ►security to management or ►underwriting by a ►syndicate. This method became common in the international lending market from the 1970s, owing largely to the great increase in funds, available from members of the ►Organization of Petroleum Exporting Countries (OPEC) and demanded by non-OPEC countries, after the oil price rises that began in 1972/3. Syndicated lending, or syndicated credit, also became commonplace in the ➤Euromarkets. ➤Venture capital companies also syndicate deals so as to spread ➤risk.

system repurchase agreement (US) A ➤repurchase agreement arranged by the ➤Federal Reserve for its own account.

system RP ➤system repurchase agreement.

systemic risk A situation where problems in any one financial institution or market may spread, widely endangering the whole system.

T

Tafelgeschaft (Ger.) ➤Over-the-counter dealing.

Tagesgeld (Ger.) Day-to-day money. ➤overnight money.

Taiwan Stock Exchange Established in 1962 and regulated by the Securities and Exchange Commission. An ➤over-the-counter market was launched in 1982.

take-over The acquisition of one company by another. ➤➤corporate raider; merger; Take-Over Panel.

Take-Over Panel (UK) The Panel on Take-Overs and Mergers is a committee responsible for supervising compliance with the City Code on Take-Overs and Mergers, a non-statutory code instituted in 1968 (though with origins earlier) and revised in 1987. The code is intended to protect the interests of ➤shareholders and requires *inter alia* that any company acquiring more than 29.9% of the ➤shares in another company must make a full bid at a price not lower than the highest price paid for its shareholding.

taker The buyer of an ➤option.

TALISMAN ➤Transfer Accounting, Lodgement for Investors, Stock Management for Jobbers.

tanigata toshi shintaku (Jap.) ➤*toshi shintaku*.

tanshi **company** (Jap.) A ➤market maker in the ➤money market and the ➤foreign exchange market.

tap The staged ➤sale of a government ➤money-market ➤instrument (e.g. a ➤Treasury bill) or ➤bond over a period of time in response to demand. Also used for staged sales by other issuers.

tap CD An issue of a ➤certificate of deposit (CD), normally in very large ➤denominations, by arrangement with a specific purchaser.

tap stock (UK) A government ➤bond issued formerly by the ➤government broker and now by a number of ➤market makers. The issue is not made all at once, and its supply can be adjusted like a tap to influence prices in the ➤gilts market.

TARGET Trans-European Automated Real-time Gross Settlement Express Transfer. After the proposed European Monetary Union (➤Maastricht Treaty), this system will allow banks to transfer ➤euros instantaneously between accounts held at their ►central bank. At present instantaneous transfers can only be made for domestic currencies, e.g. via CHAPS (►clearing house).

targeting (US) The adoption and application by the ►Federal Reserve of measures to bring about given levels of banking system ►reserves, ►credit growth and ►money supply growth.

tariffs Taxes imposed on imports. They may be levied on an ►*ad valorem* basis or as a specific amount per unit of imports.

TAURUS ►Transfer and Automated Registration of Uncertified Stock.

taux d'intérêt (Fr.) ►Rate of interest.

tax, *ad valorem* A tax expressed as a proportion of the price of a good or service; hence it is by *value*. ►Value added tax is an *ad valorem* tax, as is ►sales tax.

tax allowance ►tax credit.

tax avoidance (UK) Legal means used to take advantage of tax concessions to reduce or eliminate tax liabilities. US = ►tax shelter. ►►tax evasion.

tax credit An amount of tax deemed to have been paid that may be offset against a tax liability or reclaimed by the taxpayer if they have no liability (Fr. = *avoir fiscal*). To be distinguished from a *tax allowance*, the value of which will depend upon the taxpayer's tax bracket or marginal rate of tax. In the UK, tax credits are given on dividends, equivalent to the lower rate of income tax (►►corporation tax). Under ►double taxation agreements, a tax credit against US tax liability may be given, for example, to a US citizen who pays UK income tax. ►►capital allowance; investment credit.

tax deposit certificate (UK) Individual or corporate taxpayers may deposit funds with the Inland Revenue in advance of tax liabilities. Interest accrues daily, varying with market rates.

tax evasion Adoption of illegal measures to reduce or eliminate tax liabilities. ►►tax avoidance.

Tax-Exempt Special Savings Accounts (TESSA) (UK) A ►tax shelter savings plan open to all individuals aged 18 or over for money held on deposit in a ►bank or ►building society. Interest is not taxable provided no withdrawals are made during the five-year plan. The total sum invested may not exceed £9,000, of which not more than £3,000 may be deposited in the first 12 months. After five years investors may roll their investment into a second TESSA and continue contributions, if appropriate, up to the overall limit of £9,000. TESSAs are to be replaced by ►Individual Savings Accounts (ISAs).

tax haven A financial centre that offers a more favourable tax environment than that enjoyed in their home territory by the non-residents who invest there. Tax havens called offshore financial centres provide a base for offshore funds (e.g. ➤unit trusts or other forms of managed ➤portfolio investments). Other attractive features of tax havens may include banking secrecy and other favourable aspects of the legal environment. The essential characteristic of offshore banking is that its business is conducted in foreign currencies and on behalf of non-residents. A number of small countries have built up substantial offshore financial business, such as Bermuda, the Cayman Islands, Hong Kong, Singapore, Liechtenstein, Monaco and Luxembourg. The Channel Islands and the Isle of Man are used as tax havens by residents of the UK and other countries.

Tax Reform Act 1986 (US) This important legislation increased thresholds for personal ➤income tax and reduced or eliminated various deductions for both personal and business income taxes so as to allow major reductions in income tax and ➤corporation tax rates without significantly affecting total tax revenues. The number of personal income tax brackets was reduced from 14, with rates ranging from 11% to 50%, to two rates of 15% and 28% (though the highest effective rate is 33%, because some concessions are withdrawn for high-income taxpayers). The scope for ➤tax shelters was greatly reduced, e.g. by the limitation of deduction of interest on borrowings secured by first and second residences; and the exclusion of long-term gains from ➤capital gains tax was repealed. Maximum corporation tax rates were reduced from 46% to 34%. The ➤investment credit was eliminated. ➤Depreciation deductions were revised, and other business deductions reduced or eliminated for both incorporated and ➤unincorporated business. Subsequent legislation has affected some of the provisions of the Act.

tax shelter (US) Legal means used to take advantage of tax concessions to reduce or eliminate tax liabilities, e.g. the purchase of tax-free ➤savings bonds, the use of ➤pensions schemes (➤Keogh plan) or opting for a corporation to be taxed as a partnership. ➤➤tax havens; Tax Reform Act.

taxation A compulsory transfer of money from private individuals, institutions and commercial enterprises to finance government expenditure. It may be levied upon wealth or income, or in the form of a surcharge on prices. In the first case it would then be called a *direct tax* (e.g. ➤income tax), and in the second an *indirect tax* (e.g. ➤value added tax). ➤capital transfer tax; corporation tax; double taxation; excise duty; local taxation; sales tax; stamp duty; tariffs; tax credit; tax deposit certificate; tax shelter; wealth tax.

taxe d'émission (Fr.) The tax on ➤security issues.

taxe professionelle (Fr.) ➤local taxation.

Tea Brokers' Association of London A ➤physical commodity market, dealing in tea. Two million chests of 50 kilograms are sold annually on the market, equivalent to half the consumption of the UK, which is itself 40% of world consumption. The association is the main tea trading centre of the world. World tea production was estimated in 1993 at 546m kg.

technical analysis The study and prediction of price movements in ►security and ►commodity markets, based on the analysis of charts of ►share prices and trading volumes; hence the practitioners' title: *chartist*. Contrasted with practitioners of *fundamental analysis*, which involves the study of financial accounts and other information about companies, the chartist tends to believe that all the necessary information is in the share price. ►►efficient market hypothesis.

technical reserves A collective term used for the various reserves held by insurance companies against claims, namely ►unearned premiums reserve, ►unexpired risks reserve, ►claims outstanding reserve, ►incurred but not reported claims reserve.

teigatu (Jap.) A 10-year deposit certificate issued by the Japanese Post Office, encashable after six months, yielding interest after one year, such interest rising to a higher rate after three years.

Tel Aviv Stock Exchange The largest exchange in the Middle East (there are exchanges in Amman, Kuwait and Tehran; ►►Istanbul Menkul Kiymetter Borsasi). In its present form dates from 1953. There is also an ►unlisted securities market.

Telefonverkehr (Ger.) ►*geregelter Freiverkehr*.

telephone banking The facility to be told of bank account details and to give oral instructions for payments, account movements and other services by telephoning a special telephone number and quoting an identification code. ►►electronic banking.

Telerate (US) A majority-owned ►subsidiary of the Dow-Jones Corporation, providing news and financial information, to some extent in competition with ►Reuters. Particularly strong in the provision of data on US Treasury ►bonds and ►bills.

teletext ►viewdata.

Teletext Output of Price Information by Computer (TOPIC) (UK) A ►viewdata system provided by the ►London Stock Exchange for subscribers. It includes company information. ►►Stock Exchange Automated Quotation System.

TEMs ►*titulos de estabilización monetaria*.

10-K ►Form 10-K.

Ten Oever case ►equalization of pensions.

tender 1. Generally, to offer a payment, as in a written offer to purchase. 2. To offer a service in response to advertisement. 3. To offer to buy Treasury bills (►Treasury bill tender) issued by the ►Bank of England. 4. To offer for an issue of ►securities on the ►stock exchange (►►offer for sale; tender offer). **5.** To deliver a ►commodity to the buyer.

tender offer (US) A public offer to purchase ►securities of one company by another at a fixed price, usually at a ►premium over the current market price. Also used to refer to a public ►offer for sale of a specific portfolio of securities, normally for cash.

tender panel ►Euronote facility.

tenor The ►term or duration to maturity of a ►bill of exchange.

TEPs ►traded endowment policies.

term 1. The period of duration of a ►security until ►maturity or ►redemption. ►long term; medium term; short term. **2.** An ►insurance policy, particularly in ►life assurance, having a limited period of validity.

term insurance ►insurance; life assurance.

term loan A bank advance for a specific period (normally three to 10 years), repaid, with ►interest, usually by regular periodical payments. Term loans are made by ►commercial banks and other institutions for business finance. For large borrowings the ►loan may be syndicated (►syndicate), and it is quite common for loans to large corporations to be unsecured.

terminable annuity An ►annuity whose payment is made for a specified number of years.

terminal bonus ►life assurance.

terminate date The date of expiry of a ►futures contract in the ►commodity market.

terminal market A ►futures market in ►commodities, so called because futures contracts expire on a ►terminal date.

terzo mercato (It.) The third-tier ►unlisted securities market in Italy.

Texas hedge Any ►derivatives transaction having the effect of increasing risk, e.g. the purchase of two ►instruments adding to each other's risk. The opposite of a true ►hedge.

TGRs ►tigers.

Third Market (UK) An ►over-the-counter market set up by the ►London Stock Exchange to trade in securities of unlisted companies and with less stringent entry requirements than either the ►unlisted securities market or the ►official list or main market. It opened in January 1987 and was phased out in 1990.

Third World countries ►developing country.

thrifts (US) A general term covering non-bank institutions receiving ►deposits and making loans. ►credit union; mutual savings banks; savings and loan associations.

TIBOR (Jap.) Tokyo interbank offered rate. The Japanese equivalent of ►London interbank offered rate (LIBOR).

tick The observed minimum price movement of a ►derivative.

tigers 1. The first four ►newly industrialized countries in Asia: Hong Kong, Singapore, South Korea and Taiwan. ►►dragons. **2.** (US) The colloquial name for Treasury investment growth receipts (TGRs), ►zero coupon bonds issued by the US Treasury.

tighten A ►bond is said to *tighten* in the ►aftermarket if the interest ►yield is lower than the rate at which it was issued (►issue).

Tilgung (Ger.) ►Redemption.

till money (UK) Notes and coin held by banks. ►►vault cash (US).

time and distance policies The practice, chiefly by ►Lloyd's ►active underwriters, and chiefly in respect of ►long tail business where the ultimate claim is uncertain, of taking out an insurance policy maturing at some time in the future, rather than setting aside reserves; and of obtaining a letter of credit in respect of the maturity value of the policy. In this way, the underwriter can meet their ►solvency obligations without the sacrifice of profits for their members that a diversion of funds into reserves would entail. After the major losses of the late 1980s and early 1990s, the practice lost favour.

time deposit ►bank deposit.

time draft ►banker's acceptance.

time policy A policy for the ►insurance of a ship, applicable for a fixed period of time, regardless of the movements of the ship.

time value The difference between the market price of an ►option and the ►intrinsic value. ►►discounted cash flow.

times covered ►income gearing.

titre (Fr.) A ►certificate, or other documentary title to a ►security; also used to refer to the security itself.

***titulos de estabilización monetaria* (TEM)** (Venezuela) Monetary stabilization notes. ►Securities issued by the ►central bank of Venezuela to absorb the excess lending capacity, stemming from oil revenues of the Venezuelan banking system.

tobashi (Jap.) A practice of Japanese companies designed to conceal losses.

tokkin (Jap.) Literally, 'special investment fund'. A privileged investment fund made available in the late 1980s to Japanese companies having heavy liquidities that they wished to place in the stock market. Such companies already faced large taxable capital gains on existing holdings bought at historically low cost; further investment in such holdings would have added to the tax liability. Companies were therefore permitted to place their new resources in the new *tokkin* funds, valued at current book prices.

Tokyo dollar call market (Jap.) The ➤call market in dollar-denominated funds; dealing also in other ➤currencies.

Tokyo Grain Exchange A ➤commodity market established in 1957 for trade in US and Chinese soya beans and red beans.

Tokyo Round ➤General Agreement on Tariffs and Trade (GATT).

Tokyo Stock Exchange (TSE) One of the three largest ➤stock exchanges in the world and one of the three central Japanese exchanges; Osaka and Nagoya are the other two, and there are ➤regional stock exchanges in Fukuoka, Hiroshima, Kyoto, Niigata and Sapporo. Tokyo accounts for well over 80% of all the transactions in Japan. Tokyo, Nagoya and Osaka have two main sections – a first section (*ichibu*), which deals in the most actively traded companies, and, since 1961, a second section (*nibu*), which has less stringent listing requirements – as well as a third section for foreign stocks. Some 1,200 companies are listed on the first section and 400 on the second. There is also an ➤over-the-counter market, originally based in Osaka, which has an automated quotation system called JASDAQ and modelled on the ➤National Association of Securities Dealers Automated Quotation System (NASDAQ). The main Tokyo Stock Exchange has used an ➤automated screen trading system called CORES (Computer-Assisted Order Routing and Execution System) since 1982 on the second section and since 1985 on the first section, but some 200 actively traded shares are still bought and sold on the ➤trading floor. The Japanese exchanges are preparing for a ➤Big Bang which will deregulate ➤commission and are streamlining trading procedures and upgrading computer systems. Non-Japanese dealing firms were permitted to become members of the exchange in 1986. ➤➤Nikkei Stock Average; *saitori*; Topix.

tombstone ➤lead manager.

TOPIC ➤Teletext Output of Price Information by Computer.

Topix (Jap.) A ➤share index of some 1,200 ➤stocks quoted on Japanese stock markets. The index is capital weighted and forms the basis of a ➤futures contract listed on the ➤Tokyo Stock Exchange.

Toronto Stock Exchange (TSE) Incorporated in 1878, the TSE accounts for about 75% of trading ➤volume on the Canadian exchanges. Montreal is second in importance, followed by Vancouver, and there are also local exchanges in Calgary and Winnipeg. The Computer-Assisted Trading System (CATS) allows entry and automatic execution of ➤orders and carries market information. Reforms that began in 1987 allowed foreign dealers, banks and other financial institutions to own ➤brokers. The Toronto 35 Index of leading ➤stocks forms the basis for ➤options and ➤futures contracts. There is also a TSE 300 Composite Index. The TSE 100 ➤share index was launched in 1996. The TSE is regulated by the Ontario Securities Commission (OSC).

toshi shintaku, tanigata toshi shintaku (Jap.) ➤Investment trusts, which may take the same form as in the UK or may, in effect, be ➤unit trusts.

touch The difference between the highest ➤bid price and the lowest ➤offer price in a market for ➤securities or ➤commodities, i.e. the largest available ➤spread.

touch screen A computer monitor screen on which operating instructions can be given by touch as well as by the keyboard. For example, a dealer touches a small square on a video screen, and the computer will dial the number on the square with almost instant connection.

town clearing ➤clearing house.

tradable ➤negotiable; trade.

trade 1. To buy and sell, e.g., ➤negotiable instruments, ➤commodities, ➤currencies. **2**. Of the ➤commodity markets, business in a particular commodity.

TRADE ➤Stock Exchange Automatic Execution Facility.

trade balance ➤balance of payments.

trade bill A ➤bill of exchange accepted by a party other than a bank.

trade credit The ➤credit extended by business firms to other businesses, usually arising from the delay of receipts and payments for services performed. ➤➤factoring.

trade investments (UK) Shareholdings of one company in another. ➤➤consolidated accounts.

traded endowment policies (TEPs) Endowment policies (➤life assurance) which are sold in the open market before maturity.

traded months Months for which deliveries are quoted in ➤futures markets for ➤commodities. Standard months in the year are usually set for each market.

traded option ➤option.

trading floor The area of space in a ➤stock exchange where members gather to deal face to face in securities. Trading floors operate in most stock exchanges, though no longer on the ►London Stock Exchange, but are gradually giving way to ►automated screen trading.

trading position ►commodity market; traded months.

trading post ►specialist.

trading risk ►currency risk.

tranche A predetermined section of a financial transaction (from the French, meaning 'slice'). Thus:1. Of the ►International Monetary Fund (IMF), instalments of foreign currency that member countries may obtain, in exercise of their ►drawing rights, against their ►quota. 2. Of the ►securities market, an instalment in the progressive ►issue of a security. 3. Of the ►money market, a stage in the provision of a loan or in the issue of a money-market ►instrument, such as a ►certificate of deposit (CD).

tranche CD A ►certificate of deposit whose issue is divided into a number of smaller amounts and usually sold through a ►placing by a bank. ►tranche.

transaction risk ►currency risk.

transactions balances ►money supply.

transfer 1. The passage of money across national frontiers for non-commercial purposes, e.g. for the payment of legacies or pensions. 2. The physical delivery of certificates attesting ownership following sale of a ►security.

Transfer Accounting, Lodgement for Investors, Stock Management for Jobbers (TALISMAN) (UK) A semi-automated ►equity settlement system for the ►London Stock Exchange. Under the TALISMAN system, ►market makers transfer ►shares that they sell into ownership by a central pool (Stock Exchange Pool Nominees – SEPON) and meet buying orders from the same pool. SEPON therefore provides a clearing system. ►►CREST; Transfer and Automated Registration of Uncertified Stock (TAURUS).

transfer agent ►registrar.

transfer pricing The adjustment of prices on sales of material between members of a multi-company group so as to distribute financial burdens between the members in accordance with central financial policy. The term is most common in reference to multinational companies, where transfer pricing is suspected as a method of evading national taxation and customs duties.

Transfer and Automated Registration of Uncertified Stock (TAURUS) (UK) A project for a computerized ►share settlement system that was intended to reduce the need for handling ►share certificates on the ►London Stock Exchange. TAURUS, which was abandoned in 1993, acted as a clearing house by making book entry changes in the ownership of shares and issuing confirmation notes to buyer and seller. This would still not have been a full book entry transfer system, since the companies would need to maintain share registers (►registrar) and issue share certificates. A new system, ►CREST, has been introduced.

transferable ►negotiable.

translation risk ►currency risk.

transparency The extent to which transaction prices and ►volumes in a ►securities market are visible to all market operators. Transparency is an important condition for full and fair competition. ►►audit trail; fiscal transparency.

Treasury The central economic and finance department of a national government, so named chiefly in the USA and the UK, equivalent to the finance ministry of most other governments. The Treasury has responsibility for the overall economic and financial policy of the government, being chiefly concerned with domestic demand management, the balance of payments, monetary policy, taxation, public expenditure, the budget, government revenue and the issue of government ►securities, usually known as ►Treasury bonds and ►Treasury bills.

Treasury bill A ►money-market ►instrument issued (sold) by the ►central bank, chiefly in the UK and USA, in principle to supply the government's short-term financial needs, but also as a means of influencing ►credit and the ►money supply. Treasury bills are ►negotiable and in the UK are, at issue, wholly taken up by the ►discount houses. Treasury bills always change hands at a ►discount, the implicit rate of ►interest not being paid. Apart from issue at the ►Treasury bill tender, the bills are also sold through the ►tap but only to foreign government and overseas banks and as special deposits for banks that undertake not to release them to the open market. Treasury bills were first issued, in the UK, in 1877.

Treasury bill rate The implicit ►interest rate at which ►Treasury bills can be bought in the ►money market.

Treasury bill tender (UK) The offer for sale of ►Treasury bills each Friday by the ►Bank of England. The offer is of large quantities, and the bills' ►maturity is normally of three months.

Treasury bond A ►bond issued by the US Treasury. Equivalent instruments are issued in France and other countries but not in the UK.

Treasury investment growth receipts (TGRs) (US) ►tigers.

Treaty of Paris The treaty, signed in 1951, establishing the European Coal and Steel Community. ►European Union (EU).

Treaty of Rome The treaty, signed in 1957, establishing the European Economic Community. Also, a separate treaty, signed in the same year, establishing the

European Atomic Energy Community (Euratom). ►European Union (EU); Maastricht Treaty; Single European Act.

treaty reinsurance A form of reinsurance whereby the reinsurer and the *ceding insurer* (►cedant) are bound under their contract, or treaty, to accept certain risks. ►►reinsurance treaty; facultative reinsurance.

Treuhandanstalt (Ger.) An agency established by the German government in July 1990 with the task of privatizing large areas of state-owned industry in the former East Germany. Such enterprises were taken into ownership and management by the Treuhandanstalt and thereafter sold to private investors. By May 1992, 7,092 companies had been privatized, for a total payment of DM28bn. Of these, 366 had been acquired by foreign investors, apportioned between France (DM2.3bn), the UK (DM1.6bn), the USA (DM1.5bn) and the Netherlands (DM900m). However, 4,863 companies still awaited privatization.

triple witching hour (US) A familiar expression for the trading sessions when the expiry dates of ►stock index futures contracts, ►options on these contracts and options in individual stock fall together.

troy ounce The traditional unit of weight of a precious metal, equal to 1.0971428 oz avoirdupois. The term is derived from a weight used in Troyes, France, in the Middle Ages.

troc (Fr.) A ►foreign exchange swap.

true and fair view ►audit.

TRUF ►Euronote facility.

trust 1. In general, a legal device under which property, either financial or physical, is placed in the custody of a designated person, or people, named *trustees*, for management on behalf of others; the whole is regulated by a *trust deed* defining the trustee(s), the beneficiaries of the trust and the rights and duties of each. ►Unit trusts and ►investment trusts, as the names imply, are regulated by trust arrangements. **2**. A large US ►conglomerate prevalent in the 19th and early 20th centuries, largely outlawed by anti-trust legislation, the earliest instance of which was the Sherman Act of 1890.

trust bank A category of Japanese bank engaged in both banking and trust activities and also operating as savings institutions for the general public (Jap. = *shintaka ginko*).

trust corporation A corporate body (company) authorized under the legislation to act as trustee.

trust deed ►trust.

trust letter A document signed by a bank borrower who has pledged goods to the bank as a ➤security against the loan. The goods are held by the bank until the customer is due to repay the loan, whereupon the customer can obtain control of the goods, solely to sell to repay the loan, against signature of the trust letter, or trust receipt.

trust receipt ➤trust letter.

trustee ➤trust. Of ➤bond issues, a trustee is frequently appointed to supervise the discharge of the borrower's obligation to pay principal, interest and other commitments, and generally to safeguard the interests of the bond holders.

Trustee Savings Bank (TSB) (UK) A ➤savings bank movement, originally established in Scotland in 1810 to encourage saving by people with low incomes. It grew to a large number of banks that were eventually amalgamated into a single enterprise. The TSB was floated on the ➤stock exchange in 1986 (➤flotation) and is now part of Lloyds Bank.

trustee status Of trustees (➤trust), those authorized in the UK under the Trustee Investments Act 1961 to make designated investments not previously allowed, namely in ordinary shares.

Truth in Lending Act (US) Legislation, implemented by Regulation 2 of the ➤Federal Reserve, requiring full disclosure by the lender of the cost of consumer credit, such disclosure to include the ➤annual percentage rate (APR) and the nature of the costs involved. The Act also permits the borrower, in the case of ➤mortgages, to cancel the transaction within three business days of formal completion.

TSA ➤Securities Association.

TSB ➤Trustee Savings Bank.

TSE ➤Tokyo Stock Exchange; Toronto Stock Exchange.

tsuikagata toshi shintaku (Jap.) An open-ended ➤investment trust.

turn-round rate A combined charge on a ➤commodity transaction, consisting of the ➤broker's ➤commission and the ➤clearing fee.

turnover **1**. The total sales revenue of a business. **2**. The value of transactions carried out on a ➤stock exchange, defined usually as the value of ➤securities changing hands but on the ➤London Stock Exchange mainly as the total value of purchases and sales. ➤➤volume.

tweede markt (Bel.) The second-tier ➤unlisted securities market in Belgium. This is the Flemish name; in French the market is called the *second marché*.

Twelfth Directive ➤incorporation.

24-hour trading The ability to trade in ➤securities around the clock. Since some

➤blue-chip issues and ➤bonds are quoted on several ➤stock exchanges in different time zones, it is now possible, using satellite communications, to buy and sell securities at any time. Even though there are gaps in trading hours, many exchanges allow after-hours trading; i.e. ➤dealers are allowed to buy and sell outside the official closing time.

U

Übernahme (Ger.) **1.** ➤Take-over. **2.** The underwriting (➤underwrite) by a banking ➤syndicate of a ➤new issue, the syndicate also being responsible for the sale of security.

uberrimae fidei Literally, 'in the fullest faith'. The legal principle, especially applicable in ➤insurance, that all contracts are made on the basis of the fullest possible disclosure of material facts, regardless of whether this is explicitly stated in the contract.

UBR Uniform business rate. ➤local taxation.

UCITS ➤Undertakings for Collective Investment in Transferable Securities.

ultra vires Outside the legal powers of a company or official.

umbrella fund An offshore fund of funds, invested in other offshore funds. ➤tax haven.

undercapitalized A company is said to be undercapitalized if it does not have sufficient ➤capital to meet its due creditors even though it is making an accounted ➤profit.

uncommitted Of an international short-term issue, e.g. ➤Euro-commercial paper, not backed by an ➤underwriting bank ➤syndicate, i.e. with no commitment by banks to underpin the issue.

undated securities (UK) ➤Government securities not bearing a ➤redemption date or ➤option, hence ➤irredeemable securities.

Undertakings for Collective Investment in Transferable Securities (UCITS) A ➤European Union (EU) ➤directive entering into force in 1989 and governing ➤unit trusts and ➤open-ended investment companies, intended to allow them to be marketed throughout the EU.

undervalued ➤purchasing power parity.

underwrite 1. To guarantee to buy or find buyers for all or part of the issue of a ➤security. Normally done in return for a fee by a bank or group (➤syndicate) of banks to ensure sale of any part of an issue not bought by the public to which it is directed. **2.** To accept on behalf of an insuring firm or syndicate an insurance risk.

underwritten 1. Of a ►note, particularly a ►Euronote, an issue backed by a bank guarantee to buy unsold notes or by a bank ►standby credit. ►note issuance facility. 2. Of insurance, a ►risk accepted by the ►insurer and against which a ►policy has been issued.

undistributed profits ►retained earnings.

unearned income ►income tax.

unearned premiums reserve (UPR) A fund set aside by an insurance company at the end of its financial year to cover ►risks to be borne in the future, i.e. for the length of time ►premiums will be received in respect of any particular insurance policy.

unexpired risks reserve A fund set aside by an insurance company at the end of its financial year, in addition to its ►unearned premiums reserve, to cover all future ►risks insured under its policies.

unfunded ►pensions.

ungeregelter Freiverkehr (Ger.) ►*geregelter Freiverkehr*.

ungesichert (Ger.) ►Unsecured.

uniform business rate ►local taxation.

uniform reserve requirement (US) A requirement that the ►reserves of all financial institutions should conform to the same rule, i.e. broadly that they should be the same percentage of the same aggregate (e.g. deposits). A progressive approach to uniform reserves was prescribed in the ►Monetary Control Act 1980.

unincorporated business A business that has not taken the legal form of a company and may be a ►sole proprietorship or a ►partnership. ►incorporation.

unit banking ►banking.

unit-linked life assurance A form of endowment ►life assurance in which ►policy-holders receive, in return for their ►premiums, a portion, or unit, of a fund invested directly by the company in the ►stock exchange or in property or other investment outlets. The merit of the arrangement is seen to be in policy-holders' free choice of, direct knowledge of and, within limits, ability to switch the investment of their premiums, as opposed to their passive position as holders of normal endowment policies. Moreover, the existence in the UK until 1984 of tax relief on all life assurance premiums (*life assurance premium relief* – LAPR), together with the concessionary level of ►corporation tax paid by the life company in the income from the investment, produced considerable tax advantages for policy-holders, particularly those at higher levels of income tax. With the abolition of premium tax relief, an advantage only to higher-rate taxpayers remained.

Unit-linked life assurance has made major use of the *single-premium* technique, the policies then being generally known as *bonds*. Unit-linked assurance emerged in the UK in the 1960s, the pioneer company being Abbey Life, directed by Mark Weinberg (later Sir Mark Weinberg), who subsequently transferred his activities to Hambro Life, a company eventually renamed Allied Dunbar.

unit of account 1. In economic theory, one of the functions of money, i.e. a generally accepted unit of value, available to establish the price of goods, e.g. a pound, a dollar or a franc. **2.** The standard unit, usually an intangible creation, used normally by international financial organizations to measure their financial activities. Thus the ➤special drawing right (SDR) has been adopted as the unit of account of the ➤International Monetary Fund (IMF), and the ➤European Currency Unit (ECU) as the unit of account of the ➤European Monetary System (EMS).

unit trust (UK) An investment organization that invests funds subscribed by the public in ➤securities and in return issues units that it will repurchase at any time. The units, which represent equal shares in the trust's investment ➤portfolio, produce income and fluctuate in value according to the ➤interest and ➤dividends paid and the ➤stock exchange prices of the underlying securities. The subscriber to a unit trust does not, unlike the shareholder in an ➤investment trust, receive any of the ➤profits of the organization managing the trust. Management derives its income from a regular service charge as a percentage of the income of the trust's investments (normally less than ½% p.a.), and the difference (➤spread) between the (bid) price at which it buys in units and the (offer) price at which it sells them, which includes an initial charge. The trust is regulated by a trust deed, the trustees being separate from the management. Unit trusts are free to invest in any type of security and in recent years have tended to specialize, e.g. in small companies or ➤blue-chip shares, others in ➤commodities or foreign companies or countries. Some are designed to maximize income, others ➤capital growth. Many unit trusts offer the option of distributed or reinvested income (*accumulation units*), and there are also trusts incorporating ➤life assurance that can be subscribed to by regular payments. Unit trusts in the UK first appeared in the 1930s, were based upon the principle of ➤mutual funds in the USA. (Fr. = *société d'investissement à capital variable* (SICAV).) ➤➤open-ended fund; open-ended investment company.

unitary taxation (US) Under the unitary tax system some states in the USA assess ➤corporation tax not only on ➤profits arising from operations within the state but on total income, including the income of subsidiaries in other states or even overseas.

United Nations Monetary and Financial Conference 1944 ➤Bretton Woods.

United Sugar Terminal Market The London market in sugar ➤futures, established in 1888, closed during the First and Second World Wars, last reopened in 1957. A paper market only; i.e. physical deliveries are not made. The market fixes the London daily price, used by a number of producer countries as a reference for their physical contracts. The market is a member of the ►International Commodities Clearing House. The London market is about the same size as the New York market and considerably larger than the other world-ranking market, in Paris. Dealing has for long been dominated by successive International Sugar Agreements establishing quotas.

unitized property market ►property income certificate.

universal banking ►banking.

unlisted company A company whose ►shares are not admitted for trading on a major ►stock exchange. Unlisted companies, also referred to as *unquoted companies*, may none the less have their shares quoted and traded on ►unlisted securities markets. ►►over-the-counter market.

unlisted securities market(s) (USM(s)) 1. Generally, the markets for shares of public companies (►incorporation) not included in the official list for the main market (or first tier) of the ►stock exchange. Most of the larger industrialized countries have organized and regulated lower-tier markets as well as informal *placing markets* in which unlisted shares are traded. These lower stock market segments are less stringently regulated and perform an important function in providing a stepping-stone to the main markets. ►►National Association of Securities Dealers Automated Quotation System; over-the-counter market; *second marché*. 2. Specifically, a market set up in 1980 by the ►London Stock Exchange to trade in designated unlisted securities. ►Shares in well over 400 companies were dealt with by ►market makers on the USM in the early 1990s but by 1993 the number listed had fallen to 275. The market closed at the end of 1996, having been replaced by the ►Alternative Investment Market. Changes in admission and other requirements for the main market of the London Stock Exchange following the implementation of European Community/Union directives had reduced the differences between the two markets and lessened the appeal of the USM.

unquoted company ►unlisted company.

unrelieved corporation tax ►corporation tax.

unsecured Of a loan, not backed by a ►security.

unsecured debt A loan made without ►collateral or any charge on the ►assets of the borrower. Unsecured notes are ►securities issued by a company, involving no ►charge on the assets of the company in the event of default.

unvalued policy An ►insurance policy in which the sum to be paid in respect of loss of the subject of the contract is not stated but a maximum sum payable is usually stated.

unweighted ►weighted average.

up-and-in call/put option An ➤option that has no value until the price of the underlying security rises above a certain level.

up-and-out call/put option An ➤option becoming valueless when the price of the underlying security rises above a certain level.

UPR ➤unearned premiums reserve.

Uruguay Round ➤General Agreement on Tariffs and Trade (GATT).

utmost good faith ➤*uberrimae fidei.*

V

valeur (Fr.) **1.** The price of a ►security or value of a number of securities. **2.** The security itself.

valeur à revenue fixe (Fr.) A ►fixed-interest security.

valeur à revenu variable (Fr.) A ►variable rate security.

valeur au porteur (Fr.) A bearer bond. ►bearer security.

valeur marchande (Fr.) The market value of a ►security.

valeur non-cotée (Fr.) An ►unlisted security.

value Of ►foreign exchange transactions, the date on which a transaction must be paid for. ►►settle.

value added tax (VAT) A general tax on consumption applied at each point of exchange of goods or services from primary production to final consumption. It is levied on the difference between the sale price of the goods and services (outputs) and the cost of bought-in inputs. At each point of exchange the tax is passed on in the form of higher prices. Businesses do not bear any VAT included in the invoices for the inputs that they buy from suppliers. Being at the final point in the chain of exchange, the final consumer bears the whole of the tax in the same way as if it were a ►sales tax levied at the retail level. Exports are *zero rated* and bear no VAT. The tax is at present added in the country of destination (*destination principle*), but an alternative method is for exports to countries in the EU to bear VAT of the country of origin (*origin principle*). VAT was introduced in the UK in 1973 because it is the form of indirect ►taxation applied in the ►European Union (EU) and is the basis of contribution to the Union budget. It is levied in all EU member states, in Japan and in many other countries but not in Australia or the USA, which have sales taxes. VAT in the EU uses the invoice method; in Japan the tax is calculated from company accounts.

value investing ►investment approaches.

Vancouver stock exchange ►Toronto Stock Exchange.

variable life insurance (Jap.) ►Life assurance where the sum payable varies in relation to inflation or ►exchange rates.

variable rate security A ►security for which the ►rate of interest is not fixed but varies with rates on short-term securities, such as ➤Treasury bills, according to a specified formula that adjusts rates, say, every six months. The UK government issued variable rate stock in 1977, but such issues are common in the ➤Eurobond market and in the USA, where they are known as ➤floating rate notes (FRNs) or, more generally, *floaters.*

variabler Kurs (Ger.) The continuous quotation allowable for large company ➤shares on the ➤German stock exchanges. ➤*Einheitskurs.*

variation margin The losses and gains attributable to ➤derivatives in the light of their ➤marking-to-market values.

VAT ➤value added tax.

vault cash (US) Money held at banks in the form of banknotes and coins (UK = *notes and coin*).

VC ➤venture capital.

VCTS ➤venture capital trust scheme.

velocity Of ➤money supply, the rate at which the ➤money stock circulates within the economy. The figure for velocity is obtained by dividing the money stock into the ➤gross domestic product (GDP). ➤➤monetary school; money.

vendor placing Where a ➤listed company issues ➤shares to the sellers of another company as full or partial settlement of the acquisition price, the sellers may ask a ➤stockbroker to dispose of the shares by placing them with clients. This is known as vendor placing and may be preferable to selling them on the market, where the offer of a large line of stock might depress the price.

vente à découvert (Fr.) An uncovered sale of a ➤security, a ➤currency or a ➤commodity. ➤cover.

venture capital ➤Finance provided by a specialized institution to an entrepreneur, ➤start-up or developing business, where a fairly high degree of risk is involved. The term is also used in a wider sense to include the provision of finance for ➤management buy-outs and refinancings. In this wider sense the correct term is ➤private equity. Strictly, venture capital includes ➤equity capital, and this is often provided in a package including ➤subordinated or other ➤loans. ➤➤development capital; mezzanine; risk capital.

Venture Capital Trust Scheme (VCTS) (UK) A scheme announced in November 1993, and now in operation, to give tax-free ➤dividends and ➤capital gains for pooled investments in qualifying unquoted trading companies (➤unlisted companies).

Verfall (Ger.) ➤Redemption date.

Verkehrswert (Ger.) Market value.

vertical spread A combination of ►options: a ►long ►call option combined with a ►short call option, both with the same expiry date. Similarly a combination of long and short *put* options.

VIBOR The Vienna interbank offered rate; the Austrian equivalent of ►London interbank offered rate (LIBOR).

videotext ►viewdata.

Vietcombank The largest state-owned bank in Vietnam.

Vietnam State Securities Commission The Vietnamese supervisory body for ►securities transaction.

viewdata The provision of selected information, e.g. on ►share prices, through television screens. One example is ►Teletext Output of Price Information by Computer (TOPIC). There are two types of viewdata system: **1.** In *teletext* or *videotext* the viewer calls up pages of information by keying in numbers selected from a directory on the screen via a keyboard. Ceefax and Oracle are provided by the BBC and the Independent Broadcasting Authority respectively and are transmitted to the set by television signal. **2.** Prestel, operated by British Telecom, enables viewers to select pages of information stored on a central computer via telephone lines using their television set as a terminal. TOPIC uses this system. Viewers may also access information about their bank account and buy or sell shares (►electronic banking).

visible balance ►balance of payments.

visible trade ►balance of payments.

voice broker A ►foreign exchange ►broker making deals only by telephone.

volatility, price The extent to which security prices fluctuate, usually measured by hourly percentage changes in a ►share index.

volume **1.** The amount of any aggregate when unaffected by price changes, i.e. expressed in terms of a given period, taking no account of price changes; e.g. the volume of UK company profit margins, expressed in terms of 1980, rose by 21% between 1980 and 1987. ►►inflation; nominal; real. **2.** An indicator of ►turnover on a ►stock exchange. Volume is usually measured by the number of transactions in a ►security or in all securities during a period, e.g. a day; but on the ►London Stock Exchange volume is measured by the total number of sales and purchases – a figure twice as high.

vorläufige Dividende (Ger.) Interim dividend. ►dividend.

Vorstand (Ger.) Board of directors.

***vostro* account** A bank account maintained by a ➤correspondent bank on behalf of a depositing bank in another country; *vostro* (It.) meaning 'your'. The depositing bank will refer to *nostro account*, meaning 'our account'.

vote ➤supply expenditure.

voting shares ➤Equity shares entitling holders to vote in the election of directors of a company. Normally all ➤ordinary shares are voting shares, but sometimes a company may create a class of non-voting ordinary shares if the holders of the equity wish to raise more equity capital but exclude the possibility of losing control of the business. Bearer shares (➤bearer security) are commonly used to raise capital in some countries. Most Swiss companies register only shares held by Swiss citizens, although this is changing.

voyage policy A policy of ➤insurance of a ship, applicable only for the duration of one voyage.

W

WACC ➤weighted average cost of capital.

Wall Street ➤New York Stock Exchange.

Wandelobligation (Ger.) A ➤convertible bond.

warehouse receipt A document issued by the warehouse when a commodity is delivered to it; the document specifies the quantity and characteristics of the commodity and is confirmation, particularly in relation to ➤derivatives dealings, that the physical commodity is in safe custody. Also known as a *depository receipt*.

warrant, warehouse warrant (UK) ➤warrant of settlement.

warrant of settlement A document showing title to a specific quantity of a ➤commodity in storage, conveying responsibility for warehouse charges and insurance.

warrants ➤Securities giving the holder a right to subscribe to a ➤share or a ➤bond at a given price from a certain date. Warrants, which are commonly issued 'free' alongside the shares of new ➤investment trusts when launched, and carry no income or other rights to ➤equity, immediately trade separately on the ➤stock exchange but at a price lower than the associated security. This provides the investor in warrants with an element of ➤gearing, since, if the associated share or bond price ultimately rises above the subscription price, it will have a value corresponding to the difference between the subscription price at which the warrant rights may be exercised and the market price of the share or bond. ➤➤dilution; dividend warrant; option.

warranty The confirmation by the ➤insured party to an insurance contract that the details given as to the subject of the insurance are correct.

Warsaw Stock Exchange ➤Eastern Europe.

wash sale (US) The sale and purchase of a ➤block of ➤securities by a single investor (or investors in collusion) simultaneously or within a short period. The objective may be to establish a loss or gain or to create a false impression of ➤volume and ➤turnover in a security. ➤➤bed and breakfast.

wealth tax An annual tax on the net value of ➤assets of an individual, levied above a threshold. There are wealth taxes in a number of countries, including

Denmark, Germany, the Netherlands and Spain, but not in the UK, Japan or the USA.

weighted average An ➤average calculated by assigning weights to each item to reflect their relative importance. For example, the weighted average for a share price index calculated in this way could be arrived at by multiplying the prices of ➤securities by their traded ➤volumes (weights), adding them together and dividing by the sum of the weights. This weighted average could then be expressed as a percentage of the weighted average calculated in a similar way for an earlier, base year, to give a percentage change in prices. An *unweighted* average or index gives all its constituents an equal value. ➤➤share indices; weighted average cost of capital.

weighted average cost of capital (WACC) A measure of the average cost of a firm's capital. It is calculated for each type of capital and combining them weighted in the proportions they account for of total capital (➤weighted average). The cost of ➤debt, e.g. bank loans, is the ➤interest paid. For ➤equity it is the current rate of return on government ➤securities plus an allowance for risk. The latter consists of the historical difference between government ➤bond and market equity rates of return, plus or minus an adjustment for company-specific risk as measured by the *beta coefficient* (➤alpha coefficient).

weights ➤weighted average.

Wertpapier (Ger.) A ➤security.

Wertzuwachs (Ger.) ➤Capital gain.

Wertzuwachssteuer (Ger.) Capital gains tax. ➤capital gain.

Wheat Trade Convention (WTC) ➤International Wheat Agreement (IWA); International Wheat Council (IWC).

white knight A company subject to an unwelcome or hostile bid (➤corporate raider) may invite a second bid from a friendly company as an alternative to succumbing to a ➤take-over. That company is a white knight.

whole life policy ➤life assurance.

wholesale banking The making of loans or acceptance of deposits between banks and other ➤financial institutions, especially in the ➤interbank market. As distinct from *retail banking*, a term for the activities of the ➤commercial banks carried out with the general public and business enterprises.

wholesale deposit A ➤deposit, normally of a large amount, obtained by a bank from other banks, or from large companies or institutions, i.e. not a deposit placed directly by an individual client.

wholesale market Of banks, the ➤money market that operates between banks, dealing in interbank short-term loans in large amounts. ►interbank market.

Wig Index ►Eastern Europe.

windfall tax Specifically, a once and for all direct tax (►taxation) levied in the UK 1997 Budget on the earnings of British privatized utilities. The companies affected were the water and electricity companies, British Telecom, Railtrack, British Gas, Centrica, the British Airports Authority and British Energy. The tax was levied on the difference between the company's valuation on ►privatization and its valuation after four years of operation, the latter valuation calculated on a formula using a multiple of nine times average after tax profits in the period. The tax was once only, levied at a rate of 23% by two annual instalments. Generally, any tax imposed on persons or organizations deemed to have benefited from external events outside the normal course of their economic activities, as that imposed on oil companies following the sudden increase in oil prices in the 1970s (►Organization of Petroleum Exporting Countries (OPEC)).

winding up ►liquidation.

window A term used to describe a period, normally short, in which particular funds are available. Also applied to special lending by a ►central bank. ►discount window.

window dressing Financial adjustments made solely for the purpose of accounting presentation, normally at the time of auditing of company accounts. For example, a bank may wish to show large holdings of cash at the ►balance sheet date and may in advance of that date sell ►securities, only to repurchase them immediately afterwards.

window guidance (Jap.) Informal direction by the Bank of Japan in respect of bank lending policies.

with-profits life assurance ►life assurance.

withdrawable repurchase agreement (US) A ►repurchase agreement that can be cancelled by the dealer giving notice of termination to the ►Federal Reserve by 1.30 p.m. on the day of intended cancellation.

withdrawable RP Withdrawable ►repurchase agreement.

withholding tax ►Taxation deducted from payments to non-residents, usually in the form of a standard rate of ►income tax applied to ►dividends or other payments by companies. May be reclaimable under ►double taxation agreements.

without recourse ►resource.

won The national ►currency unit of South Korea.

work in progress Work done but not yet invoiced to a customer (US = *work in process*).

working capital The excess of current ➤assets over current ➤liabilities; that part of current assets financed from long-term funds. The ratio of current liabilities to the current assets of a business, the current ratio, is sometimes used as a measure of ➤liquidity.

working member A professional member of ➤Lloyd's carrying on the actual business of Lloyd's, either as an underwriter or as a broker.

World Bank ➤International Bank for Reconstruction and Development.

World Gold Council An international non-profit association of gold producers with the task of stimulating demand for gold in major end-use markets. Founded in 1987 by 16 gold-mining companies from four countries, in 1993 the council had 50 member companies from nine countries, representing about half of world gold production. In 1992, among other activities, the council established the Central Bank Advisory Board to promote understanding of the role of central banks in the gold market and began publication of the quarterly review *Gold Demand Trends* for the use of market analysts and commentators.

world indices ➤Morgan Stanley Capital International World Index.

World Trade Organization (WTO) The World Trade Organization was set up in Geneva in 1995 following the conclusion of the ➤Uruguay Round of trade negotiations. It replaced the ➤General Agreement on Tariffs and Trade (GATT). The WTO is charged with the further development of and the policing of the multilateral trading system along the principles followed by the eight Rounds of Trade Negotiations concluded under its predecessor. It provides the resources and the legal status for the resolution of trade disputes through independent disputes panels. A member may appeal to the WTO Appeals Tribunal but must accept its ruling. The failure of a member country to accept the WTO ruling would subject it to ➤trade sanctions. In 1996, there were 122 member states. In 1997, agreement was reached for the liberalization of the telecommunications market world-wide with effect from 1998, which had not been achieved as planned under the Uruguay Round.

writer The seller of an ➤option.

writing-down allowance ➤capital allowances.

written back ➤provisions.

written off ➤provisions.

WTC Wheat Trade Convention. ➤International Wheat Agreement (IWA); International Wheat Council (IWC).

X

xd ➤ex-dividend.

Xetra ➤German stock exchanges.

Y

yankee bond (US) A dollar-dominated ►bond issued in the USA by foreign banks and corporations. A ►foreign bond.

year of account A business year of a ►Lloyd's syndicate.

yearling bond (UK) ►Stock issued by municipal authorities with ►maturity within a year.

Yellow Book (UK) A publication of the ►London Stock Exchange, setting out the regulations governing admission to the ►official list and subsequent procedures for reporting. ►►Green Book.

yellow sheets ►pink sheets.

yield The income from a ►security as a proportion of its current market price. This is the *current yield*. The *dividend yield* is the current ►dividend as a percentage of the market price of a security. The *earnings yield* is a theoretical figure, based on the last dividend paid as a percentage of the current market price. For ►fixed-interest securities, the *running yield, interest yield* or *flat yield* is the interest rate as a percentage of the price paid for the ►stock. For example, a ►bond with a nominal or issued value of £100, but bought for £50, and with an interest rate of 5%, has a running yield of 10%. Where it is a ►redeemable security the return will also include any ►capital gain on ►redemption. This is the *redemption yield*, which takes into account the purchase price, the interest payments, the redemption value and the time remaining to maturity. The initial yield is the estimated income that an investor in a new ►unit trust or other form of managed investment, such as an ►investment trust, may expect to receive. It is based upon the present yield of the underlying investments and expressed as a percentage of the ►offer price.

yield curve The normal tendency of ►yields to rise with the increasing ►maturity of the ►security. When the opposite effect occurs, this is described as a *reverse yield curve*.

yuan The national ►currency unit of China, the currency being the *Renminbi*.

Z

zaibatsu (Jap.) A large interlocking grouping of Japanese companies, similar to a US ➤trust or a German ➤*Konzern*; dominated by a bank, holding controlling interests in the other members of the group. The *zaibatsu* have been largely outmoded by legislation since the Second World War, their place being taken by the ➤*keiretsu*.

zaitech (Jap.) Sophisticated financial management, normally that of the surplus funds of industrial companies; the term used to contrast financial profits with industrial profits.

Zeisei Chosa Kai (Jap.) Tax System Research Council. A Japanese state body concerned with tax reform.

zero coupon bond, zero coupon fund A ➤bond issued at a discount (i.e. below ➤par value), earning no ➤interest but redeemable at its par value, thus providing a guaranteed ➤capital gain. ➤➤rolled-up coupon.

zero dividend preference shares ➤Preference shares that pay no ➤dividend but a fixed sum at a ➤redemption date. ➤investment trust.

Zins (Ger.) ➤Interest.

Zinssatz (Ger.) ➤Rate of interest.

Zinsschein (Ger.) ➤Coupon.

zloty The national ➤currency unit of Poland.

Zurich Stock Exchange ➤Swiss stock exchanges.

Zwischenhandler (Ger.) Intermediary, ➤broker.